The Deep Reach of Amazing Grace

BY STEPHEN N. JOHNSON

© 2013 Nurturing Faith Inc.

Published in the United States by Nurturing Faith Inc., Macon GA, www.nurturingfaith.net.

ISBN 978-1-938514-26-5

All rights reserved. Printed in the United States of America

Unless otherwise noted all Scripture quotations taken from the New American Standard Bible®, Copyright © 1960, 1962, 1963, 1968, 1971, 1972, 1973, 1975, 1977, 1995 by The Lockman Foundation Used by permission." (www.Lockman.org).

Scripture quotations taken from the New English Bible, copyright © Cambridge University Press and Oxford University Press 1961, 1970. All rights reserved.

Endorsements

Steve Johnson is a compelling and moving voice for rescuing Christianity from the ravages of the contemporary church. The reader is not left to read between the lines. Indeed, he writes with candor and stunning clarity. His description of God's grace will be startling to many because of his refusal to allow human boundaries and an array of performance requirements and expectations, which the institutional church tries to impose, to undermine or to veil the sheer wonder and simplicity of the grace embodied by Jesus and which carries no conditions or limitations.

—R. Kirby Godsey
Chancellor, Mercer University

Steve Johnson belongs to the Baptist tribe. We talk grace and walk works. Johnson, on the other hand, talks and walks a grace so revolutionary that it offends us religious. Read this book, and I promise that you will at some point murmur: "Come on, Steve, you don't really believe . . .", "Yeah, but . . .", "Are you actually saying that . . .?". And, yes, he actually has his heart wrapped around a sweeping, drastic, radical grace. It is a radical grace that issues into radical works.

—Walter B. Shurden
Minister at Large
Mercer University

The Deep Reach of Amazing Grace is a powerful and inviting exploration of the "God of outlandish grace." Johnson combines meticulous analysis of scripture, with a willingness to look at his own beliefs and behavior with humility. He tells powerful stories from his experiences and calls on a vast range of sources—literary, philosophical, and Biblical—to carefully examine contemporary issues of religion and faith. The result is a compelling book. While I am neither a Christian nor a religious person, Steve Johnson writes in a way to make Jesus most appealing and the Christian faith both intellectually understandable and personally winsome.

— Jane Bolgatz, Ph.D.
Associate Professor, Fordham University, Graduate School of Education
Author of *Talking Race in the Classroom* (Teachers College Press, 2005)

About the Author

Stephen N. Johnson is an ordained Baptist minister and a veteran pastor of over forty years. He holds a Bachelor of Arts degree from Mercer University and a Master of Divinity degree from Southwestern Baptist Theological Seminary. He is the founder and president of Reformation Ministries, Inc. (www.refmin.org), begun because "It's Time For A New Reformation." Steve is dedicated to the proclamation of the wonders of God's grace. He and his wife, Connie, live in Macon, Georgia. They have one son, John Stephen and two daughters, Carrie Elizabeth and Kathryn Suzanne. Contact Steve at stevermi@cox.net.

Contents

Preface v

Foreword ix

Chapter 1
The Gospel According to Jesus 1

Chapter 2
Sola Gratia! Sola Fide! Solus Christus! 19

Chapter 3
Why Did Jesus Die? 33

Chapter 4
Hell in the Fire 51

Chapter 5
The "Way" of Salvation 69

Chapter 6
When Religion Goes Bad 89

Chapter 7
The Error of Inerrancy 107

Chapter 8
"I Believe in God the Father Almighty, 125
Maker of Heaven and Earth"...
And in Evolution

Chapter 9
God, the Gospel, and Gays   143

Chapter 10
The Greatest Challenge Facing the   161
    Church Today: Believing the Gospel

Chapter 11
Grace Above All. Then, More Grace   179

Epilogue   197

Works Cited   199

Preface

THE CHURCH IS LOSING. People on the outside consider it either irrelevant or dangerous. People on the inside are leaving. This is not always the result of contemporary and vocal atheists such as Christopher Hitchens and Richard Dawkins nor the pervasive secularism of our culture. The hard times the church faces today are largely the church's own making. The church has forfeited the message of Jesus—a message of incredible good news—for the trappings of religion that fail to win minds and meet the deep needs of the human heart. Too often, the church presents a religion that is superficial, inconsistent, and incompatible. Putting it bluntly, many find it repugnant.

The faith of Jesus Christ has remained vibrant for over two thousand years because the truths Jesus taught touch and transform the human heart, offering joy in good times and hope amid desperate times. In a harsh and hostile world, Jesus' message of God's love and grace has brought understanding, consolation, instruction, hope and peace to hearts and nations. Because of His life and message, Jesus survives the denials of popular atheists, the debates of the academy, and the distortions of the modern church.

So what is going wrong?

Survey after survey reveals that Americans take their faith seriously and value a vibrant spiritual life. These surveys, however, reveal that many of these same people are repulsed by the contemporary church, and for good reason. Summarizing an exhaustive research project, David Kinnaman, president of The Barna Group (a leading Christian research organization), summarizes:

> The research shows that Christians are best known for what they are against. They are perceived as being

judgmental, anti-homosexual, and too political. And young people are quick to point out that they believe that *Christianity is no longer as Jesus intended.* It is unChristian.[1]

The message of Jesus Christ has been eclipsed in the modern church in the United States. The New Testament gospel, the genuine "good news," is no longer the message of His church. It has substituted other things such as Christian doctrine (right belief) and Christian ethics (right behavior) and the endless ancillary demands that accompany both. The church now stresses secondary matters, emphasizes tertiary matters, and diminishes the one primary matter: the pure, unalloyed, unadulterated gospel of the grace of God. By substituting lesser stuff for the wonder of God's grace, the church has lost its greatest distinctive characteristic and a message that can transform the human heart.

Three new terms have entered the religious/sociological lexicon: "de-converts," those who have abandoned the Christian faith; "leavers," those who have been raised in the church and are now leaving; and "nones," those who when asked their religious faith answer, "None." The modern church is losing people by the millions.

John, the "beloved disciple," concluded the marvelous prologue to his Gospel with these revealing words:

> No one has seen God at any time; the only begotten God who is in the bosom of the Father, *He has explained Him*" [emphasis mine] (John 1:18).

According to John, Jesus came to explain God the Father. Read the Gospel of John and the other three Gospels. What Jesus "explained" is that above all else, God is a God of amazing and outlandish grace, a grace that reaches far down, far out, and forever. (I refer back to this pivotal verse throughout the book and when doing so render the word "explained" in quotes.)

I have been a churchman all my life. The church birthed me into knowledge of Jesus Christ and instilled in me a deep and abiding faith and spiritual strength that has enabled me to navigate life's inevitable storms. I have given my life to pastoring the church and studying and preaching the Bible. The church of Jesus Christ is the greatest single source for good and giving the world has ever seen. Yet today, because the church has left its primary message, the church is in serious trouble.

The Deep Reach of Amazing Grace reminds us how winsome the life of Jesus can be for our times. It clears away the dead brush and prickly briars of a misunderstood and misrepresented Christianity (sometimes even orthodox Christianity). It calls us to a clear understanding of the New Testament faith for this day, a faith "explained" by Jesus of Nazareth. It presents the timeless gospel that can transform our lives. For those who have left the church, I agree with you wholeheartedly that some churches need to be left. For those disgusted with the church, I urge you to hang in there and help make the Christian church more Christ-like. To those rejected by the church, I apologize that we were not more like Christ. To all my fellow "ragamuffins" needing "a handout of amazing grace," *The Deep Reach of Amazing Grace* explores the profound richness of the outlandish grace of God. I pray that you will feast at His table and find strength, hope, insight, and encouragement.

[1] David Kinnaman and Gabe Lyons, *unChristian: What a New Generation Really Thinks about Christianity...and Why It Matters* (Grand Rapids: Baker Books, 2007) dust jacket.

Foreword

Steve Johnson is a compelling and moving voice for rescuing Christianity from the ravages of the contemporary church. The reader is not left to read between the lines. Indeed, he writes with candor and stunning clarity. His description of God's grace will be startling to many because of his refusal to allow human boundaries and an array of performance requirements and expectations, which the institutional church tries to impose, to undermine or to veil the sheer wonder and simplicity of the grace embodied by Jesus and which carries no conditions or limitations.

The Deep Reach of Amazing Grace offers a radically personal and explicit statement on the meaning of grace and the tragic distortions of the gospel within the contemporary Christian church. With both courage and grace, Steve Johnson approaches and addresses some of the most difficult and controversial issues that have plagued and often crippled the church and driven away countless believers—for example, the meaning of hell, the church's abhorrent history of failure with respect to gays and lesbians, and the tragic failure of leadership of broad segments of the established church in dismantling the evils of segregation.

Only a person who has experienced the "deep grace" that sets you free could compose such an intelligent and passionate description of the meaning of God's grace.

Dr. R. Kirby Godsey
Chancellor, Mercer University

Chapter 1

The Gospel According to Jesus

A PROSTITUTE IN ABSOLUTE DESPERATION seeks help from a counselor in Chicago. She pours out her horrible and pitiable story confessing that she rents out her two-year-old daughter to help finance her drug habit. She has no shelter, food, or money to care for herself and her daughter. She has nowhere to turn, and says there is not one person who cares if she even lives or dies. The counselor asks her if she ever thought about going to church.

> I will never forget the look of pure, naïve shock that crossed here face. "Church?!" she cried. "Why would I ever go there? I was already feeling terrible about myself. They'd just make me feel worse."[1]

For most of my ministry, I was that Christian and preacher who would have made this prostitute feel worse. Had she heard my sermons, she would have heard the evils of her lifestyle—as if she already didn't know—along with the evils of other selected sins and sinners. What she would not have heard was the message of God's unconditional love for her, and that God had already offered forgiveness for her of all her sins. Oh, sure, in a three minute "invitation" at the end of my evangelistic sermon, I would have talked about God's love and forgiveness. But how could she have heard it after a thirty-minute harangue about her evils?

The story of this prostitute begins Philip Yancey's *What's So Amazing About Grace?* The story and the book changed my life. It forced me to see how unlike Jesus I was (and still am), how unlike Jesus my preaching was. It caused me to probe for the first time the message of God's grace seen in the life, message, and ministry of Jesus of Nazareth. In the process, I experienced a Copernican revolution in my own life and in my understanding of the Christian faith. All that I now believe about God, my interpretation of the Bible, my understanding of Christian theology, the message of the New Testament, the Christian life, and the message and calling of the church revolves around the grace of God. God's grace has become the theological and functional fulcrum of my life. At the center of the universe is a God of amazing, outlandish grace.

From personal experience I understand how the church of Jesus Christ has gone from "Come to Me, all you who are weary and heavy-laden, and I will give you rest...for I am gentle and humble in heart, and you will find rest for your souls" (Matt 11:28-29), to making this prostitute feel so unwelcomed and condemned that she is stunned at the suggestion that she might find help and understanding at a church. I was part of the problem: I had never truly understood the grace of God. Many believe that the reason our culture is slipping morally is because, "the church doesn't preach on sin anymore." I disagree. The problem is that the church doesn't preach or practice grace as often as it should. Grace is the message of Jesus, and grace—as opposed to condemning people for their sins—is what offers hope and has the power to change lives. Throughout Old Testament history, the prophets condemned Israel for her sins. How did that work out? The Old Testament ends with the words, "smite the land with a curse" (Mal 4:6). The New Testament completes God's revelation to the world: "...in these last days has spoken to us in His Son..." (Heb 1:2a).

Paul's favorite metaphor for the church is "the body of Christ." As Jesus is God incarnate in this world, so the church is to be Jesus incarnate—Jesus' body—in this world. ("Incarnate" literally means "in the flesh.") The church is to be like Jesus. Sinners of notorious reputations—tax-collectors, prostitutes, those physically, morally and ceremonially unclean—experienced the warmth of God's love and acceptance from Jesus. Since the church, as the body of Christ, is to be Christ-like, why is the church today seen in such negative light? Why is the church known more for what it is against than for the love, kindness, mercy, and forgiveness Jesus taught and demonstrated His entire life? Jesus was condemned by His enemies for being "a friend of sinners." Today the church has the reputation of being an enemy of sinners. That's why the Chicago prostitute was dumbfounded at the suggestion she attend church. She had no reason to believe she would find the love, compassion, and acceptance she needed, only more scorn and condemnation.

How has this happened? What has gone wrong?

The Liability of Being the Moral Police

The contemporary church has confused its calling and mission. Standing on resurrection ground, Jesus commissioned the church, "Go into all the world and preach the gospel to all creation" (Mark 16:15). *"Preach the gospel to all creation." This is the mission of the church.* The church has abandoned this vital mission (vital: Latin, *vita*, meaning "life") to proclaim good news in order to become the moral police; defining, defending, and enforcing the public morality.

The temptation to sacrifice the gospel on the altar of public morality has always plagued the church. Its roots are in Judaism with its emphasis on strict obedience to the law with its ubiquitous "Thou shalt nots." Jesus was confronted with this same temptation in John 8. "A woman caught in adultery" is brought before Jesus. The Pharisees asked Jesus, "Now in the Law Moses commanded us to stone such women; what then do You say?" The law and public morality demanded that she be stoned to death. Only the Romans could actually carry out capital punishment, so the practical alternative was to condemn her, ostracize her from the community, and pronounce the wrath of God on her for her sin. Short of death itself, that's what the public morality and the moral police demanded.

Jesus, characteristically, was not interested in the public morality. His interest was in the woman and in the hope of transforming her heart. He refused to yield to the public pressure to condemn her. Rather, He offered her the gospel, "Neither do I condemn you; go your way. From now on sin no more." Public condemnation, humiliation, and judgment could have forced the woman to alter her behavior. Out of fear of the moral police she might never commit adultery again, but in her heart she would remain an adulteress. In such case, we could even speculate that in the future this woman would lead the charge of the moral police, quickly and passionately condemning other careless girls discovered in a similar sins, girls who went where she really wanted to go but dare not tread out of fear of again crossing the moral police. As an aside, could this be one reason so many moral police men and women are so angry and quick to condemn others with vitriol and passion: others go where they want to go, but dare not? From personal experience, I know this is so.

You may know that this story from John 8 is not included in some of the oldest manuscripts of John's Gospel (for more detail see chapter seven in this book). It is not a stretch to understand how copyists and religious leaders, concerned with the public morality, would opt to omit this story. Believing that it is their duty to uphold the public morality, a story such as this would undercut that objective. "Publically forgive an adulteress? That's too dangerous. It undermines the Law of Moses. Why, what message would that send to the young people and to every man and woman in Israel? Best leave it out." Similar sentiments abound in the church today when we talk about forgiving sin and accepting sinners. Being gracious is just too risky; it seems like we are condoning sin. Regardless of the textual questions, the story certainly resonates with the life, teachings, and ministry of Jesus.

Jesus' response to this woman is his pattern throughout the four Gospels. The Samaritan woman Jesus encountered at Jacob's well was a serial divorcee with a live-in boyfriend. "You have had five husbands, and the one whom you now have is not your husband" (John 4:18). Yet, Jesus never condemns her, cites the law, or reads her the riot act. Rather, he offers her the water that slakes the cravings of her parched and thirsty soul. When Jesus met the chief tax-collector, Zaccheus—liar, cheat, thief, traitor that he was—Jesus put aside the prevailing public morality and offered life to Zaccheus. "Zaccheus, hurry and come down, for today I must stay at your house" (Luke 19:5). Such social interaction in the culture meant acceptance and approval. Even when Jesus did cite the law to the moral policeman known as The Rich Young Ruler, His intent was to point him beyond his rigorous obedience to the law and reveal the condition of his heart: "One thing you lack..." (Mark 10:21).

Jesus consistently refused to join the hue and cry of the moral police. His most intense conflicts were with the moral police, because in stumbling over their morality, they had no interest in or love for people. What mattered to them was the law. It still does. In contrast, Jesus gave no indication that He was concerned about public morality. What mattered to Jesus was people. He loved the people and sought to change their lives from the inside out, one heart at a time.

Chapter 1

The stark contrast between Jesus and the moral police is visibly portrayed when Jesus accepts the invitation of the Pharisee, Simon, to dine with him in his house. Here is the story from Luke 7:37-50:

> [37]And there was a woman in the city who was a sinner; and when she learned that He was reclining at the table in the Pharisee's house, she brought an alabaster vial of perfume,
> [38]and standing behind Him at His feet, weeping, she began to wet His feet with her tears, and kept wiping them with the hair of her head, and kissing His feet and anointing them with the perfume.
> [39]Now when the Pharisee who had invited Him saw this, he said to himself, "If this man were a prophet He would know who and what sort of person this woman is who is touching Him, that she is a sinner."
> [40]And Jesus answered him, "Simon, I have something to say to you." And he replied, "Say it, Teacher."
> [41]"A moneylender had two debtors: one owed five hundred denarii, and the other fifty.
> [42]When they were unable to repay, he graciously forgave them both. So which of them will love him more?"
> [43]Simon answered and said, "I suppose the one whom he forgave more." And He said to him, "You have judged correctly."
> [44]Turning toward the woman, He said to Simon, "Do you see this woman? I entered your house; you gave Me no water for My feet, but she has wet My feet with her tears and wiped them with her hair.
> [45]You gave Me no kiss; but she, since the time I came in, has not ceased to kiss My feet.
> [46]You did not anoint My head with oil, but she anointed My feet with perfume.
> [47]For this reason I say to you, her sins, which are many, have been forgiven, for she loved much; but he who is forgiven little, loves little."

⁴⁸Then He said to her, "Your sins have been forgiven."

⁴⁹Those who were reclining at the table with Him began to say to themselves, "Who is this man who even forgives sins?"

⁵⁰And He said to the woman, "Your faith has saved you; go in peace."

One statement by Simon and two questions by Jesus reveal the difference between Jesus and Simon, between the gospel and the moral police. Simon's revealing statement is: "If this man were a prophet He would know who and what sort of person this woman is who is touching Him, that she is a sinner." Tradition says, and it can be assumed, since her hair was unbound, that she was a prostitute. Simon says if Jesus knew what sort of person *she* was, He wouldn't allow her touch Him. The statement, however, reveals that Simon did not know. First, he did not know what sort of person *he* was, that his spiritual life was like a "white-washed tomb," looking good on the outside but inside he was dead as bleached bones. Jesus knew both him and her. Eschewing the public morality, Jesus explains the gospel to this keeper of the law with the parable of the two debtors in verses 41-42.

Applying the parable to Simon, Jesus poses two questions. First, "Which of them will love him more?" Though reluctant to acknowledge it ("I suppose"), Simon had to give the obvious answer. He didn't suppose at all. He knew he had been trapped, but in a way that is never understood by the moral police, then or now. He knew that a prostitute's sin was greater than his. Or was it? Here is another thing Simon didn't know. He didn't know that his arrogance and self-righteousness blinded him from the deeper truth: that his sin was greater than that of the prostitute. Prostitutes weren't a barrier to the kingdom of God, but Pharisees were. Jesus would later say, "Woe to you, scribes and Pharisees, hypocrites! For *you* [not prostitutes] lock people out of the kingdom of heaven" (Matthew 23:13 NRSV). The moral police still do.

Jesus' second question was, "Do you see this woman?" Jesus didn't wait for Simon to reply; this answer, too, was obvious. No, Simon didn't see the woman. What he saw was her "sort," her type, her kind. He didn't see her because he cared nothing about her. What he cared about was the law and her violation of the public morality; a dirty prostitute was touching a prophet. Therein is the difference between Simon and Jesus, between the moral police and the gospel. Alfred Edersheim amplifies the contrast in his beautiful translation:

> You gave me no water to wash my feet, she washed not with water but tears. You gave no kiss to my cheek, she has not stopped kissing my feet. You offered no oil, she has given perfume, not for my head, but for my feet. And yet it is into your house that I came.[2]

This is why Jesus said to the moral police, "Truly I say to you that the tax collectors and prostitutes will get into the kingdom of God before you" (Matt 21:31).

The moral police care more that the public morality be maintained than they do for the lives of people they eagerly condemn. Jesus has a passion for people; the moral police have a passion for laws and rules. Jesus wants hearts to be changed; the moral police want laws to be obeyed. I cannot recall a single time Jesus condemned individual sinners. His condemnation was aimed at the moral police—the religious authorities of His day—who, like Simon, could not see the logs in their own eyes because of their obsession with the splinters in the eyes of others. Time and time again, encounter after encounter, Jesus refused to side with the demands of the public morality. Rather, He sought to change people's hearts and lives with the message of grace He came to embody. To this woman whom Simon readily condemned, Jesus said, "Your sins have been forgiven.... Your faith has saved you; go in peace" (Luke 7:48, 50). What a gospel! What good news!

What then is the gospel, the good news, the message of Jesus?

The Gospel

The Apostle Paul put it this way in Titus 2:11-14:

> [11]For the grace of God has appeared, bringing salvation to all men,
> [12]instructing us to deny ungodliness and worldly desires and to live sensibly, righteously and godly in the present age,

> ¹³looking for the blessed hope and the appearing of the glory of our great God and Savior, Christ Jesus, ¹⁴who gave Himself for us to redeem us from every lawless deed, and to purify for Himself a people for His own possession, zealous for good deeds.

The Greek word rendered here for "appeared" is also our English word for "epiphany." It means, *"a sudden manifestation of something heretofore unseen."* When the term appears in the New Testament Greek, it is referring to the dawn of a new day when the sun leaps over the horizon. So, for our use then, we can say that in Jesus there has been "a sudden manifestation of something heretofore unseen." The New Testament writers were agreed that in Jesus of Nazareth something radically new has burst forth on the horizon, and it is a whole new day. Don't miss this new sunrise that has turned midnight darkness into noonday light: "The grace of God has appeared." Literally, it reads: "Appeared ("epiphany"): the grace of God." What appeared in Jesus that had never before been realized is *that God is a God of outlandish grace.*

Yes, grace can be found in the Old Testament. The Hebrew word *"hesed"* (God's steadfast love) can be found approximately 250 times in the Old Testament and was lived out by the prophet Hosea. But its impact had been missed. For most of the Old Testament, God seems to bless the worthy and punish the unworthy. This is how the Pharisee, Saul of Tarsus, had been trained: the hope of Judaism was in strict obedience to the Law of Moses. God would come to those who earned His favor through obedience. Yet in Jesus of Nazareth, Saul encountered One who didn't wait for people to become worthy through obedience—Jesus' entire ministry was with the disobedient and unworthy. Now this same resurrected Jesus appears to Saul who was zealous to destroy the name of Jesus and His followers. "Why are you persecuting me?" (Note that he did not say "the church," but *"me."*) Jesus comes to Saul, but not in judgment and condemnation as if to kill Saul as he was trying to kill the church. Rather, Jesus comes in love and forgiveness, compassion and understanding. So dazzling is this revelation that it knocks Saul off his horse and blinds him for three days. Having encountered Jesus, Saul the moral policeman comes to regard himself as the foremost of sinners (see 1 Tim 1:15). Indeed, Paul the Apostle writes, "For the grace of God has appeared, bringing salvation to all men" (Titus 2:11).

Not what Paul instructs in Titus 2:12, "to deny ungodliness and worldly desires and to live sensibly, righteously and godly in the present age." It is not the demand for obedience to the law as the moral police believe. Demanding that the law be kept is not the way vices are overcome and virtues are ensconced. Twenty-five hundred years of Old Testament history and "thou shalt nots" are enough proof. Jesus knew the answer and He embodied it. Paul experienced the answer and proclaims it. *The grace of God*—not the demands for morality—is what instructs us to "deny ungodliness and worldly desires and to live sensibly, righteously and godly in the present age." Amazing, this grace!

All too often, this is not what the church believes or teaches, not practically anyway. Too often the message today is a demand for keeping the law rendered with threats of judgment and punishment, both temporal and eternal. The intent is to force us to walk the straight and narrow. This is what passes for the Christian faith today. It is true that the demands of the law can be more expedient than grace. Threats of judgment and the fear of punishment can make us clean up our act, for a while anyway. The problem, however, is that it leaves the heart and life unchanged. Jesus wants to transform hearts by filling them with love. He knows that love, not the demand of the law, is what produces the fruits of righteousness. He knew that in time behavior always follows the heart.

What do you get when you squeeze a lemon? If your answer is lemon juice, you might be wrong. What if I had extracted the lemon juice and filled the lemon with vinegar? When the lemon is squeezed, vinegar would then pour out. My point here is that whatever is on the inside ultimately will come out. What comes out of you *when you get squeezed?* Resentment? Anger? Vengeance? Whatever comes out, reveals what is on the inside. The only way the love of God can come out of us when we get squeezed is for the love of God to be inside of us. And the only way God's love gets inside of us is for God to fill our hearts with His love day by day. It is by experiencing His love daily that love comes out when we are squeezed. This is what instructs us to "live sensibly, righteously, and godly in the present age."

There is an irony in grace: the grace of God achieves what the moral police demand; yet the demands of the moral police can never achieve the inner transformation of the heart required for true righteousness. Ironically, through the grace of God the external objectives of the moral police can ultimately be achieved. The law commands, the moral police demand, but only the gospel empowers us to obey. Martin Luther writes:

> The promises of God give what the commandments of God demand and fulfill what the law prescribes so that all things may be God's alone, both the commandments and the fulfilling of the commandments. He alone commands, He alone fulfills.[3]

This is the effect of grace.

The Grace of God

Years ago a conference on comparative religions occurred at Oxford University. One topic was the similarities and dissimilarities between Christianity and the other religions of the world. After some debate, C.S. Lewis entered the room and was asked, "Jack, is there anything unique in the Christian faith?" Lewis answered immediately, "Oh, yes. Grace."[4]

In Old Testament Judaism, God's grace (*hesed*) is overshadowed by the demand to keep the Commandments, the Law of Moses. In Islam, Allah can be merciful and is often called "Allah the merciful," but the God of Islam is not a God of grace. The Koran says, "Allah *loves not* the prodigal." Mercy and grace are different. Mercy says, "I'll give you another chance to get it right." Grace says, "I'll love you even if you never get it right." *Standing alone in the history of world religions is the grace of God.*

Grace is the defining, definitive, distinctive truth of Jesus' ministry and of the Christian faith. Grace should be the message of the Christian church. The church, however, gives little indication that it understands grace.

The secular culture has so co-opted the word "grace" that it has lost its meaning. Sportscasters speak of a star athlete "moving with such grace." Moves with such grace? Grace then means agile, coordinated, and able to slam-dunk a basketball or run a race without waste of motion. A good hostess is called "a gracious hostess." Now grace means charming, delightful, knowing how to throw great parties with tasty hors d'oeuvres. High clergy in certain ecclesiastical traditions and royalty in many monarchies bear the title "Your Grace." So grace now means wearing ermine

Chapter 1

robes and looking pious, or wearing jeweled crowns and acting "high falutin'." It's no wonder the New Testament term "grace" falls on deaf ears.

Grace is understood little better in the church. Many of us have the sense that the definition of graces places it somewhere between being nice and acting religious. Jesus was nice; we should be nice. Jesus did good things; we should do good things. Many learned the GRACE acrostic as children in Sunday school: Gods Riches At Christ's Expense. This, we were told, meant that Jesus died on the cross for us. We were taught that grace means "God's unmerited favor," but it was rarely explained or comprehended.

Actually, to children attending Sunday school and church, we often portray God as a bit schizophrenic. In Sunday school we have pictures on the walls and in our study materials of a kind, nice, and smiling Jesus holding some of the children gathered around Him, or of Jesus carrying and leading the little lambs. These sorts of images make you want to snuggle up to Jesus. However, somewhere between Sunday school and church, someone must make God mad as hell. By the time we get to church God is as mad as fire and holds us over the abyss into which He is ready, even anxious, to drop us because of our sins. How does one snuggle up to that kind of God? Grace gets lost in the fear of the fire. For many today, childhood impressions of God remain adult formations of God. Until, through emotional exhaustion and spiritual frustration, many give up ever hoping to please God. They abandon the church, the Christian faith, and sometimes God altogether.

Aldous Huxley wrote in *The Perennial Philosophy* that familiarity with Scripture can lead to "a reverential insensibility, a stupor of the spirit, an inward deafness to the meaning of the sacred words."[5] The church has become so familiar with the word "grace" that our senses have been dulled to the significance of this magnificent word. We have a "reverential insensibility" to grace. Insensibility means a lack of feeling or perception. We hear the term "grace" but there is no feeling associated with it. There is a "stupor of the spirit" regarding grace. Our spirits, hearts and minds are no longer stirred over grace. We have developed an "inward deafness" to its meaning.

Allow me to provide a working definition of grace with some practical applications. Both definition and application are biblically sound and theologically defensible. For me, grace has come to mean three things:

1. God loves you unconditionally.

2. God has already forgiven you of every sin you have ever or will ever commit.

3. God accepts you just as you are.

What does it mean to be loved unconditionally? It means no matter what you have done, said, or thought in the past, present, or future, God loves you. This grace is for you; it is for all humanity. You are held by "the furious love of God"[6] that will never let you go. Unconditional love means that God's love for you is not determined by your behavior. No matter what, even if you never get it right, God always loves you. No exceptions. No exclusions. This is grace.

Grace means that we are forgiven of every sin we have ever or will ever commit. The good news is that God resolved all His issues with us and our sin long before we ever sinned, long before we were ever born. "He chose us in Him before the foundation of the world" (Eph 1:4). There are those who want to restrict the chosen to the church, but nowhere in Scripture are we told that Jesus died for the church. What Scripture does say is, "He Himself is the propitiation for our sins; and not for ours only, but also for those of the whole world (1 John 2:2). God forgives because of who He is, not because we jump through religious hoops. We don't repent in order to be forgiven, we repent because we already are forgiven. Through faith and repentance we experience the forgiveness that has been there all along. But it's important to be careful: faith is not something we do to achieve salvation.

Consider the following example. My house is falling down for lack of repair. Boards are rotted and need replacing. It needs a new roof, windows, and screens, not to mention a complete paint job. In working on my house, I fall off a ladder, break my back, and can no longer do the work. A group of my friends gets together and completely repairs the entire house. They replaced rotted wood, install new windows and screens, put on a new roof, and finish with a fresh coat of paint. The house is like new. They take pictures of the house, come to the hospital, and show me the pictures of all the work they have done. I have one of two choices: I can either look at the evidence and believe that my house is fixed and just relax and enjoy it knowing all is well with my house, or I can doubt the evidence and continue to fret and worry about my house.

My point is this: either way, believe it or not, the house is fixed and I did nothing to fix it.

This is how grace and faith work. Because of God's grace we are forgiven. He forgave us long before you we ever born. He has forgiven us whether we believe it or not. When we choose to believe it we enter into the peace that comes by knowing we are forgiven. We enjoy the forgiveness of God that has been there since before the creation of the world. Faith is not a work on our part that wins us forgiveness or salvation. The faith enables us to enter into the joy of the salvation that has been there all along. This is grace.

Grace means that God accepts you just as you are, no matter where that is: spiritually, ethically, morally, mentally, emotionally, or physically. Evangelicals in the South have enjoyed singing about it for decades:

Just As I Am
Just as I am, without one plea,
But that Thy blood was shed for me,
And that Thou bidd'st me come to Thee,
O, Lamb of God, I come! I come![7]

How do we come? We come just as we are, without one claim of worth or righteousness. We don't have to clean up our act before God accepts us; He accepts us just as we are. We don't have to obey the law before God accepts us; He accepts us disobedience and all. We don't have to become moral, stop sinning, and live righteously before He accepts us. He accepts us in our immorality, sin, and unrighteousness. Wherever we are, God accepts us. He accepts murderers as they murder, rapists as they rape, adulterers in the act of adultery, thieves as they steal. He accepts the lying politician, the scheming extortionist, and yes, He accepts the radical terrorist in their acts of terror.

One of the many things that makes the "good news" so good is that it works right here in the midst of the bad news. The good news works amid the muck, misery, and mess of our lives. To paraphrase Episcopal priest, Robert Farrar Capon: God loves the murderer at the moment he plunges the knife in the victim's chest, and He loves the victim as the knife punctures her heart.[8] All of this is hard to accept, of course. It's even repugnant. Offensive! Staggering! Unbelievable! Not your everyday religion! This can't be right, can it? It sure doesn't sound right! It isn't what we've always heard. It sounds unjust, immoral, unfair, un-American, even ungodly.

Yes, it is difficult to believe. No, it doesn't sound right. This is certainly not what we've always heard and not what I always preached. Yet, this is what makes Jesus unique and His grace so amazing. Every pagan god of antiquity promised to bless their supplicants if they would obey and sacrifice to them: rain for the crops, healthy children, old age for parents. If, however, the supplicants didn't obey and sacrifice, the gods would curse them: drought, famine, plagues, sick children, and early death for parents. Is this who Jesus is, who our God is? Does our God bless the worthy who obey Him and keep His law and send judgment, wrath, and punishment to the unworthy who disobey Him? If so, *Jesus is no different from the other pagan gods of antiquity.* But this is not who Jesus is! Jesus "explained" (see John 1:18) that God is a God of grace: loving, forgiving, and blessing us regardless of merit. God loves, forgives, and accepts us not because of what we do, but because of who He is. This is grace.

If you think such an explanation of grace is radical, just wait until you see the forthcoming application.

Practical Applications of the Grace of God

At the heart of the universe is a God of outlandish grace. Of the many applications of radical, New Testament grace, I mention ten. A Scripture passage accompanies each claim along with brief comments where necessary.

> 1. There is nothing you can do to make God love you more. There is nothing you can do to make God love you less. God's love for you is not based on your performance. It is based in His character (see 1 John 4:16-17).
>
> 2. God is not angry with us. If the term "propitiation" indicates God's anger as many theologians believe, Jesus resolved that anger (see 1 John 2:2). Also, both Ephesians 2:4-5 and Romans 5 say that God loved us while we were sinners, even His enemy.

3. God does not count our sins against us. Colossians 2:13-14 says God has erased all our sins, obliterated them, carried them away, nailing them to the cross. They are gone as far as east is from west (note Ps 103:10-12).

4. True followers of Christ will never be condemned. "Therefore there is now no condemnation for those who are in Christ Jesus" (Rom 8:1).

5. The Christian faith is not about getting our act together or living a sinless life. It's about trusting in God's love, forgiveness, and grace even when we don't have our act together. Jesus said that God is like the father of the prodigal son (see Luke 15).

6. We don't have to run on a religious treadmill to earn God's favor. His favor is ours already by faith (see Titus 3:5-7).

7. The gospel is about all that God has done for you. Religion is about all you need to do for God (see Gal 3:1-3).

8. Jesus didn't come into this world to judge sinners (see John 5:17).

9. Jesus didn't come to make us nonsinners. (If He did, He failed miserably.) He came to tell us that we are forgiven sinners (see Eph 2:1-9).

10. God doesn't abandon us when we sin. From the Garden of Eden to the manger of Bethlehem, God is always coming to fallen sinners (see Gen 3:8-9; Luke 2; Mark 2:17).

This is grace!

A king falls in love with a woman and decides to marry her. There is, however, a problem: the woman is a prostitute. Despite this, the king is determined in his resolve to marry her. So, over the objections of most and the consternation of many, the king takes the prostitute as his wife. Though a prostitute, the moment he marries her, she becomes the queen. According to the protocol of court, she is accorded all the honors and privileges of a queen, and all that the king has is now hers. Correspondingly, all that she had is now his.

This story is the gospel. The king is Jesus and we are the prostitute. Jesus, the bridegroom-king has made us the bride and queen. Though we come to the altar as a prostitute, the moment we say "I do," something happens. By the marriage vow the prostitute is made pure: "having cleansed her by the washing of water with the word, that He might present (her)...in all her glory, having no spot or wrinkle or any such thing; but that she would be holy and blameless" (Eph 5:26-27). This is how God sees us. This is who we are. (I cover this in more detail later in chapter eleven.) All that is His—love, forgiveness, mercy, goodness, kindness, righteousness, honor, prestige, respect, and the wealth of the kingdom—is now ours. All that was ours—sin, sins, guilt, condemnation, judgment, wrath—is now His.

This analogy was a favorite of Martin Luther. In describing the power of the gospel and radical reach of the grace of God, he writes:

> Here this rich and divine bridegroom Christ marries this poor, wicked harlot, redeems her from all her evil, and adorns her with all His goodness. Her sins cannot now destroy her, since they are laid upon Christ and swallowed up by Him. And she has all that righteousness in Christ, her husband, of which she may boast as of her own and which she can confidently display alongside her sins in the face of death and hell and say, "If I have sinned, yet my Christ, in whom I believe, has not sinned, and all His is mine and all mine is His," as the bride in the Song of Solomon 2:16 says, "My beloved is mine and I am his."[9]

This is the wonder of the grace of God: the prostitute has become the queen. "My Beloved is mine, and I am His." This is the gospel according to Jesus.

[1] Philip Yancey, *What's So Amazing About Grace?*, (Grand Rapids: Zondervan, 1997) 11.

[2] Alfred Edersheim, *The Life and Times of Jesus the Messiah*, vol. 1 (Grand Rapids: William B. Eerdmans Publishing Company, 1969) 586.

³Martin Luther, *Three Treatises: An Open Letter to the Christian Nobility; the Babylonian Captivity of the Church; the Freedom of a Christian* (Philadelphia: The Fortress Press, 1960) 283.

⁴Scott Hoezee, *The Riddle of Grace: Applying Grace to the Christian Life* (Grand Rapids: William B. Eerdmans Publishing Company, 1996) 42.

⁵Aldous Huxley, *The Perennial Philosophy: An Interpretation of the Great Mystics, East and West* (NY: HarperCollins Perennial Modern Classics, 2009) 4.

⁶Brennan Manning, *The Ragamuffin Gospel: Embracing the Unconditional Love of God* (Sisters, OR: Multnomah Books, 1990) 18.

⁷Charlotte Elliot, "Just As I Am" (1840).

⁸Robert Farrar Capon, *The Mystery of Christ and Why We Don't Get It* (Grand Rapids: William B. Eerdmans Publishing Company, 1993) 66.

⁹Martin Luther, *Three Treatises*, 287.

Chapter 2

Sola Gratia! Sola Fide! Solus Christus!

MY AUNT ELIZABETH was the most godly person I've ever known. She consistently embodied the love, forgiveness, acceptance, kindness, goodness, and gentleness of Jesus. She was an outstanding, self-taught student of the Bible, which she studied daily in part to teach her Sunday school class. She believed in the life-changing power of prayer. When she died, her daughter, Darien, gave me her excellent library, including the complete series of *The Interpreter's Bible Commentary*. Most pages of the twelve volumes have passages underlined, with her check marks and notes written in the margins. All of her books were similarly marked-up. She read, studied, and could quote the theologians: Augustine, Luther, Calvin, and Wesley. She was a well-read Methodist laywoman and public speaker. "Aunt Lyba" was a wonderful example of what it means to follow Jesus every day.

Aunt Lyba was a theological liberal. At least she was far more liberal than I am. Given that terms like "liberal" or "conservative" are relative, here are a few examples; you decide. She believed Jesus was the Son of God, but she didn't believe in the virgin birth. She didn't believe in a devil and demons. She said there was enough meanness in the human heart that there was no need for a devil. (After pastoring for several years, there were many times I was inclined to agree.) She thought the first eleven chapters of Genesis were stories containing profound truth but not historical accounts of actual events. She believed that the Bible contained errors, that God never told Abraham to sacrifice Isaac, or commanded the slaughter of men, women, and children in the Old Testament. She loved the Old Testament book of Jonah and knew what Jesus would later say about the prophet to Nineveh, but she did not believe he was swallowed by a big fish, lived in its belly for three days, after which he was disgustingly deposited on dry land. She believed in the resurrection, though I'm not sure her belief included a physical, bodily resurrection. She did believe in the second coming, though I'm not sure in what way, and absolutely did not believe in the premillennial, pre-tribulation rapture of the church, which was almost required for membership in my home church.

Though her views deeply troubled me in my earlier years, I could not deny her personal holiness, her devout and Christ-like life. Her love for people was certainly broader and deeper than my own and every other Christian I knew. I marveled at her capacity to love and accept people as they were and to forgive when she had been wronged. Aunt Lyba demonstrated that a person could be quite liberal theologically and still have a profound, practical faith, a deep love for God and people, and be a saintly follower of Jesus. Having been raised to sincerely believe that anyone who disagreed with my church's conservative, fundamentalist doctrine was certainly wrong and probably lost and hell-bound, Aunt Lyba was both an incongruity and a conundrum to her nephew, a young seminary student and preacher.

Unbeknown to Aunt Lyba and to me, she had sown into my formative theological mind the seeds of a Christian faith and an intimate walk with God that were neither dependent on nor cultivated by an orthodox Christian doctrine. It would, however, take years for those seeds to germinate. Can people like Aunt Lyba be "saved," love God, and have the fruit of the Holy Spirit embedded in and flowing from their lives and yet reject the orthodox doctrines of the church? Aunt Lyba was living proof that we can. Can people be orthodox in doctrine and yet be arrogant, hateful, mean, unforgiving, and vengeful? Many church members and some ordained to preach the gospel are proof that we can.

Being a faithful Christian is not about having an orthodox theology or following the rules of religion. Being a faithful Christian means following Jesus of Nazareth. Did you know that nowhere in the four Gospels does Jesus ever tell us to believe in a single theological principle? What He asks is that we believe in Him and the Father who sent Him. Similarly, did you know that nowhere in the New Testament did Jesus ever tell us to worship Him? Instead, what He constantly commands is that we follow Him. Twenty-one times in the Gospels, Jesus says, "follow me." The best description of what it means to follow Jesus (and the best description of Jesus' life) is given by Paul in what is known as the "fruit of the Spirit" passage found in his letter to the Galatians (5:22-23). "The fruit of the Spirit is love, joy, peace, patience, kindness, goodness, faithfulness, gentleness, self-control." That beautifully describes the life of Jesus, and what it means to live a Christian life. How different would your home, neighborhood, community, and church be if everyone who worshipped Jesus on Sunday followed Jesus on Monday and every other day, living out the fruit of the Spirit? What difference would it make in your own life? What matters most is following Jesus.

Today Christianity is often defined by two things: (1) what a person believes (theology) and (2) how a person behaves (ethics). If you have the right beliefs—accept the orthodox theology of the church—and the right behavior—behave according to established ethics—you must be a Christian. Neither theology nor ethics, however, are good barometers of a person's relationship with God or the measure of their spiritual life. According to the orthodox theology of the church, Aunt Lyba didn't believe right, yet she lived right: she followed Jesus. The Pharisees of Jesus' day were quintessential legalists who believed right (according to their theology) and lived right. Yet the Son of God was standing in front of them and they failed to recognize Him. In fact, they thought they were doing right when they had Him crucified. Here's the heart of the matter: we are saved neither by believing right or by behaving right. *We are saved altogether by faith in the sheer grace of God.*

Many believe that a Christian is someone who keeps the Ten Commandments, the Golden Rule, and is a good family member, neighbor, citizen, and attends church regularly. Christians don't (and here the prohibitions vary widely) drink alcoholic beverages, gamble, curse, tell dirty jokes, look at pornography, dance, play cards, pierce various body parts (ear lobes accepted), or violate any of the "thou shalt nots" in the aforementioned Ten Commandments. Oh, and women don't cut their hair or wear cosmetics. Such beliefs are greatly enhanced Sunday after Sunday by the ordained clergy who demand that we do what is right and refrain from what is wrong. Surely this is what makes a Christian! Too many preachers harp on all the things we need to do or not do for God while too few proclaim all that God has done for us. The dos and don'ts easily win out. The good news of the Gospel gets lost.

It is understandable, then, that many Christians sitting in the pew conclude that *what we do* is what makes us Christians. What's more, it then follows that it is our obedience or disobedience, keeping or not keeping the laws of God, that determines our relationship with God. If we do the do's and avoid the don'ts, we are walking close to God; if we don't do the do's and do the don'ts, we are in a spiritual wilderness and God is far away from us. You may have heard this very belief expressed in a different context when, following a misfortune or tragedy, someone says, "What *did I do to deserve* that? I go to church, pray, read the Bible, and am a good person. Why did God let this happen to me?" Millions of Christians sincerely believe that their relationship with God is based on what they do and what they deserve. After all, this is the American way: in a performance-driven society, we get what we deserve, even from God.

In passionate reaction against the meritorious, performance Christianity of the Medieval Catholic Church, the Reformers (Martin Luther, John Calvin, John Knox, Ulrich Zwingli, et al.) went to great lengths to say that we are not saved either by an orthodox belief system (our theology) or by our religious performance (baptism, confession, penance, communion, obedience to the law, etc.). Rather, they emphasized, we are saved by the grace of God. Our relationship with God is all of grace. The well-worn phrase of the Protestant Reformation taken from Pauline theology is: "justification by grace alone through faith alone." More recent translations of Paul's letters translate the term "justification" as "righteousness." For example, Romans 1:16-17 says,

> For I am not ashamed of the gospel, for it is the power of God for salvation to everyone who believes, to the Jew first and also to the Greek. For in it *the righteousness* of God is revealed from faith to faith; as it is written, "But *the righteous* man shall live by faith."

Salvation/justification/righteousness is the gift of God that becomes ours by grace through faith, not by an orthodox theology or by religious performance.

No better understanding of the contrast between a salvation or a righteousness that we seek to achieve on our own (either by good beliefs and/or good behavior), and the salvation or righteousness that is God's free gift to us, can be found than the overwhelming struggle Martin

Luther experienced during his own efforts to be a righteous man before a holy God. Here are Luther's own words:

> I greatly longed to understand Paul's Epistle to the Romans and nothing stood in the way but that one expression, 'the justice of God,' because I took it to mean that justice whereby God is just and deals justly in punishing the unjust. My situation was that, although an impeccable monk, I stood before God as a sinner troubled in conscience, and I had no confidence that my merit would assuage him. Therefore I did not love a just and angry God, but rather hated and murmured against him. Yet I clung to the dear Paul and had a great yearning to know what he meant.
>
> Night and day I pondered until I saw the connection between the justice of God and the statement that "the just shall live by his faith." Then I grasped that the justice of God is that righteousness by which through grace and sheer mercy God justifies us through faith. Thereupon I felt myself to be reborn and to have gone through open doors into paradise. The whole of Scripture took on a new meaning, and whereas before the "justice of God" had filled me with hate, now it became to me inexpressibly sweet in greater love. This passage of Paul became to me a gate to heaven....
>
> If you have a true faith that Christ is your Savior, then at once you have a gracious God, for faith leads you in and opens up God's heart and will, that you should see pure grace and overflowing love. This it is to behold God in faith that you should look upon his fatherly, friendly heart, in which there is no anger or ungraciousness. He who sees God as angry does not see him rightly but looks only on a curtain, as if a dark cloud has been drawn across his face.[1]

When Luther came to see that we are justified, made right with God, by grace through faith, he was "reborn," the Protestant Reformation was on, and the history of the world turned a corner. Justification by grace through faith is the teaching that God loves us and forgives us because He is a God who loves and forgives. There is never anything we can do to earn it or be worthy of it. It is free to all. He loves, forgives, and accepts us just as we are because of who He is. He is not persuaded or impressed by our futile and frustrating attempts to prove our goodness and thereby earn our salvation.

In recent years, however, "the righteous shall live by faith" has come to mean having faith in the doctrines of the church. It's fine to believe the various doctrine about the nature of the Bible and revelation, the Trinity, the person and work of Jesus (who He is and what He has done, principally on the cross), the sinful nature of humanity, the way of salvation, and of course, obedience to the biblical laws and following Christian ethics. If you really are saved, so the argument goes, you will believe the teachings of the church. If you don't, you cannot be saved or you certainly cannot be in a right relationship with God. Just as the Roman Catholic Church in Luther's time had its list of things we must do for God to redeem and love us (baptism, confession, communion, penance, indulgences, etc.), so the modern Protestant church in our time has its lists (baptism, regular attendance in church, giving of your "time, talent, and tithe," and abstaining from your church's particular prohibitions). Both the Medieval Catholic Church then and the modern Protestant church now have their lists of what we must *do* to be righteous. The only difference is what appears on their respective lists.

The Reformers took great pains to distinguish justification by grace through faith from the idea that one is justified either by believing correct doctrine or by their good works. John Calvin writes in his *Institutes of the Christian Religion*:

> We do not obtain salvation either because we are prepared to embrace as true whatever the church has prescribed, or because we turn over to it the task of inquiring and knowing. But we do so when we know that God is our merciful Father, because of reconciliation effected through Christ, and that Christ has been given to us as a righteousness, sanctification, and life. By this knowledge, I say, not by submission of feelings, do we obtain entry into the Kingdom of Heaven.[2]

Chapter 2

For the Reformers, justification was grounded in God's grace, not in a belief system or ethical behavior. The faith that saves is believing—not in the doctrines of the church—but that God is the kind of God "explained" (see John 1:18) by Jesus; believing that God is a God of unconditional love, forgiveness, and acceptance, a God of profound grace. Righteousness, both our initial salvation and the ongoing relationship with God, is grounded neither in our doctrine nor in human efforts but in God's grace alone. Grace means we are *freely* forgiven.

To say that God is gracious means that His love for His children is not based on what the children deserve. A gracious God does not give us what we deserve. He does not count our sins against us, and neither does He count our good deeds for us. Justification by grace through faith means that God has forgiven our sins because of His grace, not because we perform certain acts deemed religious (confession, repentance, baptism, obedience) or bear characteristics that could mark anyone (be a good citizen, be honest, truthful, or virtuous) or avoid certain no-no's. Only when grace is understood can faith be understood. Saving faith is not believing in the doctrines of the church. Faith is trusting that God is this kind of God, the kind of God who, because of love and grace, always freely forgives. Always! *This is the faith that saves.*

For Jesus, salvation/justification/righteousness was a matter of a relationship. Jesus' most frequent term for God is not "King," "Master," "Sovereign," "Yahweh," or even "God." His favorite term for God is "Father." His relationship with God is deeply intimate and personal. The basic characteristic of the relationship is expressed in the intimate term "love." Just read Jesus' prayer in John 17. Beginning in the Garden of Eden, God has always desired an personal relationship of love with His children, sinners though they be. He still does.

Jesus gave us the best description of how God relates to His sinful children in the Parable of the Prodigal Son in Luke 15. The son asked for his inheritance early (as much as telling his father, "Drop dead!"), received it, wasted it, and then wanted to return home willing to *earn* his way back into his father's favor as a hired servant. His father saw him while he "was still a long way off his father saw him." (Whenever we leave home, God is always watching for us to return.). He ran to meet him and absolutely had no interest in his confession. Rather, catch the father's excitement. He embraced him and kissed him. He told the servants, "Quickly bring out the best robe (the father's own robe) and put it on him." He placed a ring on his finger (the signet ring of authority), and shoes on his feet (a sign of sonship; slaves didn't have shoes). Then he threw a party in his honor. Honor *him*? This profligate son? Why? The elder brother had a point: this son didn't *deserve* any honor. But the father was not interested in merits or demerits. He loved his son. His son had returned home. That was enough. "Yes, I will honor him. Why? I love him." Such is the way of grace.

One of the most captivating aspects of this revealing parable is the first word the father utters: "Quickly." Oh, how quickly God wants to extend to us His love, forgiveness, mercy, and grace to us! No reprobation. No rebuke. No probation. No lecture. No condemnation. Just pure, intense love.

What a God!

The late Roman Catholic priest, Henri Nouwen, suggests that the real prodigal is God revealed in Jesus. He, too, left His home for the far country of sin, and there spent all that He had on us. The term "prodigal" is defined as "*given to reckless extravagance and unrestrained spending.*" Not only does the parable describe the son's reckless, extravagant, and unrestrained sin, but more, the story is about the reckless, extravagant, and unrestrained love, forgiveness, mercy and grace God spends on us.

Why honor this son? Because the father wanted his son, not a servant. The Father still does. We are all prodigal sons and daughters who to varying distances have left the Father for the far country of sin. Yet God is always the prodigal God who spends all that He has to win us back; never as slaves and servants, always as children. Nouwen puts it this way:

> I am loved so much that I am left free to leave home. The blessing is there from the beginning. I have left it and keep on leaving it. But the Father is always looking for me with outstretched arms to receive me back and whisper again in my ear: "You are my beloved, on you my favor rests."[3]

Such personal relationships cannot come through demands for obedience to the law, working to achieve God's favor and our righteousness. The law compels, cajoles, and demands. It is incompatible with a love relationship. Seeking to earn that relationship by faithful service is as futile as it is frustrating. How many prayers must we pray? How long must we fast or study the Bible every day? How many verses must we memorize? After we sin, how long must we repent, and what must we do to prove the sincerity of our repentance? How much church must we attend, and how much service must be rendered before our relationship with God is restored? None of this makes possible a close intimate relationship with God as Father. Any or all of it can even hinder that relationship causing further guilt and condemnation when we fail to *do* enough.

A doing-our-duty relationship with God is cold, rigid, and stagnant. It is contrary to the intimate, personal relationship Jesus desires. Suppose on our wedding anniversary I really want to impress my wife, Connie, with how much I love her. So I buy flowers, a box of chocolates, and an expensive gift. In wanting to add a touch of romance, rather than just barging into the house, I ring the doorbell. She opens the door, and I smile widely and say, "Happy Anniversary!" and give her the beautiful flowers, candy, and gift. She smells the fragrance of the flowers, takes the box of candy and gift and responds, "Oh, Steve, how beautiful! You didn't have to do all this." And I reply, "Yeah, Honey, I did. It's my duty, and if I didn't you would make me pay for it for weeks on end and make my life miserable." Her reaction? "Steve, you are a wonderful, *dutiful* husband, and I appreciate it." No way! She would throw the flowers and gift back at me and slam the door in my face. (Not really, Connie, my wife would smile and receive the gifts, but her heart would be broken.) How would this make her feel? Loved or disgusted? I did what I did because *it was my duty*? To win her favor so she would be nice to me?

Is that love? Is that how love expresses itself: by doing our duty, by trying to con someone into being good to us? Duty is what one does when in military service. I work on my job because it is my duty. I pay my bills because it's my duty. I cut my grass and paint my house because it's my duty. But in an intimate and personal relationship, we do what we do not out of duty but because it is our delight to serve and honor the one we love, be it a spouse or God. The difference is huge. God wants us to follow Him and serve Him because we love Him, not because it is our duty or because we are seeking to curry His favor or avoid His wrath.

As a young person I memorized Psalm 1. I was told that it contained "The Marks of a Godly Man." I so wanted to be that kind of person. Yet, the verse that both puzzled and bothered me was the second, "His delight is in the law of the Lord." *Delight* in the law of the Lord?

I did the law, or at least did my best, because I wanted to be a good Christian, I wanted to be a man of God. But *delight* in it? It was a burden, a chore, a duty in which I found no delight. I wanted to stay home on Sunday nights and see Elvis, and later the Beatles, on "The Ed Sullivan Show," but nooooooooo, I had to go to church. I wanted to laugh at the locker-room jokes and have some locker-room stories of my own to tell, but nooooooooo, I was a good Christian. I did the law, but there was no delight in it. It chafed.

Many years later, when I discovered the wonder of God's grace, His law did become a delight. When it finally dawned on me that even if I didn't go to church Sunday night, and even if I did laugh at the locker-room stories, or did far worse, God's love for me would never change. God loves me unconditionally, and no matter what I do or don't do, His love for me would never waiver. That revelation set me free. Then I was able to obey Him with delight and serve Him with joy. It was no longer a duty. It was love responding to love. Grace enables us to do what the law demands but lacks the inner transforming dynamic that makes it possible. Oh, the wonder of grace!

When I discovered the meaning of God's grace, it was literally as if a light switch suddenly got flipped on. Midnight turned to noonday. The light didn't always stay on. I would revert to old ways of thinking and acting. I would still fall, and sometimes a long way. Perfection is not to be had in this life. Yet, it is grace today that holds my life and my faith together despite my failures, past, present, and future. I find Paul Tillich's words in *The Shaking of the Foundations* quite insightful:

> Grace strikes us when we are in great pain and restlessness. It strikes us when we walk through the dark valley of a meaningless and empty life.... It strikes us when, year after year, the longed-for perfection does not appear, when the old compulsions reign within us as they have for decades, when despair destroys all joy and courage. Sometimes at that moment a wave of light breaks into our darkness, and it is as though a voice were saying: 'You are accepted. You are accepted by that which is greater than you, and the name of which you do not know. Do not ask for the name now; perhaps you will find it later; do not try to do anything now; perhaps

later you will do much. Do not seek for anything, do not perform anything, do not intend anything. Simply accept the fact that you are accepted.' If that happens to us, we experience grace.[4]

"Accept the fact that you are accepted." That is New Testament faith, the faith that saves. Aside from and without knowing, understanding, or believing things like the virgin birth, the total depravity of humankind, the infallibility of Scripture, the deity of Jesus, His atoning death, bodily resurrection, and second coming, we are saved when we accept the fact that God accepts us. Without being baptized, taking communion, keeping the Ten Commandment, attending church, tithing or serving, we are saved when we accept the fact that we are accepted. Glorious, wondrous grace is this! When we grasp this reality, we begin to see that God is so much bigger than the petty god of our religious trappings. He is so much grander than a trivial, bookkeeper god keeping tally of our dos and don'ts: "making a list, checking it twice, gonna find out who's naughty and nice." Someone well said, "God created us in His own image and we returned the favor." We make God like unto ourselves: petty, grudging, insecure, vengeful, and angry. God, however, is not even remotely as we are; bargaining for petty points of orthodoxy or for spotless behavior. He is far greater in His love and grace than we can imagine.

Now, serve and obey, but not to earn what is already yours. Serve and obey because you love the One who already loves you. This is what it means to follow Jesus. This is the joy of the Christian life.

If not an orthodox theology and keeping the laws of religion, what, then, is essential for being a Christian and living the Christian life? The Reformers put it this way:

Sola Gratia. Sola Fide. Solus Christus.

"By grace alone. By faith alone. By Christ alone." Aside from the fact that there are three "alones,"—if there are three how can each be "alone?"—this emphasizes the vital (again, from the Latin, *vitalis*, meaning "life"), life-giving necessity of each.

Sola Gratia: by grace alone. Grace is essential. Without grace there is no hope for sinful humanity. Grace alone means that none of us has any claim to the slightest bit of our salvation. Salvation and living the

Christian life are all God's doing. God loves us, forgives us, accepts us, redeems us, elects us, and takes us to heaven, and not because of any achievement or merit on our part. Theologians of the Late Reform era would use the cherished and revealing phrase "unconditional election." God's election of us is not based on any condition in us, anything we have done or any perceived achievement we will ever do; it is all of God. This is the theme of both Paul's letter to the Romans and to the churches of Galatia. God in love and grace elects everyone. In *The Pilgrim's Regress*, C.S. Lewis calls God the "inveterate gambler."[5] He gambles on all of us. God creates us, loves us, forgives us, chooses (elects) us, and gambles that we will respond to love with love. Sometimes the gamble pays off, sometimes it does not. Some accept it, others do not. (See Sola Fide in the paragraph that follows.) Either way, salvation is all a matter of God's grace, because that is the kind of God He is: a God of deep and profound grace. When we get to heaven, none of us will be able to brag, "I'm here because *I*..." Rather it will be, "I am here because *He*...."

Sola Fide: by faith alone. Faith is essential. Not faith, however, in the doctrines of the Church of the Behavior of the Redeemed. Faith is believing that God accepts us just as we are, that He is the God of grace "explained" (see John 1:18) by Jesus. Without faith we never experience the blessings of salvation God has prepared for us such as love, forgiveness, acceptance, kindness, goodness, joy, peace, and other blessings. How important is faith? The only type of people in heaven are those who have been forgiven of their sins by the grace of God. The only type of people in hell are those who have been forgiven of their sins by the grace of God. What makes the difference? Those in heaven believe it, and those in hell do not. The author of Hebrews in what's commonly referred to as the "heroes of faith" chapter writes, "Without faith it is impossible to please Him, for he who comes to God must believe that He is and that He is a rewarder of those who seek Him" (Heb 11:6). God is pleased when we believe "that He is," that He is the kind of God Jesus "explained" (see John 1:18) to us. Think of that: *God is pleased with us.* (I dwell on this topic further in chapter eleven.) His pleasure is not because we keep the Ten Commandments, attend church, follow the religious rules, or believe the church dogma. He is pleased when we believe that He is the God revealed through Jesus. That is *amazing grace*!

Understand that God does not forgive us *if* we have faith. That would turn faith into a religious work that Paul so vehemently condemns in Galatians. Rather, faith in the revelation of God through Christ Jesus enables us to experience and enjoy the love, forgiveness, and acceptance of God that has been there all along. What then is our reward for having faith? Not stuff: crowns, robes, mansions, streets of gold, gates of pearl, and the like. The reward is God. *We get God!* Desiring anything other than God is idolatry. This brings us to the final "alone."

Solus Christus: by Christ alone. Christ is essential. In the pre-Reformation church there were so many add-ons that Jesus Christ was not thought to be sufficient for salvation. It was Christ plus baptism, plus confession, plus indulgencies, plus righteousness, and so on. For many in the church today—church leaders, the moral police, modern-day Pharisees—real, genuine, bona fide, "sho' nuff" (a favorite expression of Aunt Lyba) salvation is proved through religious performance: baptism, church membership, regular church attendance, serving in the church in some capacity (choir, teaching, keeping the preschool, committee work), obedience to the Ten Commandments, tithing, daily devotion including Bible study and prayer, and righteous living. These are absolute indicators of "sho' nuff" redemption. Without these "fruits of repentance," it is concluded that one is not saved. Like the church prior to 1517, Christ alone is no longer enough.

We can hear the echo of the Reformers still shouting at us, "No! No! No! Salvation is *solus Christus*, by Christ alone." God has worked in Jesus Christ to reveal His heart to us, and what is revealed is that God is a God of amazing, outlandish, unbelievable grace. Through Him, and Him alone, is revealed the wonder of a God who loves, forgives, and accepts us without conditions. Remember the brief explanation of Titus 2:11-14 from chapter one of this book? "For the grace of God has appeared...." Epiphany! "In Jesus there has been 'a sudden manifestation of something heretofore unseen.'" In Jesus, we see the heart of God in wondrous grace as it had never been seen before. Without the revelation of God seen in Jesus, we might have gone on thinking that God was angry, vengeful, threatening, judging, and condemning. What Jesus reveals is that, above all else, God is a God of grace: unconditional love, forgiveness, and acceptance. Will there be a judgment? Yes. The Bible and Jesus speak often of it. Judgment, however, will be quite different from what we often imagine. We will reflect more on judgment in chapter five, "Hell In The Fire."

When I first began preaching, I heard what I thought was a great illustration of salvation. "When you invite Jesus into your heart and ask Him to save you, He wipes the slate clean. The past is forgiven, gone, forgotten." Then I thought of a way to sharpen up the illustration. "When you get saved, God throws away the old slate with its residue of erased smudges of all your past sins and He gives you an entirely new slate. The old record is forgiven and forgotten. You start all over again." Later, the depths of God's grace finally dawned on me: *God does not have slates, because God doesn't keep score.* He is not making lists or recording accounts. He is forgiving, always forgiving. Understand this: God is not a bookkeeper; He is a lover. He does not keep a running tally of our sins and failures. He does not He keep a record of our good works. He does not reward or judge us by our religious performance. If that were the criteria for salvation or hope, there would be neither. But performance is not the criteria. The sole criteria for salvation is *faith* in God, that He is, in truth, the God of *grace* as revealed in *Christ Jesus: Sola Gratia, Sola Fide, Solus Christus.* This alone gives us hope. Nothing else.

[1]Roland H. Bainton, *Here I Stand: A Life of Martin Luther.* (NY: Penguin Books, 1977) 49.
[2]John Calvin, *Institutes of the Christian Religion,* vol. 2, ed. John T. McNeill, trans. Ford Lewis Battles (Philadelphia: Westminster Press, 1960) 545.
[3]Henri J. Nouwen, *The Return of the Prodigal Son: A Story of Homecoming* (NY: Doubleday, 1992) 44.
[4]Paul Tillich, *The Shaking of the Foundations* (Eugene, OR: Wipf and Stock, 2012) 163.
[5]C.S. Lewis, *The Pilgrim's Regress: An Allegorical Apology for Christianity, Reason and Romanticism* (Grand Rapids: William B. Eerdmans Publishing Company, 1992) 180.

Chapter 3

Why Did Jesus Die?

Well, this train carries saints and sinners
This train carries losers and winners
This train carries whores and gamblers
This train carries lost souls

I said, this train, dreams will not be thwarted
This train, faith will be rewarded
This train, hear the steel wheels singing
This train, bells of freedom ringing

I said, this train carries broken-hearted
This train, thieves and sweet souls departed
This train carries fools and kings thrown
This train, all aboard

You don't need no ticket
You just get on board
You just thank the Lord

("Land of Hope and Dreams," Bruce Springsteen)[1]

As a young pastor I vividly remember Newman McLarry coming from Oklahoma to preach a revival in my church. I had experienced

Newman's powerful and effective preaching at our state's evangelism conference. At twenty-one years old, Newman had been the youngest soldier ever to receive a battlefield commission to the rank of captain in the army of General George S. Patton in the European theater during World War II. He received the commission, he said, because every other officer in his unit had been killed. Newman was ordered to lead a nighttime reconnaissance mission behind enemy lines. Because of the danger of such missions, regulations required that a personnel rotation be followed. One particular soldier, a young family man (like thousands of others), was scheduled to be relieved of duty in a couple of days and taken off the front lines for much needed R & R. Sergeant Beck found Captain McLarry and asked if this soldier could be excused from the rotation and another sent in his place. Following orders Captain McLarry refused, and said the soldier had to take his place in the rotation. Sergeant Beck persisted, finally telling Captain McLarry that he would take the soldiers place in the rotation. Newman relented, and Sergeant Beck went in place of that soldier.

The reconnaissance team was discovered and came under withering fire. They did the best they could to carry out the mission and make it back to the American lines. Once back to relative safety, Newman began the roll call of the soldiers on the mission. "Kelly." "Here, Sir." "Swartz." "Here, Sir." "Dąbrowski." "Here, Sir." Etc. "Beck." "BECK!" "SERGEANT BECK?" "He didn't make it, Sir. He was killed." Newman had prided himself in protecting his men, especially on the dangerous reconnaissance missions. Flushed with both anguish and fury, he ran through the bivouac area until he found the solder whom Sergeant Beck had replaced. Newman told us that he wrestled the soldier to the ground, and began shouting in his face, "He died in your place. He died in your place. He died in your place."

The soldier-turned-evangelist then explained in an unforgettable way that this is exactly what Jesus had done for us. "Like Sergeant Beck," Newman preached, "Jesus died in your place. Because Jesus died in your place and paid the penalty for your sins, you can have life everlasting." It was a gripping story, and decades later I still remember it. That evening had a deep and lasting impact on my understanding of Jesus and the cross.

This is the foremost understanding of the death of Jesus: He died in our place.

Chapter 3

The title of this chapter is not unlike many others penned by numerous authors. Christianity's prevailing tradition teaches that Jesus died on the cross for us. As a result, we can be forgiven, saved, and know the promise and hope of everlasting life in heaven. In the academic discipline of theology, this concept is referred to as the atonement. Despite human sin, through the cross of Jesus, sinful humankind can once again be "at-one-ment" with holy God. Since the earliest days of Christianity, the nature of the atonement has been a major topic of debate. While contemporary scholars consider the entire life and ministry of Jesus as the basis for atonement, the purpose of this chapter is to look again at the death of Jesus, and answer the much debated question, "Why did Jesus die?"

Three Theories of Atonement

Explanations of exactly how and why the death of Jesus makes it possible for God to forgive and save us are called "theories of the atonement." Historically, three theories have dominated Christian theology: the ransom theory, the satisfaction theory, and the substitution theory, or more precisely the penal substitution theory. All three theories are intricately more complicated and detailed than this abridged description, and hundreds of volumes have been written (and many more sermons have been preached) attempting to explain the rationale for each view. What follows is a very brief synopsis of three theories of atonement.

First, Jesus said He came "to give His life a ransom for many" (Mark 10:45). Because of our sins, we are held for ransom. Who or what holds us for ransom is never stated. Some early theologians unfortunately said we were held ransom by the devil, and the price was paid to him. Whoever or whatever holds us ransom, if we are to be saved, the ransom price must be paid. The ransom theory of atonement says that Jesus' death on the cross is the ransom price which redeems us and enables God to save us.

Second, our sins have offended God's honor, and His anger has been kindled. God's honor has to be satisfied and His anger has to be "propitiated." John writes, "He Himself is the propitiation for our sins; and not for ours only, but also for those of the whole world" (1 John 2:2). The word propitiation means the removal of a deity's wrath by means of a sacrifice. On the cross Jesus was the sacrifice Who restores the honor of God and absorbs the anger of God, thus enabling God to forgive and

35

save us. This is known as the satisfaction theory of atonement because Jesus' death for our sins satisfies both the honor and anger of God.

Third, the Apostle Paul wrote, "The wages of sin is death" (Romans 6:23). The penal substitution theory of atonement claims that on the cross Jesus died in our place, paying the penalty of death for us. Because Jesus is our substitute in death (as exemplified in Newman McLarry's WWII account), we can be forgiven and have life everlasting. Given that Jesus is God incarnate (that is, God in human flesh), not only did God demand the penalty, what's more, in the incarnate Jesus, God Himself paid the penalty He demanded. What a dramatic picture of both incarnation and atonement! It's a concept that has intrigued the minds and tugged at the hearts of millions throughout the history of the church!

The church fathers wisely called these attempts to understand the cross "*theories*" of the atonement because they understood that the Biblical writers never explained exactly what did happen while Jesus was on the cross. Perhaps they realized something inexplicable had occurred. Still, in an effort to explain the cross and clarify our understanding, these theories have been meticulously developed through the centuries.

Are these theories what Paul, John, Peter, and a host of others had in mind when they wrote about the death of Jesus? To be perfectly honest, this chapter troubles me greatly. As I wrote, rewrote, edited, and reviewed it all many times, it troubled me. It's unsettling not because I question the validity of what I've written, but because it goes against what I have been taught and what I have believed for most of my Christian life. It runs against what I have preached for most of my ministry, and against the traditional teachings of the church to which I am committed and which I love dearly. Yet, I am convinced that this is the truth of who God is, who Jesus is, and what the cross reveals. This chapter has a message of profound understanding for us today. So, even though the message of this chapter goes against what you may have been taught and believed all your life, I hope you will consider the thoughts and claims. If it troubles you, know that it troubles me, too. And after considering it, if you think I've gone over the edge, that's okay. I still think I'm right, and thanks for at least considering it. Now, allow me to step into the jaws of the lion.

Chapter 3

An Evaluation of Atonement

One common aspect of all three theories of atonement is that God is both just and moral. Thus, the argument goes, God cannot merely turn His head or wink at sin, "let bygones be bygones," and still be a just and moral God. The ransom has to be paid, God's wrath has to be assuaged, His honor has to be upheld, and the sinner has to be punished. Since the law says death is the penalty for sin, death must be the payment and punishment. The theory is that it is morally impossible for God to forgive sin without these moral necessities first being met. To do so would compromise the righteousness, justice, and morality of God Himself. The theories of atonement describe with precise reason and detailed specificity exactly why Jesus' death enables God to forgive our sins and remain just and moral.

There is, however, a critical contradiction at the very heart of the explanation. There is nothing just or moral about an innocent person being punished and the guilty going free. What is moral or just about a sinless Jesus paying the penalty for our sins while we get off scot-free? Does punishing an innocent Jesus for the sins of the human race somehow meet the moral requirements of God? *How exactly? Based on what kind of moral reasoning? This enables God to remain just and holy? In what way? How is that in any understanding of the terms moral or just?* Even with the understanding that God Himself pays the penalty He demanded in the incarnate Jesus, in what way is that either just or moral? The innocent still dies and the guilty still go free. God cannot be so callous as to claim a death penalty must be paid and that it doesn't matter who pays, someone must, even if He pays it Himself. Just and moral? How can that be? There is nothing just or moral about it. If the law must be followed and the penalty must be applied, the only way it can be done justly and morally is for the guilty to be punished. But then, we would all be in hell or bound for it.

There is a second, basic, biblical problem with sacrificial atonement. Throughout the Old Testament we find Israel's ubiquitous and meticulous sacrificial system. From the animal sacrifice of Abel, just east of Eden, to the covenant God "cut" with Abraham, through the Law and Prophets, reaching all the way into the New Testament, animal sacrifice was a dominant part of religious practice. As prominent as sacrifices were in Israel, however, human sacrifice was strictly forbidden by the Mosaic law on pain of death (see Deut 12:31). The prophets called it "an abomination." At the spiritual nadir of the Southern Kingdom, "the people" went to pagan shrines "to burn their sons and daughters in the fire" in the valley of Hinnom (see Jer 7:30-32). The association of the valley of Hinnom with child sacrifice had made the valley so despicable and reprehensible, that by Jesus' time it had been turned into the garbage dump for the city. This is the valley to which Jesus referred as "the fiery hell." (I discuss this further in chapter four, "Hell In The Fire"). Jeremiah and Ezekiel condemned human sacrifice in the strongest language (see Jer 32:35ff and Ezek 16:20-21). Does God now, in the New Testament—under a *new covenant* no less—demand human sacrifice, the sacrifice of His own Son before He can forgive? Is God then guilty of the "abomination" described by the prophets? This cannot be!

Punishing an innocent person for the transgressions of another is blatantly immoral and unjust, even if it is God in Christ taking the punishment He demands. Such substitutionary death is more akin to primitive human sacrifices made to pagan gods in order to curry favor and assuage anger. In order for the guilty tribe to escape divine wrath, you better believe *someone* has to die. It really doesn't matter who (young virgins seemed preferable), but someone must die. Is this the meaning of the cross of Jesus? Is this why Jesus dies? Killing the innocent so the guilty can go free is beneath the God Jesus "explained" (see John 1:18) to us. Does this sound like the God Jesus presents to us in the four Gospels, a God of abounding and unconditional love, mercy, forgiveness, and grace? Jesus did die for us, but not to make it possible for God to forgive us and not as a ransom, a satisfaction, or as our substitute.

Understanding salvation or the Christian gospel in terms of atonement, for all practical purposes, renders the *life* of Jesus unimportant. The salvation story goes immediately from incarnation to crucifixion, from Bethlehem to Calvary, from the manger to the cross, and Jesus' life, teachings, and ministry are inconsequential. Jesus may offer us instructional ethics like the Sermon on the Mount and the Golden Rule, but His rich life between birth and death is inconsequential. One respected theologian says that reducing the gospel to atonement produces "vampire Christians, who only want a little blood for their sins but nothing more to do with Jesus until heaven."[2] While that criticism seems far too harsh, it truthfully exposes that for many little else matters than "Christ died for our sins." The life of Jesus presented in the four Gospels is far richer and more meaningful to us today than such neglect suggests. The Apostle

Paul said to the church in Rome, "For if while we were enemies we were reconciled to God through the death of His Son, *much more, having been reconciled, we shall be saved by His life*" (Rom 5:10). In neither his letters nor his living, did Paul sacrifice the life of Jesus, even for the sake of the cross.

A Fresh Look at the Death of Jesus

How then are we to understand the atonement and sacrificial language of the New Testament? The New Testament was written during a time of momentous spiritual transition. Many Jews were embracing the crucified Christ as the promised Messiah, and Gentiles were accepting Jesus as the crucified Savior. How did the New Testament writers explain to the Jews that Jesus was their Messiah, and how did they explain to the Gentiles that Jesus was their Savior? In part, it was through an appeal to the Old Testament and its sacrificial system.

> For if the blood of goats and bulls and the ashes of a heifer sprinkling those who have been defiled sanctify for the cleansing of the flesh, how much more will the blood of Christ, who through the eternal Spirit offered Himself without blemish to God, cleanse your conscience from dead works to serve the living God (Heb 9:13-14)?

Yom Kippur, (The Great Day of Atonement) is the holiest of days for Jews. Leviticus 16 describes it in detail. Atonement required two goats for a sin offering and a ram for a burnt offering. The High Priest, Aaron (and those after him), offered the ram as a burnt offering for his own sins. One goat was a sacrificial offering for the sins of the nation. The second goat was referred to as the "scapegoat." The priest placed his hands on this goat, confessing the sins of the nation and laying those sins on the goat before sending it away into the wilderness. Did the blood of goats and bulls actually sanctify and cleanse Israel? No. God did. Did God actually, mystically, supernaturally transfer the sins of the nation onto a goat and then send those sins into the wilderness on the head of a goat (see Lev 16:20-22)? No! That would be pagan superstition, not Biblical revelation.

The entire sacrificial system was a picture, a symbol, an analogy, an acted out metaphor demonstrating that God had forgiven, forgotten, and removed the sins of Israel. Their sins were "scaped" away into the wilderness, never again to be seen. The psalmist writes in Psalm 103:12, "As far as the east is from the west, so far has He removed our transgressions from us." God forgave because of His love for Israel. The sacrificial system did not enable God to forgive nor was it intended to do anything for God. It was for Israel. It reminded them and symbolized to them both the seriousness of sin (the rams and goats *were* killed), and that God had actually forgiven them of their sins (they saw the scapegoat sent away into the wilderness). The metaphor presents profound and much needed truth: God forgives, forgets, and removes our sins. He does this because this is the kind of God He is, not because animals are sacrificed or scapegoats actually carry our sins into the wilderness.

Jesus as the Jewish Messiah and Gentile Savior is presented in the same way. Following the Old Testament analogy, if God forgave sins through the blood of goats and bulls, "how much more will the blood of Christ...cleanse your conscience from dead works to serve the living God?" (Heb 9:14) Requiring the death of rams and goats in order for God to forgive sins, is symbolic. It is a picture, an acted out metaphor used to explain that our sins are forgiven. The death of Jesus is used to explain how Jesus is the Jewish Messiah ("Behold the Lamb of God who takes away the sins of the world" from John 1:29) and Christian Savior who forgives us of all our sins ("He made Him who knew no sin to be sin on our behalf, so that we might become the righteousness of God in Him" from 2 Cor 5:21). The image of the scapegoat is evident: Jesus is "made to be sin (the goat put to death) and He "takes away the sins of the world" (the scapegoat). This notion is also depicted in Colossians 2:13-14. He is the "Lamb of God" who died for our sins. The language of atonement in the New Testament—ransom, satisfaction, and substitution (like the language of sacrifice in the Old Testament of bulls, lambs, and scapegoats)—is graphic, symbolic imagery used to communicate the profound truth that the God of love and grace has forgiven all our sins.

The argument is further made that, because God is so holy ("Holy, Holy, Holy is the Lord of hosts" from Isa 6:3; see also Rev 4:3), He cannot simply forgive sin without demanding a penalty and still remain holy. Who says so? Why not? How does the innocent God forgiving the guilty sinner make the holy God less holy? If a judge forgives a criminal, does that make the judge less honorable? It does not. If we forgive an offence done to us, does that in any way corrupt us? It does not. Paul says in Ephesians 4:32 that forgiving makes us like Christ. The analogies admittedly are flawed. We ourselves and the judge are far from holy; but these examples hint at the truth. In Jesus, divine holiness, unlimited power, and infinite compassion are joined together to forgive. Because of this combined, inviolable holiness, omnipotence, and deep compassion, He can forgive sin without demanding a ransom, a satisfaction, or a penal substitution and still remain holy. This is El Shaddai—God Almighty—not your garden variety god keeping account of wrongdoings like brawling children in a street fight. "God is love," and because of this, God forgives. He forgives without theories, dogmas, and doctrine. Over the centuries these would be developed, *and they have clouded the simplicity of God's love and forgiveness.*

There is a spiritual and transcendental sense in which Jesus did die for us, a sense in which He did take our sins to Himself. Jesus is the Suffering Servant of Isaiah 53:

> ⁴Surely our griefs He Himself bore, And our sorrows He carried; Yet we ourselves esteemed Him stricken, Smitten of God, and afflicted.
> ⁵But He was pierced through for our transgressions, He was crushed for our iniquities; The chastening for our well-being fell upon Him, And by His scourging we are healed.
> ⁶All of us like sheep have gone astray, Each of us has turned to his own way; But the LORD has caused the iniquity of us all To fall on Him.

Paul in Romans alludes to the Isaiah 53 passage in describing the suffering of Jesus on our behalf (see below, Romans 5:6, 8; 8:32). In the incarnate Jesus, God bears in His own heart the grief, sorrow, suffering, and affliction of our sins. How so? When a bank forgives a debt of $5,000, the bank releases the debtor of responsibility and bears the cost of forgiving that debt. When you forgive a deep injury done to you, you choose to release the offender from their indebtedness to you, and you bear in your heart the cost and pain of that injury. In a far more profound and inexplicable sense, when God forgives us of our sin (or "debts" as in the Lord's Prayer), He releases us from the debt and bears in His heart the costs of our sin. In the terms of Isaiah, He bears our grief and carries our sorrows and afflictions. He bears the crushing, scourging, and sufferings of our sin in His heart. This is demonstrated literally and ultimately when God bears the costs and suffering of our sin in the cross of Christ. German theologian Jürgen Moltmann in *The Crucified God* expresses it well:

> When the crucified Jesus is called the 'image of the invisible God,' the meaning is that *this* is God, and God is like *this*. God is not greater than He is in this humiliation. God is not more glorious than He is in this self-surrender. God is not more powerful than He is in this helplessness. God is not more divine than He is in this humanity.[2]

God does not, however, bear the grief and sorrow *to enable* Him to love and forgive us. He bears the grief and sorrow *because* He loves and has *already* forgiven us. He does not bear the grief as our substitute; He bears the grief as our Savior. The grief and suffering on the cross is neither a ransom price, nor a satisfaction of God's honor or justice. He does not bear our sins in order to balance some scale of justice in a theological construct called "forensic justification"—legal action on God's part which, in some manner, enables Him to declare the sinful righteous. The cross and atonement are best understood not in legal terms but in personal terms. Paul did not write that "God was in Christ satisfying legal transactions." He wrote, "God was in Christ reconciling the world to Himself, not counting their trespasses against them"(2 Cor 5:19). Because of His love for us, He forgives us, and in forgiving us, He bears the cost of forgiving—even unto death. More surely than we can understand or ever explain, "our griefs He Himself bore, and our sorrows He carried" (Isa 53:4). That is what it cost God to love us. *That is what it cost God to forgive us.*

In his own efforts to understand atonement, C.S. Lewis realized that all doctrines about God are always "less true" than the truths themselves because, the doctrines...are translations into our *concepts* and *ideas* of that which God has already expressed in a language more adequate, namely the actual incarnation, crucifixion, and resurrection.[4]

In trying to clarify the inexplicable, theories of atonement have clouded and distracted us from the very character of God that Jesus came to reveal. They are "less true" than the truth itself. The truth is: God loves, and because He loves, He forgives and redeems. This is the "good news." This is the deep reach of amazing grace.

Why Was Jesus Crucified?

Jesus' unconditional love for all people compelled Him to live and teach in such a way that, from the earliest days of His ministry, He drew the animosity of religious and political leaders alike. As the Gospel of Mark puts it, "The Pharisees went out and immediately began conspiring with the Herodians against Him, as to how they might destroy Him" (3:6). Animosity became hostility, hostility flamed into outrage, and outrage led to the pragmatic decision to "put Him to death" (Luke 22:2).

Why did they hate Jesus so? Because He loved people. Because Jesus loved people, He healed the sick on the Sabbath and that broke the Law. Because He loved people, He frequently dined with high profile sinners and that offended the moral police. In the ancient world reclining at a meal with someone was a symbol of full acceptance and friendship. Nice people aren't supposed to hang out with sinners. Jesus offered the parable of the prodigal son in response to religious leaders who grumbled, "This man receives sinners and eats with them" (Luke 15:2). His enemies condemned Him as "a friend of tax collectors and sinners" (Luke 7:34). When was the last time you, your church, or your pastor was condemned for being a friend of sinners? How much, then, are we genuinely similar to Jesus?

Jesus honored women. That violated established tradition. Women had never been held in high esteem in the ancient world; they were little more than property. He permitted "a woman...who was a sinner" to anoint Him (see Luke 7:37). He welcomed their following and ministry to Him. He conversed publicly with a half-breed Samaritan woman who was a serial divorcee with a live-in boyfriend. He told a woman caught in the act of adultery, "I do not condemn you" (John 8:11). It was in Martha's house (not Lazarus') that Jesus spent time and found respite from the rigors of ministry.

As mentioned in the first chapter of this book, Jesus befriended the despised tax collectors, spending the night with Zaccheus and calling Matthew the tax collector to be His disciple. Jesus loved the multitudes of the sick and diseased. He touched the lepers, literally the most despised and rejected people in society and metaphorically the most despised and worst of sinners. He loved them all: tax-gatherers, prostitutes, half-breed Samaritans, women, the unclean, lepers, and Gentiles. He often made lawbreakers, asocial, and immoral people the champions of His stories.

Jesus embodies the unconditional love of God for all people. Pure love. Unqualified love. Unconditional love. No agenda. No rules. No discrimination. No exceptions. No exclusions. No one is left out. He loves us all. John said in his Gospel that Jesus "explained" God to us (see John 1:18), and in his epistle—after a lifetime of contemplation and wonder—his considered explanation of God is simply: "God is love" (1 John 4:8, 16).

Because He loves people, Jesus announces to them, "Your sins are forgiven." He gives no complex theories of atonement, no explanation of how God can do such, no explanation of "forensic justification," protecting the moral nature of God, or safe-guarding the holiness of God. There is simply the profound and welcome truth: "Your sins are forgiven...go in peace." So simple. Jesus "explained" (see John 1:18) so we could see the love of God.

Because of all this, the religious establishment hated Him and made the decision to kill Him. An entire religious order was built on rules that had to be followed and laws that could not be broken. There were specified threats of judgment and warnings of wrath or punishment for those who disobeyed. Then an untutored, unlettered outsider came along. ("'Where did this man get these things, and what is this wisdom given to Him...Is not this the carpenter...?' And they took offense at Him." Mark 6:2-3) He spoke of unconditional love for the very people they were criticizing and threatening with divine condemnation and eternal damnation. It simply was not acceptable. If such teachings took hold of the people, at the least the religious leaders could lose their tactics of intimidation and manipulation, and at the most it could bring down the entire social order (their religion was profoundly entwined in the culture). The religious leaders could not permit either to happen. By no accident, John records that it was following the resurrection of Lazarus that the religious leaders concluded that, "it is expedient for you that one man die for the people, and that the whole nation not perish" (John 11:50). Because Jesus did things like give Lazarus life, the religious authorities masterminded His death. If the religion of the fathers was to stand, Jesus had to fall. Because Jesus was uncompromising in living and teaching this radical love of God, He was crucified.

Did the Father Kill His Son?

The short answer is, No. The cross is not deicide (meaning, "the killer of a god"). It is legally sanctioned homicide. Fearful and angry religious leaders and Pilate, a politically devious Roman governor, crucified Jesus. Having said that, the New Testament writers use the crucifixion to reveal God's love for all humankind.

> Romans 3:24-25. Being justified as a gift by His grace through the redemption which is in Christ Jesus; whom God displayed publicly as a propitiation in His blood through faith.
> Romans 5:6. For while we were still helpless, at the right time Christ died for the ungodly.
> Romans 5:8. But God demonstrates His own love toward us, in that while we were yet sinners, Christ died for us.
> Romans 8:32. He who did not spare His own Son, but delivered Him up for us all, how will He not also with Him freely give us all things?
> Ephesians 5:2. Walk in love, just as Christ also loved you and gave Himself up for us, an offering and a sacrifice to God as a fragrant aroma.

Either expressed or implied in all these verses is the truth that God is a God of outlandish and amazing grace who loves and forgives. The love and forgiveness is not made possible because of sacrifices on Old Testament altars or a New Testament cross. Love and grace exist because that is the kind of God He is. Paul says as much in Ephesians 1:3-4,

"Blessed be the God and Father of our Lord Jesus Christ, who has blessed us with every spiritual blessing in the heavenly places in Christ, just as *He chose us in Him before the foundation of the world*" [emphasis mine]. God blessed us and chose us before the altars of Aaron, before the cross of Christ, and eons before the creation of the world. Why? Because God loves us. Rather than compromise on unconditional love, Jesus willingly went to the cross. God is like a third grade teacher who provides us the greatest object lesson ever: the cross is the historic testimony to the eternal love God has for all humankind. The testimony is historic: it happened at a place and time identifiable with a map and a calendar. The love is eternal: the everlasting God in the incarnate Jesus, "the Alpha and the Omega...who is and who was and who is to come, the Almighty" (Rev 1:8), gave his life for love. Jesus even loved the ones crucified with Him ("Truly I say to you, today you shall be with Me in Paradise." Luke 23:43) and those crucifying Him ("Father, forgive them; for they do not know what they are doing" Luke 23:34). Though humankind crucified Him, He still loves us. What greater evidence could He give of His love for humankind than His own life?

The Cost of Loving People

Had Jesus simply not loved the unlovely (tax-collectors, prostitutes, adulteresses, thieves, the sick and diseased, the dead, and Gentiles), avoided doing the things He did because of love (dine with sinners, allow a prostitute to anoint Him, heal on the Sabbath, touch the untouchable, and raise the dead), and said the things He said because of love ("Your sins are forgiven" from Matt 9:2 and "I do not condemn you" from John 8:11), He would have been fine. Had He been another teacher or prophet like John the Baptist, laying down the law, calling people a "brood of vipers" (Matt 3:7, 12:24, 23:33; Luke 3:7), threatening them with "the wrath to come" (Matt 3:7; Luke 3:7), the religious leaders would have accepted Him, tolerated Him, or ignored Him. Either way, they would have let Him alone. But He didn't, and they didn't. He loved all without exception, and they crucified Him because of it.

Love people. That sounds innocuous enough, doesn't it? I mean, what can be bad about simply loving people? That's what we all want deep down, to be loved. Dionne Warwick had it right a long time ago: "What the world needs now is love, sweet love."[5] But now, as then, seriously loving all people can create tremendous problems and turmoil.

Love those of another race or color or ethnicity? Love liberals? Love conservatives? Love Republicans? Love Democrats? Love Catholics, Jews, Palestinians, Moslems? Love gays and lesbians? (For further discussion, see chapter nine of this book.) Love those our culture despises most: terrorists, pornographers, sex offenders, convicts, criminals? Love abortionists? They don't need to be loved, they need to be jailed, or worse. Loving such people can sound strange, even wrong and immoral to those within the church, and utterly crazy to those outside the church.

Research consistently reveals that Bible-believing, evangelical Christians are among the most ardent supporters of capital punishment, of taking the nation to war, and of anti-gay and lesbian action. Is there a disconnect here? Where is the love, forgiveness, and mercy of Jesus from those who claim most loudly to be followers of Jesus? Spend some time at the next church social or community barbeque talking about how we should love people like those I've described. Or better yet, invite some of them to the next neighborhood cookout and watch the reaction to them *and to you.* Or best of all, become friends and invite them to dinner at a restaurant or to your house. It's just as risky today for you and me to love people unconditionally as it was for Jesus in his era. We will not be put to death for it, but we may certainly be vilified, maligned, and ostracized for it.

But that's not the issue, is it? The issue is not how others respond to us, but how we respond to those despised by the culture and even by the church. How do we think or talk about people so radically different from us? How do we relate to them, or do we simply choose not to relate to them at all, and if so what does that say about our brand of Christianity?

Why did Jesus die? As a ransom price? No. As a satisfaction for an angry and offended God? No. As a substitute for us? No. Given the religious, political, and cultural climate in which Jesus lived, it is not difficult to see why His unconditional love for people led to His crucifixion. He was crucified so quickly because He loved so deeply. His entire ministry spanned but three years, and He had not killed anyone, stolen any money, or advocated the overthrow of Roman authority. How much does God love us? He refused to compromise His unconditional love for all humankind even if it meant death. Therefore, His enemies pursued Him to the cross where He endured the pain of human sin and there reveals the depth of God's love. *The death of Jesus Christ on the cross is the eternal testimony to the furious love and resolute forgiveness of God for all people.* Because of God's love,

> Well, this train carries saints and sinners
> This train carries losers and winners
> This train carries whores and gamblers
> This train carries lost souls
>
> I said, this train, dreams will not be thwarted
> This train, faith will be rewarded
> This train, hear the steel wheels singing
> This train, bells of freedom ringing
>
> I said, this train carries broken-hearted
> This train, thieves and sweet souls departed
> This train carries fools and kings thrown
> This train, all aboard
>
> You don't need no ticket
> You just get on board
> You just thank the Lord
>
> ("Land of Hope and Dreams," Bruce Springsteen)[6]

Long before "The Boss" so graphically expresses the gospel for this generation, Charles Wesley expressed it for those of his era (and ensuing generations):

> And can it be that I should gain
> An int'rest in the Savior's blood?
> Died he for me, who caused His pain
> For me, who Him to death pursued?
> Amazing love! How can it be
> That Thou, my God, should die for me?[7]

Chapter 3

[1] Bruce Springsteen, "Land of Hope And Dreams," *Wrecking Ball* (2012).
[2] Dallas Willard, *The Divine Conspiracy: Rediscovering Our Hidden Life in God* (San Francisco: HarperCollins, 1998) 403.
[3] Jürgen Moltmann, *The Crucified God: The Cross of Christ as the Foundation and Criticism of Christian Theology* (Minneapolis, MN: Fortress Press, 1993) 205.
[4] Alan Jacobs, *The Narnian: The Life and Imagination of C.S. Lewis* (San Francisco: Harper San Francisco, 2005) 149.
[5] Dionne Warwick, lyrics by Hal David, "What the World Needs Now Is Love," *Here Where There Is Love* (1966).
[6] Springsteen, "Hope and Dreams," 2012.
[7] Charles Wesley, "And Can It Be That I Should Gain?," *Psalms and Hymns* (1738).

Chapter 4

Hell in the Fire

WE HAD ALREADY BEEN SINGING for about half an hour when the old-time Southern evangelist from Myrtle, Mississippi walked into the little sanctuary. He looked every bit the part: mid-sixties, white hair, a bit of a paunchy stomach, and high cheekbones, with a stout, reddish face. Neil Diamond pegs it when singing, "Brother Love's Travelling Salvation Show" from the album of the same name:

> Room gets suddenly still
> And when you'd almost bet
> You could hear yourself sweat, he walks in
> Eyes black as coal
> And when he lifts his face
> Every ear in the place is on him
>
> Starting soft and slow
> Like a small earthquake
> And when he lets go
> Half the valley shakes.[1]

With white handkerchief in hand to dramatize the fateful event, lifting it high and lowering it down, he describes what it will be like falling forever and ever and deeper and deeper. And the deeper you fall the hotter it gets, the darker it gets, blacker and blacker. "The demons come-a-dartin' out atcha from the darkness, and you can see their twisted and hideous faces as they scream, *'Forever! Forever! Forever!'* Deeper and deeper, hotter and hotter, darker and darker, louder and louder: *'Forever! Forever!! FOREVER!!!'* You fall down and down and deeper and deeper into the pit that has no bottom, where there is weeping and gnashing of teeth. Where the worm dieth not, where the fire is not quenched, forever and forever and forever." As the evangelist shrieks the "forevers," he contorts his voice, changing pitch, tone, and timbre to mimic the infinite number of hideous demons who for all eternity will be screaming their tortuous, eternal damnations at you. I was there. It was memorable.

This was the evangelist's graphic description of the horror of the bottomless pit of Revelation 9:1-2, his description of hell where all who aren't saved will go for eternity. And the people flocked to the altar to repent, to get saved, to do anything to avoid such terrifying torture. Who wouldn't? This is the opposite end of the broken spectrum from the burning bush that confronted Moses on Mt. Sinai. Like the bush that was never consumed by the flames, those in hell burn and burn, yet are never consumed by the flames. This is the "hellfire and brimstone" preaching on which I, and much of the church-going Bible-belt South, was raised. It is a description of hell many evangelicals ardently believe and passionately defend today.

Is this what Jesus wanted us to understand about hell, that it is a bottomless pit of eternal terror and torture? Is this what Jesus wanted us to understand about the God He "explained" (see John 1:18) to us in the Gospels?

For all the emphasis on hell (religious and profane), would it surprise you to know that the term "hell" is found only thirteen times in all of the New Testament? On all but two occasions it is used by Jesus, and four of those times are in parallel passages of the synoptic Gospels. Jesus actually provides very little information about hell, though the imagery He uses on those occasions is arresting. His consistent warning seems clear: be sure you don't go there. Would it surprise you further to know that in none of these instances is Jesus referring to a bottomless pit of fire and brimstone in the center of the earth; to some sort of abode for Satan and his demonic followers?

The term translated in many of our Bibles as the English word "hell" is in every instance the Greek word, *Gehenna* (*ge*, meaning "valley" and *henna*, referring to a location named Hinnom). Gehenna was an actual place that existed during the biblical era. The Valley of Hinnom was located just outside the southwest walls of Jerusalem. Jeremiah called it the "valley of slaughter" where, during the reigns of Old Testament kings Ahaz and Manasseh, the sons of Judah sacrificed their own children causing them to "pass through the fire," burning them alive or first killing them and then burning their dead bodies (see 2 Chron 28:3). It is almost inconceivable that God's chosen people could be capable of such heinous acts. Yet Jeremiah found it necessary to warn them that in this valley, "The dead bodies of this people [Israel] will be food for the birds of the sky, and for the beasts of the earth" (Jer 7:33). By the time of Christ, the valley had become so cursed that it was used as the city dump where garbage, refuse, animal carcasses, and unclean corpses were discarded. Fires were always burning to consume the maggot-infested garbage, thus "the Gehenna of fire" in Matthew 5:22, and Jesus' warning in Mark 9:43-48 (the bracketed verses do not appear in some of the best available manuscripts from which the texts of our Bibles are traced):

> ^{43}And if your hand causes you to stumble, cut it off; it is better for you to enter life crippled, than, having your two hands, to go into hell, into the unquenchable fire,
> ^{44}[where THEIR WORM DOES NOT DIE, AND THE FIRE IS NOT QUENCHED.]
> ^{45}And if your foot causes you to stumble, cut it off; it is better for you to enter life lame, than, having your two feet, to be cast into hell,
> ^{46}[where THEIR WORM DOES NOT DIE, AND THE FIRE IS NOT QUENCHED.]
> ^{47}And if your eye causes you to stumble, throw it out; it is better for you to enter the kingdom of God with one eye, than, having two eyes, to be cast into hell,
> ^{48}where THEIR WORM DOES NOT DIE, AND THE FIRE IS NOT QUENCHED.

Stray dogs and wild animals constantly roamed the valley fighting over the garbage, thus the reference to the "gnashing of teeth" in Matthew 13:42. Tradition held that this valley was the "Field of Blood" or "potter's field," purchased with the money Judas had been paid for betraying Jesus but ultimately given back to the chief priests.

There are other descriptions in the New Testament that have shaped our traditional understanding of hell as a place of fire, torment, and damnation: "eternal fire" (Matt 18:8); "eternal punishment" (Matt 25:46); "outer darkness" (Matt 8:12); "wrath and indignation" (Rom 2:8); "eternal destruction away from the presence of the Lord" (2 Thess 1:9); "the lake of fire and brimstone" (Rev 14:10).

Many modern ideas about hell are from sources outside the Bible—artists and authors—rather than from the Bible. While the New Testament writers wanted to convey the appalling dread of hell, they never give the graphic descriptions of hellfire's torture depicted by the Southern evangelist. Those horrific, detailed, descriptions of suffering and torment would not come until the Middle Ages when artists portrayed the righteous taking delight in the torment of those flung into the fires of hell. The most famous of these paintings is Michelangelo's magnificent fresco of "The Last Judgment" covering the entire altar wall in the Sistine Chapel in Vatican City. The modern understanding of hell is also significantly influenced by Dante's *Divine Comedy*, which places hell, "Inferno," in the center of the earth where Satan dwells. Inferno has nine circles of suffering commensurate with the condemned's earthly sin. The deeper the circle, the greater the suffering. The inscription on the gate to the ninth circle is the famous quote, "Despair of hope, ye who enter here." The graphic descriptions of the tortures and horrors of hell are from sources other than the Bible.

Jonathan Edwards (d. 1758) is considered by some to be among the greatest theologians America has produced. His preaching was influential in the 18th century during the Great Awakening. Even today one of his sermons is still well-known, "Sinners In The Hands Of An Angry God." In it he describes both the horrors of hell and provides a rather distinctive image of God. Edwards' ideas, too, have shaped our modern concepts of both God and hell. The following quotes serve to summarize well his views on each:

Chapter 4

On God
God holds you over the pit of hell, much as one holds a spider, or some loathsome insect over the fire, abhors you, and is dreadfully provoked: His wrath toward you burns like fire; he looks upon you as worthy of nothing else, but to be cast into the fire; he is of purer eyes than to bear to have you in his sight; you are ten thousand times more abominable in his eyes, than the most hateful venomous serpent is in ours.[2]

On Hell
Consider the fearful danger you are in: it is a great furnace of wrath, a wide and bottomless pit, full of the fire of wrath, that you are held over in the hand of that God, whose wrath is provoked and incensed as much against you, as against many of the damned in hell. You hang by a slender thread, with the flames of divine wrath flashing about it, and ready ever moment to singe it, and burn it asunder.[3]

Is this the God Jesus "explained" (see John 1:18) to us? Does this sound like the God of "I do not condemn you" (John 8:11), of "Permit the children to come to me" (Mark 10:14), of "Father, forgive them" (Luke 23:34)? Does is seem like the God who loves sinners, who goes out of His way to fellowship with them? Even as Jonathan Edwards graphically warns of the reality of hell, the picture of God in his message—a God who holds us over a yawning hell threatening, almost yearning, to drop us in any moment—is so unlike the God that Jesus reveals to us. One theologian told me that while this was Edwards' most famous sermon, it was also Edwards at his worst. Regardless, the sermon has influenced greatly our society's widely understood notions of hell.

Why not just take the traditional understanding of hell at face value, that somewhere (the New Testament never hints at hell's location) there is a bottomless pit of flaming, white hot fire and sulfurous brimstone into which all who don't accept Jesus as their personal Savior will be cast and tortured for an endless eternity? After all, this has been the church's accepted interpretation for centuries. So, why would one question it? Well, because of Jesus. Because it's difficult, it's impossible to reconcile the two: a fire into which God casts the overwhelming majority of the people who have been made in His image so that they can be tortured for eternity versus the Jesus of love and forgiveness presented in the four Gospels. Why do I question the popular understanding of hell? Because it is impossible to reconcile the traditional view of hell with the God of grace that Jesus "explained" (see John 1:18) in the four Gospels.

So, what then happens to those who do not "accept Jesus" or to non-Christians? Is there a hell? There is. Do people go there? They do. These questions, then, prompt two other important questions: (1) What is hell, and (2) Who goes there? First, What is hell? When Jesus spoke of hell, Gehenna, the Valley of Hinnom, those listening to Him understood that Jesus was using a metaphor. His audience would not have thought that Jesus was speaking literally. They didn't think that when a godless person or an enemy died that their bodies literally went into the Valley of Hinnom, and the next day they could go there and find the dead bodies of their enemies in the valley, point out those bodies to their children and warn them, "This is what happens if you disobey God and break the Law." Nor would they have thought that the spirits of the godless were floating around in the valley. They understood that Gehenna—hell—was a metaphor. Jesus' listeners would have understood that He was speaking of a state or a place utterly accursed, dreadful, and damnable; a state or a place utterly forsaken by God and humankind. The message? Above all, don't go there! The Apostle Paul warns of judgment and the wrath of God, but he never speaks of hell as fire, brimstone, and burning.

Jesus does provide a description of hell in the Gospels. It's a description of a place so appalling and horrible, that it's like Gehenna, the Valley of Hinnom where ancient Israel offered their children in sacrifice to pagan idols. It's like the burning, maggot-infested garbage dump to which Jesus refers. How terrible is hell? It is an accursed place, a horrible place, compared to the agony of burning in a fire that never stops. Jesus described hell at the end of the Sermon on the Mount in Matthew 7:21-23:

> Not everyone who says to Me, "Lord, Lord," will enter the kingdom of heaven; but he who does the will of My Father who is in heaven will enter. Many will say to Me on that day, "Lord, Lord, did we not prophesy in Your name, and in Your name cast out demons, and in Your name perform many miracles?" And then I will

declare to them, "I never knew you; depart from Me, you who practice lawlessness."

The historic and orthodox position of the church is that God is both omnipresent and omniscient. Omnipresent means that God is at all times present everywhere in and beyond the known universe. The psalmist found comfort in the assurance of God's presence no matter where he was. Psalm 139:7-10:

> Where can I go from Your Spirit? Or where can I flee from Your presence? If I ascend to heaven, You are there; If I make my bed in Sheol, behold, You are there. If I take the wings of the dawn, if I dwell in the remotest part of the sea, even there Your hand will lead me, and Your right hand will lay hold of me.

Omniscient means that God knows everything. There is no thing—fact or fiction, thought, word, or deed, perception, concept or concrete, tangible reality, nothing—that God does not know. The same psalmist wrote in Psalm 139:1-4:

> O LORD, You have searched me and known me. You know when I sit down and when I rise up; You understand my thought from afar. You scrutinize my path and my lying down and are intimately acquainted with all my ways. Even before there is a word on my tongue, behold, O LORD, You know it all.

God knows all. God knows everything. God is present everywhere at all times.

Yet, Jesus says a day will come when He ("Lord," God) will say "depart from me, you who practice lawlessness." Though God is omnipresent (always, everywhere present), there is a place where God is not. A person in that place is forsaken by God. The Apostle Paul in 2 Thessalonians 1:9 defines "eternal destruction" as "away from the presence of the Lord."

Not only that, He will say on that day, "I never knew you." There is, therefore, a place or a state (I don't know that it matters) where a person can go where the God who knows everything, does not know the people who go there. John celebrated Jesus as the great Shepherd of the sheep who, "calls His own sheep by name" (John 10:3). One of the most precious truths of the Bible is that God knows us; He knows our name. We are not nameless faces amid the mass of humanity. He knows us one by one. He knows our name. Yet there is a time that will come when the great Shepherd of the sheep, who knows His sheep by name, no longer knows the names of those "who practice lawlessness." Not only does He not know their name, He no longer knows that person exists. This person is out of the mind and consciousness of God. The God who knows everything no longer knows this person, who he or she is, or even that she or he is. In the omniscient mind of God, they are not. They no longer exist. Not only that; it will be as if they have never existed. Jesus warns us to never let be said of us, "I *never* knew you."

This is hell; out of God's presence, out of the mind of God and beyond the God of love, forgiveness, goodness, kindness, mercy, and grace. This is worse than what the evangelist from my youth described. It's worse than a bottomless pit of fire and brimstone, worse than where the worm dieth not and the fire is not quenched, worse than the valley where Israel offered their children in burnt sacrifice as God looked on, and worse than Gehenna. *This is hell.*

My good friend, historian and theologian Dr. Mark Smith, says it so well: "Everybody gets what they want. You don't want God. You don't get God." Who goes to hell? If, as I argue throughout this book, God is a God of grace—unconditional love, forgiveness, and acceptance—who, then, winds up in hell, out of the presence and mind of the omnipresent, omniscient God? All those who don't want God. Jesus' answer is, "You who practice lawlessness." To whom is Jesus referring? It may not be those you think. I'll explain below, but let's first consider one more important truth.

There is at least some evidence that in the Kingdom of God, everybody is *in* until they either choose to get *out,* or get put out. Let's at least consider the evidence. In the Parable of the Ten Maidens, or Ten Bridesmaids found in Matthew 25, Jesus describes what "the kingdom of heaven will be comparable to." All ten were part of the wedding party. The failure of the five foolish bridesmaids was not that they didn't bring enough oil to last out the night. Their failure was in looking to the other five, smarmy, stingy bridesmaids who refused to share their oil, rather than trusting the goodness of their friend, the bridegroom, to take them into the wedding feast even though their lamps had gone out. They were in until they left because they didn't trust the kindness of the bridegroom. When they did return, the door was shut. In the traditional interpretation of the parable, it is the five stingy bridesmaids who get to heaven. Is that who makes up heaven, stingy little twits like this? Yes, along with foolish little twits who don't leave but trust the Bridegroom despite their foolishness or lack of preparation. The gospel is here, and I find it exhilarating!

In Matthew 13, Jesus tells seven parables, all of which deal with the kingdom of God. Jesus says the Kingdom of God is like the Parable of the Wheat and Weeds: both grow together in the kingdom of God. The weeds are in until the harvest when they are finally cast out. All are in until separated out. The kingdom of God is like the Parable of the Dragnet thrown into the sea that gathers every kind of fish, both good and bad. Only after the net is pulled onto shore are the "bad fish" cast out. All are in until they are cast out. The kingdom of God is like yeast in three pecks of meal that effect the entire measure of flour.

Even Revelation says that the one "who overcomes will thus be clothed in white garments; and I will not erase his name from the book of life" (3:5). Those who do not overcome will have their names removed from the book of life. The obvious implication is that their names are in the book of life until they are finally "erased." They were in until they were put out.

Then, there are some verses that seem to indicate that all are in.

> So then as through one transgression there resulted condemnation to all men, even so through one act of righteousness there resulted *justification of life to all men* [emphasis mine] (Rom 5:18).
>
> For as in Adam all die, so also in Christ *all shall be made alive* [emphasis] (1 Cor 15:22).
>
> He Himself is the propitiation for our sins; and not for ours only, but also for those of *the whole world* [emphasis mine] (1 John 2:2).

Is my interpretation of the parables and these verses from Paul irrefutable? It is not, and the traditional interpretation of all of these passages certainly argues against it. But would you consider that this interpretation is at least plausible? And—and here is the key for me—it fits the character of Jesus, and it magnifies the grace of God. Am I saying then that everyone goes to heaven? I am not. There is a hell, and people go there. So, back to the question: Who then, goes to hell? Jesus said, "you who practice lawlessness." What does that mean? It can't mean those who break the laws of God. If that were the case everybody would go to hell, and there would be no "good news."

Let me answer the question by a parable of my own to show who is in and who is out, a theme central to the kingdom parables in Matthew 13. The kingdom of God is like a concert orchestra. Jesus is the conductor and everyone who wants to be in the orchestra is welcome. You choose your instrument, and you are invited to participate in the orchestra. If you are a novice and cannot play well, that is fine; you will be put with the more skilled musicians who can mentor you. If you want to learn to be a conductor, you can be an understudy. If you are not musically talented but still want to be part of the orchestra, you are welcome, too. You can be a personal assistant to the conductor or help with the physical arrangements in preparation for the concert: setting the stage, arranging the music stands and director's platform, placing the music all in order on the stands, and so on. You can help with the ticket distribution (tickets are free), ushering, hosting, lighting, sound, climate-control, and cleaning the music hall before and after the concerts. Anyone who wants to be part of the orchestra is welcome. Talent and ability are irrelevant. The invitation truly is, "Whosoever will, let him come."

There is one kind of person, however, who is not welcome, and will not be permitted in the orchestra. The only people who will be forbidden from being in the orchestra or who will be "cast out" from the orchestra are *those who want to destroy the orchestra*. If you want to fight with the musicians rather than play the music; if you would rip up the sheet music, tear down the music stands, and make the performance impossible; if you would sabotage the music hall and even assault the conductor, you cannot be part of the orchestra. Such "lawlessness" cannot be permitted. Why? To give admission to such people would destroy the orchestra. The Conductor will not let that happen. People of such "lawlessness," therefore, will be cast out. It's not that the Conductor doesn't care about these people; He does. The Conductor, however, cannot permit the orchestra to be destroyed. These lawless people must be cast out in order for the orchestra to exist and to perform. In the same way, God will not permit into the kingdom of God those who would destroy the kingdom, those who practice lawlessness. These are cast out, their names are blotted out of the book of life. These go to hell. *Other than these, all are welcome.*

What does this mean practically? The traditional requirement for salvation in the Christian church is expressed in Romans 10:9 & 13 "If you confess with your mouth Jesus as Lord, and believe in your heart that God raised Him from the dead, you will be saved.... For whoever will call on the name of the Lord will be saved." This requires that people must first hear the story of Jesus. Absent of that, they cannot "confess" or "believe" or "call upon" a name they have never heard. This belief—that anyone must hear the name and story of Jesus or else go to hell—has driven the modern mission movement to send tens of thousands of missionaries around the world to tell the story of Jesus. Missionaries have poured out their lives, many in the face of appalling hardships to carry the name of Jesus around the world. Paul says in the next two verses:

> How then will they call on Him in whom they have not believed? How will they believe in Him whom they have not heard? And how will they hear without a preacher? How will they preach unless they are sent? Just as it is written, "How beautiful are the feet of those who bring good news of good things! (Rom 10:14-15)

There is, however, a serious difficulty with this interpretation. The Population Reference Bureau estimates that nearly 108 billion people have lived on the Earth from 50,000 BCE through today. Obviously, the overwhelming majority of this number never heard the name "Jesus." Today it is estimated that some 2.8 billion people currently alive have never heard the name "Jesus." If all who have never heard His name and have never converted to Christianity go to hell, the overwhelming majority of the people who have lived are in hell or are on their way there. Is this why God created us?! Are multiplied billions of people to burn forever in a hell where "the worm dieth not, and the fire is not quenched?" While it is true that "All have sinned and come short of the glory of God" (Rom 3:23), these billions have committed no greater sins than the redeemed. They just never heard of Jesus, never had a chance to "call on the name of the Lord" (Rom 10:13). Does this mean that for all eternity they must suffer in the flames and torment of hell? On the one hand, orthodox Christian theology claims that all human life is precious and created in the image of God (see Gen 1:27). Yet, on the other hand, it holds that this same God sends billions of these He created to the fires of hell because they were born at places or in times that had or has never heard Jesus' name, never had the opportunity for salvation. And, given the orthodox belief that God is omniscient, this means that from the beginning, before time began, God designed creation knowing that he would be sending billions into the torment of hell.

Can we reconcile the God Jesus "explained" (see John 1:18) to us in the Gospels—a God of unconditional love, forgiveness, and grace—with a God who sends billions of people (sinners, sure) to hell, because they never heard the name of Jesus, never had a chance to repent, to believe, and never had a chance to call on His name? One justifying argument is that since all have sinned and all deserve hell, saving some magnifies the glory of God, His goodness, mercy, and grace. For the sake of argument, even if this sounds good in theory (and I don't think it does.), what if it is your spouse, your sons or daughters, your parents, your dearest friend who goes to an eternal, fiery torment, in order for God's glory to be magnified? In your heart, would it glorify God to know that, while God in His mercy and grace saved you, God created those you love to burn in hell for all eternity? The practical application of such thinking is, well, unthinkable. I cannot reconcile this with the God Jesus "explained" (see John 1:18) in the four Gospels.

Even today in Muslim countries, a child raised in a home of radical Islamic terrorists hears the name of Jesus for sure, but from infancy the child is taught to hate Christianity, Christians, and all the "unconverted" who follow Jesus Christ rather than Muhammad. For the sake of making my point, allow me to offer a different rendition of Deuteronomy 11:19. The children are taught to hate non-Muslims when they sit in their house and when they walk along the road and when they lie down and when they rise up. At home by his parents, in the midrasha (school) by the mudaris, in the mosques by the imam, the child is taught that everything about the West and Christianity is evil, opposed to all that he holds sacred, is the archenemy of his God and his faith, and all such people need to convert to Islam or be killed. Many are taught from childhood that people advance the cause of Allah by killing non-Muslims, and these will receive great rewards in heaven. That child grows to be a young man who hates Jesus and all Christians. He may even strap a bomb to himself in order to kill as many non-Muslims as possible. According to the Christian church, because he rejected Jesus and becomes a terrorist he goes to hell, all too often to the satisfaction and "Amens" of those claiming to love Jesus. (By the way, how is it in any way like Jesus to want a person to be consigned to hell?)

Did he have a choice? O, yes, I know philosophically he had a choice; not all young Muslims choose to become suicide bombers. But practically, having been taught all his life by every authority he respected to hate Christians, did he have a choice? Did he ever have a fair, reasonable, or just opportunity to "call on the name of the Lord? (Rom 10:13)." He did not. Compare his opportunity to "call on the name of the Lord" with those to whom the aforementioned evangelist preached during my youth. These people heard of Jesus from their infancy. When I was a boy Jesus was everywhere. He was in the home and in the many, many churches, one located on every corner. (My home town's claim to fame is that the city has more churches per capita than any other city in the nation—and we must need them because we are just as corrupt as any other city in the nation.) We were confronted with Jesus from the radio to the pine trees telling us "Jesus Saves" or calling us to "Repent or go to hell." Street preachers downtown warned us of the "soon coming Jesus" and after that, the judgment. As soon as television came along, Jesus was all over TV. And, while not everybody was baptized or went to church, virtually everybody believed (to some measure) in and respected, maybe even loved Jesus. What's not to love? He is loving, forgiving, good, kind, teaches us to be the same (even if we aren't) and He answers prayers. In the United States we really are free to make a choice. A young boy raised in Saudi Arabia does not have the same choice. Does this Muslim boy go to hell because he didn't pray the sinner's prayer and accept Jesus his personal Savior, the Jesus he was taught to hate all his life? I cannot believe that a just and loving God would condemn him to the kind of hell described by the evangelist and that for all eternity.

What, then, does happen to him and the majority of the billions who never heard the name of Jesus? (I discuss this further in chapter five, "The Way Of Salvation.") What about the end time judgment to which Jesus and the New Testament writers refer? Judgment is real, but the judgment at the end of time, however, will not be like Michelangelo's "The Last Judgment" in the Sistine Chapel City. The God of grace will not cease being the God of grace in judgment.

Let me raise one final question: Is the punishment in hell for the unconverted forever? The historic position of the church answers in the affirmative. We have twenty to eighty or so years to get it right: to confess, repent, and be saved. If we don't, we go to hell for all eternity. Compared to eternity, the few years we have in this life is a twinkle in the eye of time. Yet, in this *brief moment* of our lifetime, we must make the right decisions or suffer in a fiery torment of hell for *eternity*. Is this who God is? Is this the God Jesus "explained" to us (see John 1:18). Is this what the New Testament actually teaches?

There are an endless number of reasons a person may not be saved. Millions are like the example of the little Muslim boy who is taught all his life to hate Jesus. Millions are raised in other religions and are satisfied, never giving a thought to Jesus. Untold numbers simply are not raised in a religious environment of any kind and spiritual matters never become part of their lives. They don't hate or reject Jesus; Jesus is just never a factor in their lives. Some people have had a brutal and abusive father, and the idea of God as "Father," is not a winsome image. Others have consciously rejected Jesus, or more often rejected the church of Jesus, because of foolish and unfortunate things done by the church as a whole (I discuss this further in chapter six, "When Religion Goes Bad") or by local congregations who are supposed to be the body of Christ.

Ron DuPriest was a former member of the notorious Hell's Angels motorcycle gang in Southern California. He looked every bit the part: large, burly, long-haired, and tattooed all over. I can easily imagine him riding a Harley on the California interstates and highways. By the time I came to know Ron he had been gloriously converted in a Pentecostal Holiness camp meeting—and the conversion took! Ron had become a Pentecostal preacher. "The old things [have] passed away; behold, new things have come" (2 Cor 5:17). Had they ever! Shortly after his conversion Ron joined a small rural church near his home. One Sunday the pastor asked the men in the congregation to be at the church at eight o'clock on Saturday morning for a work day. A concrete slab had to be poured and men were needed to smooth and screed the concrete. Ron arrived early and was the only there when the concrete truck arrived. The driver backed up to the form built for the slab and prepared to pour the concrete. Ron told him, "You can't pour it yet. We have to wait on the other men to help screed the concrete. I can't do all this by myself." The driver told Ron, "Tell you what, Mac, I've got a job to do, and I ain't waitin' on nobody. I'm gonna pour this concrete, and you can do whatever you want to with it." Ron told me, "If that driver had called me 'Mac' a month earlier, I'da sent him to the Promised Land." So, in the hot, blistering summer sun, Ron proceeded to screed the entire slab by himself.

Working alone and pouring sweat, he took off shirt and was pretty much a mess when he later entered the church looking for a water fountain. The pastor came in, saw Ron, and said to him, "Brother Ron, this is the house of the Lord. We don't come in here looking that way." Just imagine. There was no "Thank you for being here" or "Thanks for your hard work." There was nothing more than, "Brother Ron we don't come in here looking that way." Ron told me that when the Hell's Angels called a gang member "brother" it meant something. It meant you would take a knife or a bullet for him. You would lay down your life for him. On that day and in that church, however, it was a shallow, meaningless reference. All it meant was that a so-called "brother" didn't come into the church looking that way. Ron left that church, never to return. Had he been less determined or adamant about following Jesus, he might have left both the church and Jesus altogether, concluding that it means nothing. Men and women of God have said and done many unfortunate things that have turned away many people from both the church and Jesus. Yet, we are supposed to believe that these very same people are going to be sent by God to a fiery, tortuous hell for all eternity because Christians do and say stupid things that repulse thousands, turning them away from the church and from Jesus?

Think about that for a moment. For all eternity—*for all eternity*—the God "explained" (see John 1:18) to us by Jesus of Nazareth is going to consign these people to hell because they didn't "call on the name of the Lord" (Rom 10:13), a Lord whose name they might never have heard or one they rejected because of the poor witness of believers? (Interestingly, Gandhi is reported to have claimed that he might have become a Christian had it not been for the Christians he knew.) Can we reconcile this with the God of love and grace Jesus "explained" to us? Is this what the New Testament teaches? I know New Testament speaks of "eternal fire" (see Matt 18:8, 25:41), but can that mean that the place is eternal, not necessarily that all who go there are condemned to remain there for eternity? The Apocalypse of John does say that the devil, the beast and the false prophet "will be tormented day and night forever and ever" (Rev 20:10).

Following closely after the Parable of The Prodigal Son, Jesus tells the Parable of the Rich Man and Lazarus where he speaks of "a great chasm fixed" (Luke 16:26). This is a favorite proof text many use to establish that once a person is in hell, they remain there forever because the chasm between heaven and hell is "fixed." This is an unfortunate misunderstanding of Jesus' intentions. The parable was spoken to the Pharisees who loved privilege (see 16:14). Jesus explained that it's a new day and new world in the kingdom of God (16:16). No longer are the economically, academically, socially, and religiously privileged, (e.g., the rich man in the parable) giving orders to the poor and underprivileged (Lazarus). Even though the rich man is in Hades, he still considers Lazarus his servant and orders Abraham to "send Lazarus" (the Greek here is rendered in the imperative mode, the mode of command) so that he can bring water. This same type of imperative command from the rich man occurs again in verse 27: "send him to my father's house." Lazarus, however, is no longer the rich man's servant. The dynamics have changed. The privileged are no longer superior to the poor and cannot command servants. This is one of Jesus' many descriptions of what the Kingdom of God is like. The "great chasm" that has been "fixed"—that can never again be bridged—is not between heaven and hell. The great, fixed chasm is that the social, intellectual, or religious elite are no longer superior to the poor, the sick, and the less fortunate. In this type of world (the Kingdom of God), the poor, sick, and less fortunate can be greatly blessed far beyond their former so-called betters. The rich man is in hell, the servant is in heaven. The story has nothing to do with or to say about the eternality of the damned.

For some reason, and I'm not sure why—perhaps more psychological than Biblical—the church has always been enamored with hell. Could it have more to do with our own insecurities or our desires to manipulate and control other people? I know this to be true for me during the early days of my ministry. One deacon (who was not as circumspect as I thought he should be) told me one Sunday, "Steve, you preach on hell like you wish I was already there." He was right. I hoped that my threats of impending hell would make him shape up. Too often, the church is far more hell-focused than grace-focused. In characteristic clarity, Robert Farrar Capon writes:

> As a preacher, I can with the greatest of ease tell people that God is going to get them, and I can be sure they will believe every word I say. But what I cannot do, without inviting utter disbelief and serious doubts about my sanity, is proclaim that He has in fact taken away *all* the sins of the world and that He has, accordingly, solved all the problems He once had with sin.... Their one pressing worry is always, "What have you done with the hell we know and love?"[4]

Is your reaction to this chapter something like, "What have you done with the hell we know and love?" Is the idea of grace reaching all the way to the depths of hell an atrocious idea for you? I ask you to consider that it is possible. Is the idea completely unbiblical? Or is it that we have not thought enough about the deep reach of amazing grace? What if some people genuinely want to play in God's orchestra and would make outstanding members, but never knew who the Conductor was until they stood before Him in judgment? Or perhaps they never even knew there was an orchestra until just that time. Will the Conductor described to us in the Gospel Symphony turn these down and consign them to the tortures of eternal fire? Given what is revealed about Jesus in that Symphony, I cannot believe He would do such a thing. What Jesus presents for us all, is after all, *The Symphony of Good News*.

I am aware that I cannot quote a biblical chapter and verse that clearly and definitively states or proves what I describe above. I do, however, confidently stand with the totality God's nature and character and with Jesus' message: God is overwhelmingly a God of love, mercy, forgiveness, and grace to all humankind. For me it is more than possible. I believe that is who God is. Otherwise, if the few get it right, if we know enough, if we were born in the right family, in the right nation, under the right circumstances, and we "call on the name of the Lord" (Rom 10:13) and are saved, all is well: we go to heaven. But for those who don't get it right, if for one or a mixture of an infinite number of reasons, they don't "call on the name of the Lord" like the evangelist said, they fall forever and forever into a bottomless pit—darker and darker, hotter and hotter, blacker and blacker—suffering for all eternity in the flaming torments of hell. Or even worse (if such could be worse) according to some, God "elected" them to eternal damnation. Either way it means that billions and billions of people were created by God in order to burn in a tortuous hell for ever and ever, without ever having any chance of redemption. Where is the "good news" in that sort of message? That is not the God of Jesus Christ.

Hell? Yes. Fire? No. For whom? Not whom we may think. For eternity? Don't be *too* sure. Consider, at least consider *the deep reach of amazing grace.*

[1]Neil Diamond, "Brother Love's Travelling Salvation Show," *Brother Love's Travelling Salvation Show* (1969).
[2]Jonathan Edwards, "Sinners in the Hands of an Angry God," *Electronic Texts in American Studies Libraries at University of Nebraska-Lincoln* (Lincoln, NB: University of Nebraska-Lincoln) 15.
[3]Ibid, 16.
[4]Robert Farrar Capon, *The Parables of Judgment* (Grand Rapids: William B. Eerdmans Publishing Company, 1989) 7.

Chapter 5

The "Way" of Salvation

I WAS RAISED TO BELIEVE that evangelism—getting the lost saved—was the *summum bonum* (Latin, meaning "the highest good") of life. This was the purpose of Jesus, the Bible, the church, and the Christian life. It was the consistent emphasis and the constant message of my church: "Who have you told about Jesus today?" As teenagers we took "soul-winning" courses, were taught how to present God's plan for salvation and were given tracts (small pamphlets explaining the way of salvation) to assist in the all-important task of soul-winning. Annual themes for my Baptist denomination's national convention always focused attention for the upcoming year on one inevitable point: evangelism. In 1953, Southern Baptist Convention churches added nearly a million people to its Sunday school rolls, prompting the theme for 1954, "A Million More In '54." With characteristic, rapier insight, Southern Baptist revivalist Vance Havner, replied, "God help us if we get another million like that million." And, "We Southern Baptists are many, but we're not much." We memorized the salvation formula from Romans 10:9, "If you confess with your mouth Jesus as Lord, and believe in your heart that God raised Him from the dead, you will be saved."

In my days of stormtrooper evangelism, I would do all I could to convince (i.e., coerce) my "prospect" to say a prayer and "confess the Lord Jesus." I believed it was my job as a Christian to do this long before I entered ministry as vocation. If the "prospects" were not comfortable praying themselves, I was coached on how to lead the prayer, asking the "prospect" to repeat what I said word-for-word. If they did, I had hit a homerun; they had been saved. Later as a pastor, I would urge them to confess publically, join the church, and get baptized. If they were baptized, they could be counted in the annual report to the Southern Baptist Convention. The number of baptisms was singularly the greatest measure of a church's or a pastor's success. If they did all of this, I had hit a grand slam: getting saved (one run), joining church (two runs), getting baptized (three runs), and becoming involved in the church (grand slam). We didn't have much time for follow-up. The important thing was moving on and getting the next one saved.

Actually living like Jesus taught—feeding the poor, caring for the homeless, defending the helpless, demanding justice for all—was what the "social gospel" people did, and we didn't like them. They were probably Methodists or Episcopalians anyway. They may have been nice people, but they spent a lot of time and energy missing the main thing: the cross and getting people saved. What is bizarre to me now, is that I distinctly remember that the Methodists I knew, like Aunt Lyba and her church friends, seemed to have a peace I knew I did not have. It was a peace for which I longed and did not have as a young person or even much later as a preacher. We didn't know any Episcopalians. As far as we were concerned, they drank liquor so we really didn't want to know or like them. Honestly, the pressure always to "witness for Jesus" made me fearful (talking with complete strangers about something as personal as their lives, redemption, and future), guilty (no matter how much I witnessed, it was never enough), and therefore miserable. If I really loved God I would "win souls." If I didn't win souls, people would go to hell, and it was my fault. I was the watchman on the wall who failed to blow the trumpet (see Ezek 33:1-6). I suppose it is no wonder I was never an effective soul winner: "Come on and get saved, so you can be as miserable as me." I compensated effectively, but I do remember times when I wanted to escape the unrelenting pressure to "win souls for Jesus."

One reason for this constant emphasis on evangelism was our atonement theology. What mattered was the cross. I believed then (as I do now) that we are saved "by the blood of the Lamb."

There Is a Fountain Filled with Blood
There is a fountain filled with blood
Drawn from Immanuel's veins;
And sinners, plunged beneath that flood,
Lose all their guilty stains:[1]

Alas! And Did My Savior Bleed?
Alas! and did my Savior bleed,
And did my Sovereign die?
Would he devote that sacred head
For sinners such as I?[2]

The Old Rugged Cross
On a hill far away stood an old rugged cross,
The emblem of suff'ring and shame;
And I love that old cross where the dearest and best
For a world of lost sinners was slain.[3]

I have sung these songs with deep emotion and great gusto so often that I have all the stanzas memorized. Even now they still tug at my heart and stir my emotions. I still love these old hymns.

What mattered was incarnation (who Jesus was) and crucifixion (what Jesus did). We talked about the life between those two points, but it was never the focus. Regardless of the sermon topic or scriptural text, the message was always the same: if you are not saved, get saved right now:

Oh, Why Not Tonight?
Tomorrow's sun may never rise
To bless thy long deluded sight;
This is the time, oh, then be wise,
Be saved, oh, tonight.[4]

If you are saved, get somebody else saved:

Rescue the Perishing
Rescue the perishing, care for the dying,
Snatch them in pity from sin and the grave;
Weep o'er the erring one, lift up the fallen,
Tell them of Jesus, the mighty to save.[5]

Thus armed with Bible passages in our minds, tracts in our pockets, and guilt in our hearts, we went out soul-winning.

The Need For Salvation

Anyone with a modicum of awareness can agree that something is dreadfully wrong with the human race. We are a mess, and we have made a mess of the world. Crime occurs on Wall Street and Main Street, violence happens on side streets, criminals and offenders clog court dockets, and we cannot build prisons fast enough to house those found guilty. Child abuse, battered women, and human trafficking are an international disgrace. There is war after war in every generation and all over the world. Take, for example, Eric Bogle's gripping ballad that reveals the utter waste of war in telling the story of a young Willie McBride, a nineteen-year-old soldier killed in France during WWI. No one knows how Willie was killed. No one remembers. The chorus of the ballad painfully and piercingly expresses the piteous dichotomy between the useless killing of this young man (and the thousands who lie buried with him) and nugatory efforts to sugarcoat irresponsible killing by the reverent way nations bury their dead. Did those who sponsored the war honor Willie? Perhaps the drums beat, and the fife, band, and bagpipes played the songs a military plays when a soldier is killed and buried. Perhaps, but maybe not. There were so many dead and wounded to care for after the battle. No one knows, no one remembers. Note especially how the final verse of the ballad expresses the gut-wrenching agony and futility of all wars. (It's worth a few moments of your time to search for and listen to the Irish version of this song on YouTube.com.)

Green Fields of France
Well, how do you do, Private William McBride,
Do you mind if I sit down here by your graveside?
And rest for a while in the warm summer sun,

I've been walking all day, and I'm nearly done
And I see by your gravestone you were only 19
When you joined the glorious fallen in 1916,
Well, I hope you died quick and I hope you died clean
Or, Willie McBride, was it slow and obscene?

[chorus]
Did they Beat the drum slowly, did they play the pipes lowly?
Did the rifles fir o'er you as they lowered you down?
Did the bugles sound "The Last Post" in chorus?
Did the pipes play the "Flowers of the Forest"?

The sun's shining down on these green fields of France;
The warm wind blows gently, and the red poppies dance.
The trenches have vanished long under the plow;
No gas and no barbed wire, no guns firing now.
But here in this graveyard that's still No Man's Land
The countless white crosses in mute witness stand
To man's blind indifference to his fellow man.
And a whole generation who were butchered and damned.

And I can't help but wonder, no Willie McBride,
Do all those who lie here know why they died?
Did you really believe them when they told you "The Cause?"
Did you really believe that this war would end wars?
Well the suffering, the sorrow, the glory, the shame
The killing, the dying, it was all done in vain,
For Willie McBride, it all happened again,
And again, and again, and again, and again.

We know two things for sure. First, nineteen year old Willie McBride is dead; taken from family, maybe a young wife or a sweetheart. Second, war occurs again, and again, and again, and again, and again. The solemn, manicured military cemeteries are silent testimony to one thing: something indeed is dreadfully wrong with the human race. The Bible calls it sin, and the solution is the Savior through whom is found salvation.

What Say the Scriptures?

The Apostle Paul presented his view of the problem and solution around 56 C.E. in a letter to the church at Rome. Representing the Christian church's understanding of the need for and way of salvation, Romans has become the manifesto of the Christian faith. In Romans, Paul lays out four major premises.

First, through the creation of the world God has revealed enough of Himself that all of the world should acknowledge Him and worship Him. This is known as "general revelation," the revelation known to all of the human race through nature. (Revelation that comes through the Bible and ultimately through Jesus Christ is referred to as "special revelation.")

> Because that which is known about God is evident within them; for God made it evident to them. For since the creation of the world His invisible attributes, His eternal power and divine nature, have been clearly seen, being understood through what has been made, so that they are without excuse (Rom 1:19-20).

Second, humanity rejected God and worshipped the creation rather than the Creator.

> For even though they knew God, they did not honor Him as God, or give thanks; but they became futile in their speculations, and their foolish heart was darkened. Professing to be wise, they became fools, and exchanged the glory of the incorruptible God for an image in the form of corruptible man and of birds and four-footed animals and crawling creatures (Rom 1:21-23).

Third, in one of the most scathing denunciations of the human race found in all literature—sacred or secular—Paul says that the entire human race stands condemned.

> There is no one righteous, not even one. There is no one who understands; there is no one who seeks God. All have turned away; all alike have become useless. There is no one who does what is good, not even one. Their throat is an open grave; they deceive with their tongues. Vipers' venom is under their lips. Their mouth is full of cursing and bitterness. Their feet are swift to shed blood; ruin and wretchedness are in their paths, and the path of peace they have not known. There is no fear of God before their eyes. (Rom 3:10-18 HCSB).

Fourth, God offers salvation and the forgiveness of sin to all who look in faith to Jesus Christ:

> If you confess with your mouth Jesus as Lord, and believe in your heart that God raised Him from the dead, you shall be saved; for with the heart man believes, resulting in righteousness, and with the mouth he confesses, resulting in salvation" (Rom 10:9-10).

Millions of people through the centuries have been exposed to the good news of God's love, forgiveness, and grace and have heard the name of Jesus. Millions have received His salvation when they place their faith in the God of grace revealed to us through Jesus of Nazareth. "Whoever will call on the name of the Lord will be saved" (Rom 10:13). They have called on the name Jesus and have received His salvation.

In the previous chapter, I raised the question of what happens to the billions of people who have lived on Earth who never heard the name of Jesus. Does God intend for His salvation to be restricted to the relative few who hear the gospel of grace? Is it axiomatic that every one of the 109 billion people who have lived on earth worshipped the *creation* rather than the *Creator*? Is Paul giving an absolute principle, true for all people at all times? Or could Paul be giving a general principle that is true most times? Could there be some exceptions? Paul acknowledges that people can know God without knowing God's name: "...that which is known about God is *evident within them*, for God made it *evident to them*" [emphasis mine] (Rom 1:19). Is it possible that some have seen "His eternal power and divine nature" and "understood through what has been made" limited though their understanding might be to general revelation? (Rom 1:20) Could some of these know that something is dreadfully wrong in their lives and they need a power greater than themselves to redeem them? They realize that deep inside they have a propensity for destructive hatred and vengeance, for debilitating bitterness and jealousy, a yearning for corruptive greediness and meanness, and the impulse to lie, cheat, steal, and even kill. They do not know why or what is wrong, but they know that something within is corrupting and destroying their lives, families, and folk. Could some in desperation, as Paul says, look "within them[selves]" (their conscience) and look out beyond themselves at the creation and along with virtually every culture ever discovered—regardless of how primitive—realize and acknowledge that there is a power, a force, a God greater than them, a Creator? In the words of Paul they see "His invisible attributes, His eternal power, and divine nature" (Rom 1:20). Yet, in contrast to the general principle Paul describes in Romans 1, they do not turn to nature and create idols, but rather they bow before this God whom they know instinctively within and whom they see undeniably without through the creation. They give thanks to Him, and they worship Him, the Creator, rather than the creation. As best they know how, they surrender to Him. They just don't know His name.

The classic text used to prove that there is only one way to salvation is John 14:6: "I am the way, and the truth, and the life; no one comes to the Father but through Me." This verse was prominently displayed at Billy Graham Evangelistic Crusades throughout the world. This short, nineteen-word statement has driven personal evangelism and international missions for centuries. What did Jesus mean when He said, "I am the way?" What are we to understand by it? What is the way of salvation? Is it possible for people to come to the Father through Jesus even if they don't know His name?

When Jesus says, "I am the way," could He mean that *His way* is the way? Could He mean that the way to the Father is the way of love, goodness, kindness, forgiveness, and mercy, that this is the truth about life? It is not that a person acts this way to *earn* God's favor or forgiveness. Without the biblical revelation these people may not even know that they stand condemned of sin. They just know that something is terribly amiss in their lives. This is not neo-Pelagianism. (Over 1500 years ago the early church fathers deemed Pelagianism as heresy. It is the belief that humans are capable of securing their own redemption.). I am not talking about people being capable of earning their salvation. On the contrary, as noted in chapter two, salvation is *sola gratia, sola fide,* and *solus Christus.* This is the response to the promptings of God's Spirit. The Spirit cannot relate to them in the exact same way He relates to those who know His name, who have the advantage of special revelation. These have never seen a Bible, don't know the story of Jesus, and have never heard the good news of God's love. Yet they look beyond themselves to Another. They love goodness, truthfulness, kindness, and justice. They are loving toward their neighbors. They forgive others who offend them. They love God.

In a messed up world, where do people who do not know His name acquire these virtues? From the same Spirit who transforms the hearts of those who call on His name for salvation. These, too, bow in submission before Him whose name they do not know. His Spirit transforms their hearts. Their knowledge of God is limited to general revelation, but they know Him. They just don't know His name. They love the light, and they hate the evil. Just like those who know His name, these can at times shun the light and do evil. They can slip back into old habits. Yet their desire is to be where the wind of love, joy, peace, goodness, and kindness is blowing. That wind whirls around them and flows from them. Who can say that the omnipotent and omnipresent God of Jesus Christ, the God of all compassion, has not revealed Himself to them in some primitive way (at least primitive in our way of thinking)? After all, did not Jesus say, "The wind blows where it wishes and you hear the sound of it, but do not know where it comes from and where it is going; so is everyone who is born of the Spirit." (John 3:8)? The writers of Old Testament wisdom literature understood the mystery of God's workings. "Just as you do not know the path of the wind and how bones are formed in the womb of the pregnant woman, so you do not know the activity of God who makes all things" (Eccl 11:5). Or, as Paul reminds us in Romans 11:33-36,

> Oh, the depth of the riches both of the wisdom and knowledge of God! How unsearchable are His

judgments and unfathomable His ways! For who has known the mind of the Lord, or who became His counselor? Or who has first given to Him that it might be paid back to him again? For from Him and through Him and to Him are all things. To Him be the glory forever. Amen.

There is something at work here that no one fully understands. Salvation can't be reduced to a formula (The Roman Road; Four Spiritual Laws; Atonement theology). God is far greater than our theological arguments, petty religious squabbles, and has little interest in preserving our religious plans and programs. No one can rightly say God does not reveal Himself unless people carry the Bible to them and tell them the story of Jesus. To be sure, they can come to a clearer and deeper understanding of God through the Bible. But the spirit of God is blowing where we do not know and in ways we do not understanding.

There is a "plan of salvation," but it involves more than selected and memorized scriptures and a program that culminates in leading a prospect to say a prayer. The plan of salvation involves the totality of the character of God as revealed in the entire Bible, ultimately in and through Jesus of Nazareth, and the wind of God flutters throughout the entire world.

The Character of God and Our Salvation

The orthodox position of the Christian church is that salvation is sola gratia, sola fide, solus Christus (by grace alone, by faith alone, by Christ alone). So, what about the Christus? What about Jesus Christ? Of all the attributes the four Gospels reveal about Jesus, His love and compassion are chief among them. Mark isn't out of the first chapter when he records Jesus' reaction to a hopeless and diseased leper: "*Moved with compassion*, Jesus stretched out His hand and touched him" [emphasis mine] (Mark 1:41). And then just a few chapters later we note once again Jesus' heartfelt concern for people: "He saw a large crowd, and *He felt compassion* for them because they were like sheep without a shepherd" [emphasis mine] (Mark 6:34).

The Good Samaritan is commended because he felt compassion and cared for the wounded man who was left for dead. The parable of the prodigal son is more about the character of the father than the repenting of the son. When the rebellious son returned home dirty, defeated and without money, "While he was still a long way off, his father saw him and *felt compassion* for him, and ran and embraced him and kissed him." [emphasis mine] (Luke 15:19). How does Jesus portray the Father reacting to unclean sinners? He responds with compassion. Interestingly, two different times Jesus quotes from God's word to the prophet Hosea: "I desire compassion and not sacrifice" (Matt 9:13, 12:7).

For Jesus, compassion defines God. Jesus' purposefully and specifically recast the Holiness Code of Leviticus. From "Speak to all the congregation of the sons of Israel and say to them, 'You shall be holy, for I the LORD your God am holy'" (Lev 19:2) to "Be merciful, just as your Father is merciful" (Luke 6:36).

Aramaic was the language of conversation in the time of Christ. The Aramaic word for "compassion" is derived from the same word as "womb." What then does it mean when Jesus says that our Heavenly Father is compassionate? It means that God is "womb-like." What does it mean when the gospel writers say that Jesus is a man of compassion? It means that Jesus, too, is "womb-like." Think about that for a moment. I think this is a salient and significant insight into the nature of Jesus and God (and thus the nature of the Christian life). The implications are incredible. Life begins with compassion. Life is surrounded and protected by God's compassion. Life is nourished and nurtured through God's compassion. All that is alive, all that is, even the creation itself, comes from the compassion of God. God is our Father; compassion is our mother.

The idea that God is womb-like provides an interesting new perspective on Jesus' words to Nicodemus, "You must be born again" (John 3:7). A Pharisee came to Jesus for answers. He had the Law and knew it well. He was still missing something, though. His soul was barren. He needed a spiritual birth from the womb of God's compassion. The fertility of the life-giving womb must supplant the sterility of the life-quashing law (see 2 Cor 3:6). He needed a God of love and life, a God of compassion. Don't we all!

Though millions may have never heard the name of Jesus, some—whether from frustration, desperation, defeat, despair, or depression—realize the hopelessness of their own shattered life and reach out to a Name they do not know, yearning and begging for help. Can any of us who do know That Name believe Jesus would turn them away just because they have never heard of Him? I cannot and will not believe that Jesus, out of his deep love for all people would turn away someone who through no fault of their own had never heard of Him. I believe He welcomes them into the compassion of His wide and loving embrace.

When I was a little boy, momma had a songbook called *Look and Live*. The theology behind the title is that there is salvation (life) just for a look. For those who know the name of Jesus, they must look at Jesus. But for those who have never heard His name, they too can look and live. They look beyond their own resources to a force they cannot name, to a God whose name they do not know, but they know Someone is there. And because they look, they also have "washed their robes and made them white in the blood of the Lamb" (Rev 7:14). On the isle of Patmos John saw in his vision of the throne of God a universal mass of people from all places and times:

> After these things I looked, and behold, a great multitude which no one could count, from every nation and all tribes and peoples and tongues, standing before the throne and before the Lamb, clothed in white robes, and palm branches were in their hands; and they cry out with a loud voice, saying, "Salvation to our God who sits on the throne, and to the Lamb" (Rev 7:9-10).

Because of God's compassion, among the countless number of people standing before the throne, dressed in white robes and waiving palms in their hands will be prostitutes and pimps, thieves, drunkards, and drug addicts, women who have had abortions and the men who impregnated them, politicians and businessmen who have stolen, clergymen who have fallen, and the sexually abused teenager now selling his or her body on the street. There will be those defeated by life, soiled by poor decisions, bested by temptations, overcome by addictions, and bloodied by life's tribulations. These are the children of atheistic parents who see beyond the humanism of their culture and know that there is a God. These come from the bush of Africa and the jungles of the Amazon where language has not been reproduced in written characters. They come from the masses of teeming cities and the middle class suburbs, writhe with sterile secularism and materialism, yet they know that "for not even when one has an abundance does his life consist of his possessions" (Luke 12:15). These have come out of Muslim countries, yet they instinctively know that God is not a God of hate who demands conversion at the point of a sword, but that love, not hate, is at the heart of life. Some have heard His name and have called "on the name of the Lord" (Rom 10:13) and were saved. Many more are there who once bowed before pagan totems or where held in the fears of shamans and superstitions or under the spell of witch doctors. They never heard His name, but the Spirit of God was blowing. They escaped and fled it all and called on the Name they did not know until they stood before His throne, palm branches in hand, raised in praise of the Name they now hear for the first time. This is the God of grace, not the god of religion. This is the deep reach of amazing grace.

Salvation through Jesus, Though Some Do Not Know His Name

John R.W. Stott is perhaps the most highly regarded and respected preacher and expositor of the New Testament among evangelicals in my lifetime. In *The Contemporary Christian*, he raised the question: "Is there no hope of salvation...for those who belong to other religions, and who may never even have heard of Jesus?"[6] Answering "biblically," as he says, there are some things we know and some things we do not know. We are certain, of course, that there is no such thing as "self-salvation." And, as Dr. Stott continues,

> What we do not know, however, is exactly how much knowledge and understanding of the gospel people need before they can cry to God for mercy and be saved. In the Old Testament people were certainly "justified by grace through faith," even though they had little knowledge or expectation of Christ. Perhaps there are others today in a somewhat similar position. They know they are sinful and guilty before God, and that they cannot do anything to win His favor, so in self-despair they call upon the God they dimly perceive to save them. If God does save such, as many evangelical

Christians tentatively believe, their salvation is still only by grace, only through Christ, only by faith.

Something else we know is that the final number of God's redeemed people will be actually countless, in final fulfillment of God's promise to Abraham that his posterity (spiritual as well as physical) will be "as numerous as the stars in the sky and as the sand on the seashore." In the same vein we seem to be assured by Paul that many more people will be saved than lost, because Christ's work in causing salvation will be more successful than Adam's cause in ruin, and because God's grace in bringing life will overflow "much more" than Adam's trespass in bringing death.[7]

From God's promise to Abraham (see Gen 12:3) to the angels on Christmas morning, the biblical message is, "I bring you good news of great joy *which will be for all the people*" [emphasis mine] (Luke 2:10). "For if by the transgression of the one the many died, much more did the grace of God and the gift by the grace of the one Man, Jesus Christ, *abound to the many*" [emphasis mine] (Rom 5:15). A few verses later: "So then as through one transgression there resulted condemnation to all men, even so through one act of righteousness there resulted justification of *life to all men*" [emphasis mine] (Rom 5:18). Next, we find Paul saying to the church at Corinth: "For as in Adam all die, so also in Christ *all shall be made alive* [emphasis mine] (1 Cor 15:22). On the one hand, because of the sin of one person (Adam) all are condemned. On the other hand, because of the righteousness of one person (Jesus) all are given life. And finally, "He Himself is the propitiation for our sins; and not for ours only, but also for those of *the whole world*" [emphasis mine] (1 John 2:2).

Lesslie Newbigin (d. 1998), was a theologian, missionary to India for forty years, and Bishop in the Church of Scotland. In *The Gospel In A Pluralist Society*, he writes this about the Christian faith:

> Exclusivist in the sense that it affirms the unique truth of the revelation in Jesus Christ, but it is not exclusivist in the sense of *denying the possibility of salvation of the non-Christian*. It is inclusivist in the sense that it *refuses to limit the saving grace of God to members*

of the Christian church, but it rejects the inclusivism which regards the non-Christian religions as vehicles of salvation. It is pluralist in the sense of *acknowledging the gracious work of God in the lives of all human beings,* but it *rejects a pluralism which denies the uniqueness and decisiveness of what God has done in Jesus Christ* [emphasis mine].

The Christian church has been unambiguous in asserting that there is only one Savior: the Lord, Jesus Christ. All who come to God for salvation come by and through Jesus Christ, whether they know it (or Him) or not. In one of the first sermons ever preached in the newborn church, Simon Peter expressed the means of salvation for all people and for all time: "And there is salvation in no one else; for there is no other name under heaven that has been given among men, by which we must be saved" (Acts 4:12).

The church, however, has restricted salvation only to those who know enough to use the name of Jesus. Does such narrow exclusivism contradict the character of God revealed in Jesus of Nazareth and His love, passion, and compassion for all humankind? I think it does. Will God refuse salvation to billions because they never heard the name Jesus? I think He will not. Paul prayed that the Ephesians would come to know "what is the breadth and length and height and depth" of "the love of Christ which surpasses knowledge" (Eph 3:18-19). God's love is broader, longer, higher, and deeper than the human mind can conceive. This describes the dimensions of God's love for all humankind. No object is sufficient for the love of God short of the entire world. Such love reaches far beyond the Christian church. Can His love and redemption reach those who have never heard His name? It can. Can His love reach and even redeem those still involved in other religions? It can. Further, the church believes that all humankind is created in the image of God. Is it, therefore, beyond reason and biblical revelation to believe—as Newbigin so eloquently states above—that "the gracious work of God" can take place "in the lives of all human beings" even though they have not embraced the Christian religion? For me this is exactly how great God's love is. It reaches far beyond the Christian religion. God is not just the God of the Christian church. He is Lord of all who call on Him, even if they do not know His name. This is the deep reach of amazing grace.

Henry van Dyke's poetry put lyrics to Ludwig van Beethoven's *Ninth Symphony*, furnishing us with one of the most revered and well-known hymns of faith. The third stanza expresses perfectly the deep reach of amazing grace:

> *Joyful, Joyful We Adore Thee*
> Thou art giving and forgiving, ever blessing, ever blest,
> Wellspring of the joy of living, ocean depth of happy rest!
> Thou our Father, Christ our Brother, all who live in love are Thine,
> Teach us how to love each other, lift us to the joy divine.[8]

The Brothers Karamazov by Fyodor Dostoyevsky is considered by many literary critics to be the greatest novel ever written. He illumines the deep reach of God's grace in the chapter, "Cana of Galilee." As you may recall, the Gospel of John records the account of Jesus' first miracle. It occurred during a wedding feast held in the village of Cana that was situated in the region of Galilee. At His mother's request Jesus turns water to wine so that the family would not be embarrassed socially at having run out of wine. John calls the miracles of Jesus "signs" (miraculous events pointing beyond themselves to something greater than the miracle itself). It's important to remember John's assertion about Jesus: He came to *explain* the Father (John 1:18). What Jesus explains is that God has such compassion on a poor young couple from a nowhere town in a backwater region of the world that He turns water to wine so the party can continue. Take a moment to ponder what this communicates to us about God.

In Dostoevsky's chapter, "Cana of Galilee" an elderly and godly Father Zossima has died. Alyosha, one of the Karamazov brothers, loved Father Zossima who had been his kind and wise mentor. In keeping with the tradition, when a priest died, his fellow priests would read the Scriptures over his body until it was buried. Alyosha comes into the room where all of this is occurring. Putrefaction has already set in and windows have been opened to let in fresh air. Alyosha kneels to pray and soon lapses exhausted into a stupor, half-awake and half-asleep. He can hear

Chapter 5

Father Paisey reading the miracle at Cana from John 2 and in Alyosha's daze of grief and exhaustion, imagines he and Father Zossima are attending the wedding feast at Cana. Note the depth of God's love and grace as Dostoyevsky writes:

> Ah, that miracle! Ah, that sweet miracle! It was not men's grief, but their joy Christ visited, He worked his first miracle to help men's gladness.... "He who loves men loves their gladness too...." His Mother, knew that He had come not only to make His great terrible sacrifice. She knew that His heart was open to even the simple, artless merry-making of some obscure and unlearned people, who had warmly bidden Him to their poor wedding... And indeed was it to make wine abundant at a poor wedding He had come down to earth?
>
> "We are rejoicing.... We are drinking the new wine, the wine of new, great gladness: do you see how many guests?" [says Father Zossima] "I am afraid...I dare not look," whispers Alyosha.
>
> [To which Father Zossima replies] "Do you fear Him? He is terrible in His greatness, awful in His sublimity, but infinitely merciful. He has made Himself like unto us from love and rejoices with us. He is changing the water to wine that the gladness of the guests may not be cut short. He is expecting new guests, He is calling new ones unceasingly for ever and ever.... There they are bringing new wine. Do you see they are bringing the vessels."
>
> Something glowed in Alyosha's heart, something filled it till it ached, tears of rapture rose from his soul.... He stretched out his hands, uttered a cry and waked up.[9]

Alyosha begins weeping as rapturous waves of joy flood his soul. He throws himself down to embrace the ground.

> He did not know why he embraced it. He could not have told why he longed so irresistibly to kiss it, to

kiss all. But he kissed it weeping, sobbing and watering it with his tears, and vowed passionately to love it, to love it for ever and ever. "Water the earth with the tears of your joy and love those tears," echoed in his soul.... He longed to forgive everyone and for everything, and to beg forgiveness. Oh, not for himself, but for all men, for all and for everything.[10]

A miracle greater than turning water to wine had occurred. Even as his saintly old father dies, Alyosha has reborn spiritually. He understands that Christ did not come only to die on a cross, but to bring joy and love to the world. And the people keep coming "unceasingly for ever and ever." God so loved the world, and having been loved by God, Alyosha, too, loves the world.

Dostoyevsky is on record as saying that this chapter was the most important one in his book. It provides a moving example of the revelation of the God that Jesus "explained" to us: a God so compassionate that He gave a poor, young couple hundreds of gallons of wine so they could keep partying! If those whom He calls, "new ones unceasingly for ever and ever,"[11] look at "the creation of the world" (Rom 1:20) and come to understand (as much as general revelation makes possible) God's "invisible attributes, His eternal power and divine nature" (Rom 1:20) and bow down and worship Him, would such a God refuse these the joy of salvation *just because they do not know His name?* Is this the God Jesus explained to us? The good news is greater and more encompassing than we think. The last invitation in the Bible, written by John in Revelation 22:17 says, "The Spirit and the bride say, 'Come.' And let the one who hears say, 'Come.' And let the one who is thirsty come; *let the one who wishes* take the water of life without cost" [emphasis mine]. Anyone, *anyone* who is thirsty can come. All are invited to another wedding party: the marriage supper of the Lamb.

On seeing the wonder of God's love and grace, Alyosha was overwhelmed. He fell to the ground, embraced it and watered it with his tears. We go to church, sing the songs, listen to the sermon, pass the collection plate, go to lunch, and return home. We are seldom touched by the wonder of God's way of salvation and we are blind to the deep reach of amazing grace. And, rarely is the full and complete truth of what Jesus "explained" about God communicated.

[1] William Cowper, "There Is a Fountain Filled with Blood," 1772.
[2] Isaac Watts, "Alas! And Did My Savior Bleed," 1707.
[3] George Bennard, "The Old Rugged Cross," 1913.
[4] Eliza Holmes Reed, "Oh, Why Not Tonight," 1842.
[5] Fanny Crosby, "Rescue the Perishing," 1869.
[6] John R.W. Stott, *The Contemporary Christian* (Downers Grove, IL: InterVarsity Press, 1992) 318.
[7] Ibid, 319.
[8] Henry J. van Dyke, "Joyful, Joyful We Adore Thee," *Book of Poems* (1911).
[9] Fyodor Dostoyevsky, *The Brothers Karamazov* (Doubleday Book & Music Clubs, 1995) 336.
[10] Ibid, 338.
[11] Ibid, 337.

CHAPTER 6

When Religion Goes Bad

"Men never do evil so completely and cheerfully as when they do it from religious conviction."
—Blaise Pascal

"We have just enough religion to make us hate, but not enough to make us love one another."
—Jonathan Swift

HISTORICALLY, RELIGION HAS BEEN a double-edged sword. Religion has done immeasurable good throughout the world. The Christian religion has singlehandedly built more hospitals for the sick, orphanages for children, and homes for the aged than all other religions combined. International mission forces have carried the message of God's love and forgiveness to people groups from densely populated cities in Asia to remote villages in Africa where tribes can only be reached by walking for miles.

And, oh, the majestic music of the Christian church! Christian music has brought untold beauty to this world. I know of no other religion that has a history of magnificent music like the Christian church. The hymns of John Newton, Isaac Watts, Charles Wesley, Fanny Crosby, and many others are poetry set to music expressing our faith, comforting our souls, lifting our spirits, enlarging our vision, and challenge our imagination. Just one example of the many, many majestic hymns of the church is "How Firm A Foundation." Consider its content and its structure. It begins with an exclamation (note the exclamation point in first stanza at the end of the second line). Then it poses a question (note the question mark at the end of the first stanza). The remainder of the hymn answers that question. Note the quotation marks at the beginning of each stanza. This is God's "excellent Word" to us. What God has said in the third stanza has been a great comfort to me and to thousands of others who have been bruised and battered by life. The final stanza expresses God's firm and emphatic promise that God walks with us though all hell or anything else life throws against us.

How Firm A Foundation
How firm a foundation, ye saints of the Lord,
Is laid for your faith in His excellent Word!
What more can He say than to you He has said,
To you who for refuge to Jesus have fled?

"Fear not, I am with you, O be not dismayed,
For I am your God and will still give you aid;
I'll strengthen you, help you, and cause you to stand,
Upheld by my righteous, omnipotent hand."

"When through fiery trials your pathway shall lie,
My grace all sufficient shall be your supply;
The flame shall not hurt you; I only design
Your dross to consume and your gold to refine."

"The soul that on Jesus has leaned for repose
I will not, I will not desert to its foes;
That soul, though all hell should endeavor to shake,
I'll never, no never, no never forsake!"[1]

Take a moment and meditate on that final line: "I'll never, no never, no never forsake!" What great comfort and assurance is this! With whatever problems the church may have, the church of the Lord Jesus Christ has been the greatest agent for benevolence and beauty the world has ever known.

An honest evaluation of history, however, reveals the horrendous scourge religion, including the Christian religion, has fomented among the people and nations of this world. It has been so from earliest times. The first murder recorded in the Bible was over religion. The writer of Genesis doesn't tell why (and to speculate misses the truths of the story), but God accepted Abel's offering and rejected Cain's. These two religious observances were the catalysts that led Cain to murder his brother. From then until now, religion has caused incalculable suffering, pain, and death. Religion has brought the destruction of families and friendships and conflicts between nations which have gone to war over religion. When religion is good, it is very good. When religion goes bad it is horrible and exacts monstrous consequences.

I offer here two quotes to exemplify why I title this chapter as I have. The first was found among the devotional writings of one of the 9/11 terrorists. Make no mistake, 9/11 was definitely an example of religion gone bad. The second quote is from Spanish essayist, George Santayana.

> Be happy, optimistic, calm, because you are heading for a deed that God loves and will accept. It will be the day, God willing, you spend with the women of paradise.... Strike for God's sake.... Take prisoners and kill them.... Remind brothers that this act is for Almighty God.[2]

> Those who cannot remember the past are condemned to repeat it.[3]

Whenever Christian people or Christian leaders (from pastors to popes) use Christianity or the church to dominate, divide, categorize, typify, stigmatize, isolate, or condemn people, it has forgotten the gospel of the grace of God, and it is Christianity gone bad.

A Few Examples of Christianity Gone Terribly Bad

It is worth noting that some of the terrible acts in history (the Inquisition, witch-hunts, torture, execution, etc.) were not carried out by barbaric or animistic savages; they were administered by some of the most learned officials of the church.

1. In the Third Crusade, after Richard the Lion-Hearted captured the Galilean port city of Acre in 1191, he ordered 3,000 captives—many of them women and children—to be taken outside the city and slaughtered.

2. The Fourth Lateran Council in 1215 proclaimed the doctrine of transubstantiation: that the communion wafer miraculously turns into the body of Jesus during the mass. It was soon rumored that Jews were stealing the sacred wafers and stabbing or driving nails through them to crucify Jesus again. What is not rumored is that on this charge, in 1243, every Jew in Berlitz, Germany was burned alive. To avenge the tortured host, the German knight Rindfleisch in 1298 led a brigade that in six months exterminated 146 defenseless Jewish communities and massacred entire cities.

3. From the Middle Ages to modern times there has been what is known as "The Blood Libel." The rumor is that Jews captured Christian children, tortured and killed them, and used their blood in the preparation of the Passover Matzoth. What is not a rumor is that in response to "The Blood Libel," many Jews have been arrested, tortured, and killed by the church.

4. In 1209, Pope Innocent III launched an armed crusade against Albigenses Christians in southern France. When the besieged city of Beziers fell, soldiers asked their papal adviser how to distinguish the faithful from the infidel among the captives. He commanded: "Kill them all. God will know his own." Nearly 20,000 were slaughtered—after first being blinded, mutilated, dragged behind horses, or used for target practice.

5. The formal Inquisitions of the church sought to weed out heretics. Heinous methods of torture were devised by the church to force confessions out of its victims. Some of the most horrible torture and deaths came at the hands of Dominican friar Tomás de Torquemada, called "the hammer of heretics, the light of Spain, the savior of his country, the honor of his order." In the fifteenth century Pope Sixtus IV named Torquemada "Grand Inquisitor." He led the church to imprison,

torture, and burn suspected heretics at the stake. The number of victims during his tenure as Grand Inquisitor is estimated at about 2,000. He was influential in the decision of King Ferdinand and Queen Isabella to expel from Spain all Jews who would not convert to Christianity.

6. The Inquisition sought to root out those accused (mostly women) of being witches. The *Malleus Maleficarum* (Latin for "Hammer of the Witches") was written by Inquisitors of the Roman Church and first published in 1487; latter editions actually included an official papal bull (a written charter or legal instrument issued by the Pope). The manual assisted clergy and magistrates in both identifying witches and discrediting those who denied their existence. The accused were subjected to indescribable torture. If they confessed they were executed, many being burned alive at the stake. If they denied being a witch, they were killed because they denied it.

7. Following the Reformation, religious terror reigned throughout Europe in France, The Netherlands, Belgium, England, Scotland, and other areas. Unspeakable tortures were used against untold millions of accused heretics, and tens of thousands were put to death all in the name of the church, all in the name of Jesus. In the St. Bartholomew's day massacre, which actually took place over several days in sixteenth-century Paris, Catholics killed thousands of French Huguenots (Protestant Calvinists). Estimates of the number killed are imprecise and vary wildly, ranging from 5,000-30,000. Whatever the number, it is still an example of Christianity gone bad.

While exact figures are impossible, it is estimated that over the centuries all religious wars have killed some 809 million people. To put that in perspective, in the great purge of Russia, Stalin murdered 43 million of his own citizens. The total estimated number killed in Russian Revolution from 1917 to 1987 is 62 million The most recent documents now reveal that, in the Cultural Revolution, Mao Zedong murdered 77 million of his own citizens. Hitler murdered 8 million people in the concentration camps of World War II. Harvard historian Niall Ferguson reports that World Wars I and II resulted in the deaths of some 75 million people. And since WWII, organized violence by the enlightened people of the twentieth century have killed an estimated 167-188 million people.[4] All of these together total 404 million people killed in political wars in twentieth century. And that is still less than half of those killed via the religiously sponsored violence and war to which I refer above. While the

809 million are from all religions, modern critics of the church can accurately claim that more people have been killed in the name of Jesus Christ than all of those killed in the names of Adolf Hitler, Joseph Stalin, Mao Zedong, Pol Pot, and even Genghis Khan combined. (The 809 million killed are from all religions.)

When Christianity Goes Bad *Today*

What bothers me *more* than religion gone bad in history is when religion goes bad today. Yet, to again put this in perspective, the Christian church admits that all the atrocities perpetrated in the name of Jesus Christ reflects *the church at its worst. The church admits that in these horrible times, Christianity has failed.* In 1995, Pope John Paul, II asked, "How can one remain silent about the many forms of violence perpetrated in the name of the faith-wars of religion, tribunals of the Inquisition and other forms of violations of the rights of persons?"[5] The Christian church acknowledges that in the past it has failed miserably in representing Jesus Christ and His message of love and forgiveness for all humankind.

Again, what concerns me *most*, however, is *when Christianity goes bad today.*

> When the Westboro Baptist Church in Topeka, Kansas pickets the funerals of Americans soldiers with signs such as "God Hates Fags," or "God Hates X" (X being anything they not might like at the time);
> When a pastor in Florida burns a copy of the Koran;
> When two of the most public and vocal spokesmen for the Christian church (both ordained ministers of the gospel of Jesus Christ, one now deceased) say, "... the abortionists, and the feminists, and the gays and the lesbians" are the reason for 9/11;[6]
> When the Focus on the Family organization regularly co-mingles Christianity with politics;
> When the leadership of the country's largest Protestant denomination supports a President's rush to war even when the war didn't meet the classic principles of Augustine's "Just War" principle;

When Christians give *unilateral support* to the nation of Israel and have no concern for the millions of Palestinians who were dispossessed from the land that became the state of Israel;

When syndicated columnist and best-selling author Ann Coulter says, "I'm a Christian first, and a mean-spirited, bigoted conservative second, and don't you ever forget it";

When a Christian denomination forces out of its membership churches who minister to gays and lesbians;

When Churches deny baptism, membership, and communion to gays and lesbians;

When Christians say, "Gays or lesbians cannot be Christian";

When Christians at work, at a coffee shop, over lunch, at a ball game, on a golf course, or in casual conversation sound more like the vitriolic hosts of talk radio than a compassionate Jesus Christ;

When the attitude of Christians toward Islamic terrorists is, "Kill them over there, before they come over here";

When Christians consider people of a different political party or persuasion no longer opponents to be defeated, but enemies to be hated;

When Christians blame all Muslims for terrorism against the United States;

When Philip Yancey asks hundreds of people, "What comes to mind when you think of evangelical Christianity?" and they answer, judgmental, anti-abortion, Republican party, and not one time does anyone mention the love, forgiveness, mercy and grace of God;[7]

When churches and Christians do and say such things as these, it is a practical and public denial of the gospel we claim to believe. It is Christianity gone bad.

Other than the media, I don't know anyone who cares what the fifty-member Westboro Baptist Church says or does. (The church is affiliated with no national Baptist denomination.) But when a Christian denomination dismisses a member church because it ministers to gays and lesbians, when local congregations refuse baptism, church membership, and communion to gays and lesbians, and when Christians say that there is no way gays and lesbians can be "saved" and go to heaven, all together this establishes a pattern, and a message is presented. The church has learned better than to say anymore that God hates homosexuals, but rather, He hates their sin. But if the truth were told, many of these Christians want nothing to do with gays and lesbians. They hate their lifestyle, and they hate them. They certainly do not treat them as Jesus would. Members of the Westboro church say, "God's hatred is one of His holy attributes." I have often heard that excuse given when Christians denounce sin. However, it is evident that the intention is to denounce not only the sin, but the person. This is a denial of the gospel of unconditional love. It is a denial of the God Jesus "explained" to us in John 1:18. Henry David Thoreau wrote, "There is no odor so bad as that which arises from goodness tainted."[8] Far too often today, Christianity, in the name of Jesus, in the name of the Bible, in the name of goodness, emits a foul odor, and the stench repulses millions. This is Christianity gone bad.

When the church is unable to win its arguments through persuasion and seeks to use the government to try to codify its morality into law, this is Christianity gone bad. This was the attempt of the Moral Majority in the 1980s, and it created a huge set of problems. I'll mention only two. First, churches, ministers, and Christians who supported that platform of ideas subtly admitted a belief that the gospel is impotent. No longer was there a trust in the gospel to be "the power of God for salvation" (Rom 1:16). The church no longer has confidence that it can go to the market place of ideas with its gospel and trust the gospel to change the hearts and lives of people, who, in turn, will change the culture. Therefore, the church seeks to use the power of government to coerce people to accept its morality and conform to its ethics.

This presents a second problem. Such coercion by the church—using the government to try and force conformity to a code of morality and ethics—engenders massive resentment from the very people the church should be reaching with the message of God's love, forgiveness, mercy, and grace. The public, in a constitutional republic, sensitive to the provision of separation of church and state in the United States Constitution, despises the church for such injudicious and manipulative maneuvers. Many in the church see this fallacy and oppose the tactics. They realize that a low tide for one ship lowers all ships. Jesus eschewed the trappings of political power and sought to win the world one heart at a time. He knew that the government (like the moral police of His time) could force compliance to an ethical standard, but that would leave the heart completely unchanged. A person may not kill because they fear prison, but the violence of hatred can remain in their heart. Jesus sought not conformity to the law but the transformation of the heart.

One bittersweet irony of the Moral Majority is that after it swung its support from President Jimmy Carter (a born-again, evangelical Baptist Sunday school teacher) to Governor Ronald Reagan (a remarried divorcee who had signed into law a bill legalizing abortion in California), during Reagan's eight-year presidency not a single piece of legislation demanded by the religious right was passed or even given more than token support by Reagan. When members of the religious right complained to the leadership of the Moral Majority they were told they could not criticize the President. Why? It might cause the organization to lose access to the oval office. In dabbling in the trappings of power, the Moral Majority had lost its prophetic voice with the President and eventually with the nation. As British Lord Acton warned: power corrupts and absolute power corrupts absolutely. While the Moral Majority lost its prophetic voice and failed to secure passage of any legislation it demanded, the deleterious effects of the Moral Majority remain with us to this day. One reason for the enormous hostility aimed at the church for most of my adult life is that the Moral Majority worked to force its morality on the nation. This is an example Christianity gone bad.

Anytime the church does and says things that fail to represent Jesus and His message of love, forgiveness, and acceptance for all people, we do a disservice to Jesus' call to follow him. When the church fails to accurately articulate the gospel of the grace of God, Christianity eventually goes bad. I know where of I speak. I have been terribly guilty of such failures, even (to my own shame) from my pulpit. During the eight years of the Clinton presidency, I blasted President and Mrs. Clinton almost every Sunday. I even grew tired of hearing me complain about them and their policies. They gave ample fodder for my moralistic cannons. From gays in the military, females on submarines, partial birth abortion, safe-sex and condoms in schools, comments by the Surgeon General on personal pleasures, to the President's personal dalliances, and on and on and on. In those days Focus on the Family would send out a weekly "Pastor's Fax" that came to my church office before daylight every Friday morning and would be on my desk when I arrived. It covered a variety of matters addressing their concerns for the deterioration of "Christian America." That faxed information was part of an overall effort to get us back to our "Christian foundations." It always contained some juicy information I could use to punch up my Sunday morning sermons, further blasting some recent policy, position, or comment of the political administration in power. (By the way, talk to African Americans, the descendants of slaves, or to native Americans who were massacred and driven off their lands about the glories of our "Christian foundations.")

I failed to understand so much in those days. No matter how terrible the sin is—and sin is terrible—God's love and forgiveness are far greater. No matter how terrible, how many, how often the sin, God always loves and forgives. Getting my man elected to the White House would not advance the cause of Christ. The Kingdom of God will not arrive on Air Force One no matter who is riding in that airplane. The message of the church is that no one—President, pope, or preacher—can out-sin the capacity of God to forgive. "Where sin increased, grace abounded all the more" (Rom 5:20).

A preacher wrote a letter to the editor of a local newspaper citing the moral failures of the culture and the dangers of its continued demise; a letter that excoriated the church for no longer preaching against sin. In a noble effort to force us back on the straight and narrow, he concluded his letter by warning the reader, "Grace has a way of running out." I have kept this letter in my files because it is so revealing of the church's failure to understand the gospel, to understand grace. You see, if it runs out, it is not grace. By definition, grace cannot run out. God's grace, His love, forgiveness, and acceptance are *unconditional.* His grace is not tied to our behavior, our obedience, our walking the straight and narrow. God loves and forgives and accepts us because that is who He is, not because of what we do. Too often, rather than reminding the culture and the sinner of God's grace, like the preacher's letter, we want to recite the laws of God and the warnings for disobedience. How well did that work out in the 1,500 years of Old Testament history? Jesus realized that sin is overcome, *not by forbidding it, but by forgiving it.* This is grace, the gospel, the good news, the message of the New Testament, the message of Jesus. This is the message that transforms lives. When the church abandons this message, it forfeits the only unique message it has. It becomes the purveyor of just another religion, and Christianity goes bad.

The one thing that President and Mrs. Clinton would not have heard had they been sitting in my church in those eight years was the overwhelming love God has for them. They, along with everyone else who was there, would not have heard the heart of the gospel. (Ironically, we built a large congregation due in part to my political preaching.) Regardless of sins, evil, wickedness, addictions, ethical failures, immorality, ungodliness, and unrighteousness, the message of the Christian church is God's grace: His unconditional love, forgiveness, and acceptance of all people. Whenever that is truncated, Christianity has gone bad.

The Necessary Offence of the Gospel and the Needless Offence of the Church

The last thing the Christian church needs is to be offensive. The gospel is offensive enough without the ill-considered offence of bad Christianity. The offence of the gospel is a double-edged sword—it cuts two ways. One edge of the sword cuts because no matter how good, kind, sweet, loving, and so on a person is, that person does not deserve salvation and heaven. There is nothing anyone can do to merit God's love, forgiveness, and salvation. Take the sweetest person you know, the kindness and best person you know (someone like my Aunt Lyba, whom I described earlier). If they got what they deserved, they would be dead, condemned, and consigned to hell. This is insulting, impertinent, disrespectful, and impolite. It is rude. This is offensive; it is to me. Yet, *this* is the offense of the gospel. Salvation is *sola gratia, sola fide, solus Christus,* and not by anything we do or do not do.

The other edge of the sword cuts because no matter how mean, hateful, greedy, criminal, indecent, profane, vulgar, or vengeful a person is, God still loves that person and *sola gratia, sola fide, solus Christus* all their sins are forgiven. They are still welcome at the portals of heaven. To this notion I have had people remark, "How can that be?! You don't realize what they did! They killed (or lied, raped, assaulted, etc.)." Yet by faith in Christ, heaven is just as much theirs as Mother Teresa's. The hymn writer, William Cowper, wrote of this offence: "The dying thief rejoiced to see that fountain in his day; And there may I, *though vile as he*, wash all my sins away" [emphasis mine].⁹ *This* is the offence of the gospel.

Andy became a friend of mine. I didn't know Andy until two years after he brutally murdered two Mercer University students at Lake Juliette, Georgia, in 1995. Members of his family were part of my church. Andy's father, John, called me at home very early one morning and said he needed to see me ASAP. John was a no-nonsense, career agent for the Federal Bureau of Investigation. We met at my office at 7:30 that morning and he told me the story.

The Georgia Bureau of Investigation had called him the night before and asked how to get in touch with Andy. They needed to talk with him about the Lake Juliette murders. John thought it was a routine request, just running down leads and gave them Andy's beeper number. John then dialed Andy's beeper. He was already in bed for the night when Andy returned the called. "Andy, the GBI wants to talk with you about the Lake Juliette murders. Do you know what they want?" John asked. "Yes," Andy replied. "Do you know anything about those murders?" his father inquired. Andy replied once again, "Yes." John told me he has wished a thousand times he had never asked the next question: "Andy, did you kill those kids?" Andy replied a third time, "Yes."

John told me that his mind was racing like a trip hammer, a thousand thoughts screaming at him all in the brutal moments of that unforgiving time. He told Andy that he needed to turn himself in to the county sheriff. Andy refused, saying he was going to run. Amid the flood of things in John's mind, he told his son, "Andy, you cannot get away. They will track you down. You will be considered armed and dangerous. You could be shot on sight." John also told me that among the gazillion thoughts he had, he knew enough about how law enforcement works that he could facilitate Andy's getaway. "Pastor, I have given my life to the apprehension and arrest of criminals. I could do no less now."

Though it was well after midnight when John ended the conversation with Andy, before his protective instincts as a father would take him where he knew he could not go he immediately called his FBI supervisor. "I need to tell you what my son, Andy, has just told me. He has just confessed to the Lake Juliette murders." John told his supervisor that first thing the next morning he was going to the Monroe County Sheriff to tell him what his son had just confessed. His supervisor told him to

Chapter 6

wait until he could fly to Macon and the two would go together. In the meantime, John came to see me.

That same morning, a GBI agent was at Andy's mobile home and saw Andy skinning a deer he had killed out of season. Since he did not know of Andy's confession to his father the night before, he had no reason to arrest him, even though by now he was a suspect. The agent called a game warden who came and arrested Andy for the hunting violation. He was brought into the Monroe County jail at the same moment his father was on site telling the sheriff about Andy's confession. Andy was soon charged with double murder. During the trial, Andy's FBI agent father was the prosecution's star witness. In 1998 Andy was convicted and sentenced to die.

I first met Andy in the county jail just days after his arrest. He was almost catatonic. He was barely responsive and if he answered at all it was in monosyllabic sounds. Over the years in visiting Andy, he became much more conversant, and we had numerous meaningful conversations. As a minister of the gospel, I sought many times to assure Andy that God loved him regardless of what he had done. I assured him that God had forgiven him of all his sins—no exceptions—and that God accepted him just as he was.

I wish I could tell you that Andy had a great spiritual epiphany and a glorious conversion. Those make for good stories. In fact, while Andy had professed faith in Jesus Christ as a child, he was not at all religious. He said he prayed some, but didn't read the Bible. He told me that he believed in God, but he could not understand how God could forgive him for what he did. My hope for Andy, as my hope for Steve, for you, and for all born of Adam's race, was not in our religion or in our performance, be it criminal or charitable. My hope was and is in the grace of God.

Without drawing the dramatics that paint a necessary picture, Andy killed two promising young university students, both the only child in their families. When I asked Andy through the years why he did it, his consistent reply was, "Something came over me." That is it. He didn't know them, hadn't stalked them, had never met them, and didn't speak to them that night. He just killed them—for no known reason. Yet God loves Andy and always will. God has forgiven Andy. I understand that the natural thought is Andy did not deserve love and forgiveness; that he deserved death sentence rendered by the State of Georgia. Or perhaps,

"Fine, love and forgive him if you want, but he still deserves to die" (as if that is not a contradiction in meaning). I can understand that this is popular thinking. It is the thinking of many Christians who sit in church pews on Sundays.

I know that the State of Georgia has a job to do and that the courts sentenced Andy to death. I know the courts are not the church. They cannot simply say, "We forgive" and subsequently release those guilty of violent crimes into society. The state has a responsibility to protect us. The church, however, also has a job to do for those like Andy (over three thousand people sit on death row in the United States). What is the responsibility of the church when a capital crime is committed? What is the responsibility of the *ordained* clergy to the convicted, to the society, to the gospel of Jesus Christ they represent? How would Jesus treat these people? What would He say to them? The job of the Christian church is to proclaim the good news of God's grace to all those arrested, awaiting trial, or convicted. The job of the ordained Christian clergy is to explain the gospel of Jesus Christ to the church, to society, and to the convicted. The state will do its job. Will the church and clergy do their job? Will we proclaim God's *unconditional* love and forgiveness for all people, including people like Andy and all those who sit on death row? For many Christians, this is unthinkable. *This the offence of the gospel.*

When surveys consistently reveal that conservative, evangelical Christians are among the staunchest supporters of the death penalty, it says something about a failure to understand the gospel. It says something about the failure of the ordained clergy *either* to understand the gospel *or* to explain it to their congregations. The oft-repeated justification for capital punishment is, "They took a life. They forfeit their life. It is just. It is what they deserve." This is retaliatory, "eye for eye, tooth for tooth" type of thinking (see Lev 17:17-22). Certainly the legal principle *lex talionis* (Latin, *lex* meaning "law" and *talionis* meaning "retaliation") existed in both biblical and early Roman law. The penalty—taking a life—fits the crime—a life taken.

The gospel, however, is not simply about what is just, getting what we deserve, or the penalty fitting the crime. The gospel is about grace. It is about receiving the love and forgiveness we do not deserve and not suffering from the penalty and punishment we do deserve. I often wonder, "What is it about Jesus' message and ministry that Christians do not understand?" I find it unimaginable that Jesus could or would support the death penalty. What about the Jesus of "turn the other cheek" (see Matt 5:38-40)? Of "love your enemies and pray for those who persecute you" (Matt 5:44)? Of "I was in prison and you came to Me" (see Matt 25:34-40)? And to the latter, while Jesus did not specifically provide a reason to visit one in prison, I am quite sure it has nothing to do with reaffirming to the prisoner the sentence of the court. On the contrary, I believe that it is to assure the convicted criminal of God's love and forgiveness, and to be a friend to that prisoner who has been outcast by and isolated from society.

Not only did Jesus reject the notion of *lex talionis* (see Matt 5:38ff), He in fact actually spoke about the death penalty. In John 8 when the religious leaders brought to Jesus the woman who had been taken during an act of adultery they said in verse 5, "Now in the Law Moses commanded us to stone such women; what then do You say?" After outwitting them, they left and Jesus turned to respond to the woman (verse 11): "I do not condemn you, either. Go. From now on sin no more." The gospel, the "good news" is that, in the same way, Jesus loves, forgives, and accepts a man who murdered two innocent young people. Should not His church do the same? Why then does the church not obey Jesus' command to follow Him?

For many years I supported the death penalty. Two circumstances changed my viewpoint. First, there is Andy: a name, a face, a personality, a life, and a family were attached to the issue. I know Andy's family, and I have come to know Andy as a friend. The death penalty is no longer a philosophical debate for me. My connection with Andy has made it personal. We have talked and prayed together. When you know the individual and not simply a meaningless name and newspaper photo, or a type or a sort of person, or a legal argument; but when it is your friend sitting on death row, you grow to think differently. At least I do, and not just about Andy, but about the State putting to death another person.

However, second and more important, there is Jesus; there is the good news gospel of love, mercy, grace, and forgiveness. Regardless of Andy's crime and sin, God still loves Andy, forgives him, and accepts him. If this is God's response, should not this be the church's response and the Christian's response? Whatever Jesus would do, however Jesus would treat murderers, is how the church, how Christians are to treat them. If God loves and forgives, the church, the Christian, and especially the ordained minister must do the same. I understand the families of murdered victims and the public in general wanting "justice." "Justice for all" is the American way. The Christian church, however, is supposed to be different from the American public in general. The Christian faith is not about dispensing justice. It is about extending mercy, forgiveness, and grace. God has dealt with us in mercy, forgiveness, and grace—not with justice. I believe that Christians and the Christian church are responsible for extending the same. Though many will disagree (and not many years ago I, too, would have disagreed), when the church, Christians, or ordained ministers advocate the death penalty, this is an example of Christianity gone bad.

Andy was executed by the State of Georgia on February 21, 2013. I spent time with him that afternoon and assured him of God's love and forgiveness. I believe God accepted Andy. This is the offence of the gospel. This is the deep reach of amazing grace.

The Result of Christianity Gone Bad Today

Millions have concluded that the church is no longer like Jesus. Therefore they no longer want to be part of the church. Because of the dichotomy between the life of Jesus—what He taught, how He lived—and the way Christians live and act today, millions of teenagers and young adults no longer take the church seriously. They have concluded that modern Christianity does not represent the life Jesus lived. Three new terms have entered the religious/sociological lexicon:

> De-converts: Those who have abandoned the Christian faith.
> Leavers: Those who have been raised in the church and are now leaving it.
> Nones: Those who reject all religious identity and when asked their religious preference, now answer "none."[10]

David Kinnaman points out that "these young people are not an unreached people group: they are our brothers, sisters, sons and daughters, and friends. They have dwelt among us."[11] Because of bad Christianity, because the church too often forfeits the only unique message it has—the message of God's unconditional love, forgiveness, and acceptance of all people—the church has lost credibility with millions, including some who remain in the church seeking to remind the church of the gospel it claims to believe and the Jesus it claims to represent.

Why include a chapter on the horrors of religion in a book about God's grace? Because we need to know that there is a high price paid when the church forgets the gospel of grace and Christianity goes bad. Bad Christianity fails terribly to represent our God and Jesus Christ. David Kinnaman writes, that there are many people who now, "...reject Jesus because they feel rejected by Christians."[12] This is what happens whenever the church of Jesus Christ forgets the gospel of grace and its message of the overwhelming love God has for all humankind. Throughout history, world systems have sought to dominate and control people; be they the armies of the states or the popes, or the coercive efforts of religious institutions—the church and para-church organizations—with their authoritarian theology and intimidating ethical demands. Robert Farrar Capon, with characteristic, rapier insight says that the church treats people like dumb sheep, "And then we have the nerve to wonder why so many people hate themselves for being sheep, and hate the church for making them such."[13] When the church forgets the gospel of God's grace, it becomes just another system trying to dominate and control people; just another entity treating people as if they were nothing more than dumb sheep.

In contrast to the controlling tactics of religion, Jesus of Nazareth came to set us free. His assurance of God's unconditional love, forgiveness, and acceptance sets us free from fear, condemnation, guilt, and oppression. It liberates the human spirit, unshackles our hearts and minds, our emotions and our thinking, freeing us to be all that God created us to be. I wonder, can we even conceive of what that realistically means? Can we get beyond the oppression of bad religion to truly know with our minds and believe in our hearts that we are thoroughly loved, forgiven, and accepted no matter what, and that it will always be so? If we could wrap our minds and hearts around the truth that, regardless of our sins, failures, immorality, or crimes, God's love, forgiveness, and acceptance remain forever unchanged, it would transform the human heart. This is "the power of the gospel for salvation" (Rom 1:16). This is freedom! It was in a culture dominated by the oppression of the Roman Empire and to the moral police of His day that Jesus said, "If the Son makes you free, you will be free indeed" (John 8:36). Regardless of the oppression of state or religion, we can be free. It all pivots on understanding the gospel and the deep reach of amazing grace.

Dostoyevsky wrote that *within each of us* there is the "Madonna" and the "Sodom." The "Madonna" represents the good in all of us, and the "Sodom" represents the evil in all of us.[14] Martin Luther's learned phrase is *simul justus et peccator*, "at the same time righteous and sinner."[15] Although redeemed, with Madonna in us, every Christian should ever guard against the Sodom in us or we, too, will make Christianity a bad thing; dominating, manipulating, controlling, condemning, and abusing rather than liberating people whom Jesus loves.

[1] John Rippon, "How Firm A Foundation," *Selection of Hymns* (1787).
[2] Public Broadcasting Service, "Instructions for the Last Night," *Frontline* <www.pbs.org/wgbh/pages/frontline/shows/network/personal/instructions.html>.
[3] George Santayana, *Reason in Common Sense* (Amherst, NY: Prometheus Books) 82.
[4] Niall Ferguson, *The War of The World, Twentieth-Century Conflict and the Descent of the West* (NY: Penguin Press, 2006) 649.
[5] Lee Strobel, *The Case for Faith: A Journalist Investigates the Toughest Objections to Christianity* (Grand Rapids: Zondervan, 2000) 200.
[6] Jerry Falwell and Pat Robertson, "The 700 Club," *The Christian Broadcasting Network, Inc.*, 13 September 2001 <www.youtube.com/watch?v=H-CAcdta_8I>.
[7] Philip Yancey, *What's So Amazing*, 11.
[8] Henry David Thoreau, *Walden; Or, Life in the Woods* (NY: Dover Publications, 1994) 49.
[9] Cowper, "Fountain Filled," 1772.
[10] Robert D. Putnam and David E Campbell, *American Grace: How Religion Divides and Unites Us* (NY: Simon and Schuster, 2012) 23.
[11] Drew Dyck, "The Leavers: Young Doubters Exit the Church," *Christianity Today*, November 2010.
[12] Kinnaman, *unChristian*, 11.
[13] Capon, *Mystery of Christ*, 23.
[14] Dostoyevsky, *Karamazov*, 97.
[15] Alister E. McGrath, ed., "Martin Luther on Sin and Grace," *The Christian Theology Reader* (Hoboken, NJ: Blackwell Publishing, 2007) 443.

CHAPTER 7

The Error of Inerrancy

ONE OF MY EARLIEST CHILDHOOD MEMORIES is singing with great gusto in Vacation Bible School:

> The B-I-B-L-E
> Yes, that's the book for me
> I stand alone on the word of God
> The B-I-B-L-E

Then we would stand with hand over heart and promise, "I pledge allegiance to the Bible, God's Holy Word, and will make it a lamp unto my feet, a light unto my path, and hide its word in my heart that I might not sin against God." I managed to obey nearly all of that well-meant pledge. The part "that I might not sin against God" didn't work out so well, but that's another story for another time.

With whatever is second being far behind, the Bible has had the greatest, most formative influence in shaping my life. It still does. From preschool to this day, the Bible continues to sculpt my views, values, priorities, life-calling, and life-goals. Even after a lifetime of reading, studying, and believing the Bible, I still find it spiritually instructive, intellectually challenging, and emotionally comforting and thrilling. It continues to be "a lamp unto my feet [and] a light unto my path." The B-I-B-L-E, yes, that's the Book for me!

The Bible has been different things to me through the course of my life. First it was a storybook of wonderful tales of creation (Noah and the ark, David and Goliath, etc.). After that I came to understand the Bible as a rule book. With parents, Sunday school teachers, and preachers trying to keep us kids on the straight and narrow, the Bible explained the rules by which we were to live. The "thou shalts" and "thou shalt nots" were drummed into our heads and hearts providing us with rules for right and wrong. It was the measuring stick for obedience and disobedience, and for dispensing affirmation or discipline. Next, the Bible became an answer book for the most important questions: How should I live? How do I please God? How can I get to heaven? (Not to mention, "How do I avoid making God angry and going to hell?") Later the Bible became the sole factor for defining doctrine (helping us know what to believe) and ethics (telling us how to behave). Then, unfortunately and way too often as a minister, the Bible became a cudgel to bludgeon those who disagreed with my interpretation, opinion, and beliefs or who didn't measure up to my standards. I never had trouble finding the needed verses as proof-texts to justify my viewpoints and positions. I wasn't being insincere. I honestly thought that a primary reason the Bible existed was to prove what I believed. "God said it. I believe it. That settles it." While some of these uses of the Bible are legitimate, and some are not, they all miss the main purpose of the Bible and its central message.

The progressive revelation of God comes to ultimate realization in the person of Jesus of Nazareth. What it reveals is that God is supremely a God of love. "God is love," twice written in 1 John, is the message Jesus "explained" (see John 1:18) to the world. I have come to believe that above all else, the Bible is God's love letter to humankind.

However, throughout the church's history, the Bible—written to reveal to the world that God is love—has played a key role in controversy, conflict, hatred, division, and war. It is bad enough when conflicts and wars arise from governments, non-believers, atheists, or other religions; each of which might reject the Bible. It is a tragedy when the conflicts come among those who purport to believe the Bible. Some of the most intense conflicts and divisions within the culture and the church have come over the nature of the Bible itself, and no topic has been more fiercely debated than the subject of inerrancy: the belief that the Bible has no errors of any kind. Most limit inerrancy to textual matters, the words of Scripture themselves. Others claim that the Bible is inerrant in all matters including geography, history, and science.

Chapter 7

Like every chapter in this book, this one is written not from the perspective not of a biblical scholar but from the viewpoint of a pastor and with a pastoral intent: to enlighten and instruct, to correct gently where necessary, and always to encourage and comfort. For those who have been aware of the battles over inerrancy, have participated in some of those clashes, or have been wounded by those fights, I hope this chapter can shed meaningful light on the nature of this cherished Book and strengthen not only your faith in its message, but your conviction and appreciation of its truth.

The preacher holds aloft the Bible and with impassioned sweat, ardently proclaims, "I don't care what anyone says, this is the infallible, inerrant Word of God, every jot and tittle. I even believe the maps are inspired!" In unison the assembly roars, "Amen!" The assembly understands the claim that it contains no errors; not in wording, syntax, science, cosmology, history, or in any other discipline. It is today just as it was when inspired by the Spirit and written by the original authors. "If the King James Version was good enough for the Apostle Paul, it's good enough for me!" says the uninformed person who obviously isn't thinking about the fact that the KJV wasn't even written until 1611. If the preacher had known his subject, he would know full well that this is not the truth. It cannot be the truth as even a casual reading of any contemporary translation reveals. This sort of diatribe, however, rouses the faithful, offers security in uncertain times, and keeps the offering plates full. We are defending the Bible and the faith against godless liberalism that wants to destroy the Word of God. Any view other than the inerrancy and infallibility of the Bible is just an attempt to tear down the Bible and the faith. I know of which I speak. I was one of those eagerly defending the inerrancy of the Bible. I have come to understand the Bible differently, and it hasn't made be believe less. On the contrary, the Bible has become more alive and treasured than ever.

The biblical writings have been subjected to more scrutiny than any other written work of the ancient world. They should be. They claim to be the revelation of God, express the foundation of the Christian faith, and contain the path to eternal life. The life and ministry of Jesus is unparalleled in history, and His universal claims on all humankind are so far-reaching that the highest degree of scrutiny is necessary to establish the truth of His life and ministry. Sincere Christians, therefore, should always welcome scrutiny. The integrity of the Bible can withstand the most critical examination from either theological scholar or armchair atheist. It has for two thousand years. It will continue to do so.

Inerrancy and "The Autographs"

The truth is, however, that the inerrancy battle is a fierce and divisive debate over that which has never actually been viewed. Surprising isn't it? What I'm referring to are known as the "autographs." These are the actual, original documents written by the New Testament authors (John, Paul, James, Luke, Peter, etc.). As of today, not a single one of these autographs has been located. And they never will. (I explain why. Keep reading.) They have not been seen for over two thousand years.

The standard and accepted definition, defining exactly what is meant by inerrancy, is "The Chicago Statement on Biblical Inerrancy." It was written in 1978 and signed by a who's who of conservative, evangelical professors and preachers. It says, in part:

> Since God has nowhere promised an inerrant transmission of Scripture, it is necessary to affirm that *only the autographic text of the original documents was inspired* and to maintain the need of textual criticism as a means of detecting *any slips that may have crept into the text in the course of its transmission.... The copies we possess are not entirely error-free* [emphasis mine].[1]

This statement acknowledges that the Bible we hold in our hands today is not inerrant. In the words of this statement: it is "not entirely error-free." Even before this statement appears in the Chicago Statement, there are nineteen articles filled with affirmations and denials that define what is meant by "inerrancy." Is it beneficial to use a term ("inerrant") that requires nineteen affirmations and nineteen denials in order to define that term? I think not. Article Ten of the affirmations and denials acknowledges that inspiration, "strictly speaking, applies *only to the autographic text of Scripture*, which in the providence of God can be ascertained from available manuscripts *with great accuracy*," and copies and translations of Scripture are "the Word of God *to the extent that they faithfully represent the original*" [emphasis mine].[2] This acknowledges that copies may not "represent the original."

Again, this very statement acknowledges that the Bible we have today is not inerrant. "Strictly speaking" we do not have the autographs, so any assessment of them is speculation. The Bible we have today has been transmitted and translated with "great accuracy." I absolutely affirm that declaration. However, "great accuracy" does not mean perfect or "inerrant" accuracy. Copies "to the extent that they faithfully represent the original" are very reliable, but this wording acknowledges that copies may not be perfect copies representing the original autographs.

Accurate? Yes. Reliable and trustworthy? Yes. The Word of God? Yes. Inerrant? No.

How does it help to argue that the very words of the autographs are inerrant when we don't have the autographs, when they haven't been seen for 2,000 years? Not only do we not have the original autographs, we don't have the first copies of the originals. We don't even have the copies of the copies. What we have are the copies of copies of copies (and so on) made over several centuries following the original writings. And these copies differ from each other in thousands of places. As we will see, almost every one of these differences is inconsequential to our Christian faith and living. If, *if* we can take a courageous and honest assessment of how the Bible we hold in our hands today came into being, it can help our understanding of the treasured Book we call the Word of God, alleviate some of our fears, and perhaps even diminish some of the "Bible wars" so that we can turn our attention to telling the story about the deep reach of God's amazing grace.

Replicating the Autographs

These early manuscripts—which by the fourth century would be the basis for the New Testament—were vital to the Christian community. The Jews who made up most of the New Testament church had been closely attached to the Torah (Hebrew, meaning "instruction" or "guidance"). Christians refer to it as the Pentateuch and it consists of the first five books of the Bible. It is understandable that the autographs—letters, Gospels, narratives, sermons—became for the early church the instruction or guidance for faith and practice (what to believe and how to live). These autographs were a unifying force in the infant church scattered throughout the Roman Empire. Nothing was more important to the church than having them, reading and hearing them read, and preserving them.

The question has to be asked, "How did churches scattered throughout the Roman Empire from Jerusalem to Rome have access to the various writings of Paul, Luke, James, Peter, John, Jude, the Gospels, the book of Hebrews, and the Apocalypse of John?" We know that the documents were shared between the various churches. Colossians 4:16 tells us, "When this letter is read among you, have it also read in the church of the Laodiceans; and you, for your part read my letter that is coming from Laodicea." Access to these vital writings posed a problem for the rapidly growing infant church: autographs could only be in one church at a time. In addition to this obvious problem, the New Testament books were actually not books but papyrus scrolls made from the pith of the papyrus reeds that grow along riverbanks. Without near perfect conditions, these scrolls quickly deteriorated and in time disintegrated. How, then, could the church both preserve these writings and make them available to the churches scattered throughout the Roman Empire?

The answer is that copies of the autographs were made, which raises still more questions. Who was doing the copying? How proficient were the copyists? After a few years, were copyists copying originals or making copies of copies? Anywhere along the process did copyists miscopy the originals or did any of the copyists alter the text to conform to their theological views? (Is this why the story of the adulterous woman in John 8 is left out of numerous manuscripts yet included in others? See below.) It is at this juncture that claims to inerrancy become untenable.

Consider the following. The New Testament was written way before copy machines could perfectly reproduce exact multiple copies. This was all some 1,400 years before the invention of movable type. Every single copy was produced by hand: letter by letter, word by word, line by line. Early copyists were not professional scribes and mistakes were inevitable. It's easy to understand how a person could accidentally omit a letter, a word, or a line. Origen, one of the early church fathers of the third century, complained about copies of the Gospel he had in his possession:

> The differences among the manuscripts have become greater, either through the negligence of some copyists or through the perverse audacity of others; they

either neglect to check over what they have transcribed, or, in the process of checking, they make additions or deletions as they please.³

Once a manuscript left the authors' hands there was no way they could be certain future copies would be reproduced exactly as their work had been written. Most of the differences among early manuscripts were not deliberate or interpretative. They were simply mistakes in copying: a letter, a few words, or a line of text accidentally omitted from or added to the wrong place. If a copyist realized he had omitted a line or word, he could not simply erase, go back, and make the correction; so the omission was often added in the margin. How would a future copyist handle the marginal note? Would they add it back into the main text? Place it in the correct location? Omit it all together? If, then, this work was copied, the alterations were perpetuated, and the error extended to other copies along with the new mistakes of the most recent copyist.

By the fourth and fifth centuries a professional class of scribes had emerged, primarily monks working in monasteries. Though these were both trained and skilled copyists, some were less skilled than others and all were still subject to human error. In one form of reproducing a copy, a monk would read the text aloud while several others were writing what he read. If the monk reading the text missed something, every copy being made would miss it as well. Some words are similar in sound but different in meaning, and both could make sense in the context. If a word was mispronounced or misheard, mistakes were made. At times the texts were changed because the scribe thought there were mistakes in the version he was using. He would then correct the error in the manuscript he was creating. Later, his "corrected" copy was then copied. To further complicate matters, a future copyist might realize that a text had been altered, seek to correct it, and, in doing so, make his own mistakes. Several hundred years removed from the original authorship, it isn't difficult to imagine that many texts existed: maybe the original (if the papyrus had stood the test of time), a mistaken copy, a copy of that version, and a corrected copy. It is entirely plausible that each one of these versions then served as the primary source from which other copies were being made (each with the potential of more human entry errors). It is mind boggling to consider all the possibilities. There are literally thousands of examples of these altered texts copied, corrected, and miscorrected. These types of occurrences took place over several centuries, so over time the exact wording of the original got lost. There are more differences among the known copies of manuscripts than there are words in the New Testament.

Moreover, it was not uncommon for copyists to become editors, adding their own enlightened views, opinions, and comments (or omitting details with which they disagreed). Some texts were deliberately changed by copyists in order to enhance the theological position of the content. This practice was so common in antiquity that the writer warns against this practice at the end of Revelation:

> I testify to everyone who hears the words of the prophecy of this book: if anyone adds to them, God shall add to him the plagues which are written in this book; and if anyone takes away from the words of the book of this prophecy, God shall take away his part from the tree of life and from the holy city, which are written in this book (Rev 22:18-19).

When I was a child, this verse was interpreted as a warning for us to believe literally everything in Revelation exactly as it appeared. This was not John's concern, though. His warning was for future copyists not to add their opinions or delete anything he had written.

Two Obvious Examples of Mistakes Seen in Our Modern Translations

There are two decidedly obvious examples of mistakes made by ancient copyists in reproducing New Testament texts. The first is the occasion of the woman taken in adultery and brought before Jesus. I have referenced previously this event from the life of Jesus. It is found in John 7:53–8:11. These verses are not found in many of the oldest and best manuscripts of John's Gospel, and the manuscripts that do include them place this passage at varying locations in John's Gospel or even in the Gospel of Luke. Some of the manuscripts that include these verses have reference marks such as an asterisk or an obelus—a symbol used in ancient manuscripts to indicate a questionable passage. Why all these differences over these verses? Was this event included in the original writing of John's Gospel or added later by a copyist? Either way, it surely seems

Chapter 7

that these verses were not originally situated in the location we now find in our Bibles.

Consider the sequence of events in John 7-8 of Jesus' teachings. Jesus is in Jerusalem for the Feast of Tabernacles, Israel's most popular national festival during that time period. A significant part of the celebration involved the priests filling a golden jar with water from the Pool of Siloam and with grand procession carrying it to the Temple. With great fanfare and celebration, the water was poured into a silver bowl on the altar. It is during this celebration that Jesus utters His famous words, "If anyone is thirsty, let him come to Me and drink. He who believes in Me, as the Scripture said, 'From his innermost being will flow rivers of living water'" (John 7:37-38). A powerful claim at a dramatic moment! This claim had an impact on the crowd and John recorded the conflict it created among the people. If you then follow the sequence as printed in most modern Bibles, "Everyone went to his home" (7:53) and Jesus heads toward the Mount of Olives (see 8:1). Early the next morning, Jesus returns to Jerusalem where the adulterous woman is thrown down before Him (see 8:2-11). Jesus deals with the guilty woman and the accusing crowd. Then, beginning in 8:12, the debate between Jesus and the Pharisees takes up right where it left off in 7:52.

Next, after the story of the adulterous woman Jesus utters His memorable saying, "I am the Light of the world; he who follows Me will not walk in the darkness, but will have the Light of life" (John 8:12). The careful reader will note how John places back to back two of Jesus' most riveting sayings: Jesus is the water of life and the light of the world. The significance of these two claims offered one after the other is not to be overlooked. The obvious problem is that the impact of these two powerful metaphors is interrupted by the account about the adulterous woman. It seems apparent that these two teachings were placed together and without the intervening story of the adulterous woman. In fact, most commentaries place their discussion about John 7:35–8:11 either at the end of the chapter or at the end of the Gospel. Commentaries urge us not to lose the continuity of Jesus' teachings because of the insertion of the verses contained in 7:53–8:11. Further, scholars say that the style and language in these verses are unlike the rest of John's Gospel. This story simply does not fit where it is found in our modern texts.

If these verses were part of the original, why are they placed where they are? Why do some manuscripts place them at the end of John's

Gospel? Why are they omitted in later copies? Were they not part of the original, but added to later copies of this Gospel? Did later copyists omit these verses from the original because of the radical view of forgiveness, and this did not suit their view of God? Did this event never happen, and it is just an apocryphal story about Jesus added by some copyist? We may never know. (Refer to the first chapter of this book for additional treatment of the story contained in 7:53–8:11.) It seems that some copyists wanted to preserve the account because they deemed it to be authentic. They did not, however, know where to place it in the texts of the Gospels. Most modern translations put these verses in brackets with a marginal notation that they are not found in the oldest Greek manuscripts. *The New English Bible* omits these verses entirely from the text of John and begins John 8 with verse 12. These disputed verses are added after the conclusion of the Gospel with this note:

> This passage, which in the most widely received editions of the New Testament is printed in the text of John, 7:53–8:11, has no fixed place in our witnesses. Some of them do not contain it at all. Some place it after Luke 21:38, others after John 7:36, or 7:52, or 21:24.[4]

The dispute over these verses clearly reveals that in copying the original manuscripts (or during the rendering of copies of copies), mistakes were obviously made. Material was either added or omitted, or both. How then can we insist on claiming an inerrant Bible? The original autographs have long ago been lost, and the copies we do have reveal many variances.

The second example of copying errors is related to the ending of Mark's Gospel. I still recall the first time I realized the ending was in dispute. My seminary New Testament Greek class was taught the late Dr. Curtis Vaughan, a renowned scholar. One of my classmates asked our professor if he believed what Mark wrote in the closing verses of his Gospel, "They will pick up serpents, and if they drink any deadly poison, it will not hurt them; they will lay hands on the sick, and they will recover" (Mark 16:18). (This verse is referenced by some Appalachian Pentecostals to explain why they handle highly poisonous snakes during their worship practices.) Dr. Vaughan replied without hesitation, "Mark

Chapter 7

did not write that material." Yet, there it has been in plain King James English for hundreds of years!

Most modern translations indicate that Mark's Gospel ends at 16:8. The remaining material appears in brackets with a marginal notation that verses 9-20 are not found in the best available manuscripts. In addition, some ancient copies provide an optional ending to Mark which is included in some modern translations following verse 8 and in other translations can be found tacked to tend of verse 20:

> And they promptly reported all these instructions to Peter and his companions. And after that, Jesus Himself sent out through them from east to west the sacred and imperishable proclamation of eternal salvation (Mark 16:20, NASB)

If the best manuscripts conclude Mark's Gospel with verse 8, from where do the added verses in our Bible come? If Mark's Gospel ends with verse 8, it is a stark and abrupt end to the Gospel. An angel appears to Mary Magdalene, Jesus' mother Mary, and Salome at the empty tomb, announcing that Jesus has risen and telling them to report the resurrection to the disciples. The reaction of the three women? "They went out and fled from the tomb, for trembling and astonishment had gripped them; and they said nothing to anyone, for they were afraid" (Mark 16:8). There ends the Gospel of Mark. The disciples are never told of the resurrection. The resurrected Jesus never appears to anyone else. The Gospel of Mark ends with three terrified women fleeing the tomb of Jesus and saying nothing to anyone.

Most scholars, however, concur that this is not the way Mark's Gospel ended. The best scholarship contends that the original ending has been lost. Why, then, do we have various endings to Mark's Gospel? Because copyists concluded that this was not an appropriate ending to this Gospel. They could not finish their copy of Jesus' life with three scared, muted women who were too afraid to say a word to anyone. There is no gospel, no "good news" in that type of ending. Therefore, copyists added verses 9-20 and the optional ending cited above. The endings to Mark's Gospel that we have in our possession are copyists' noble efforts to add a more appropriate conclusion to a Gospel whose ending had been lost and, doing so, to preserve the "good news" of the resurrected Jesus.

These versions were then copied over and over again. The marginal notes in *The New English Bible* cite several of these endings.

It is obvious from the various endings of Mark's Gospel that copyists added their own words to the texts they were reproducing, even the handling of snakes to prove one's faith. How did Mark actually end his Gospel? What were his words? We do not know and, most likely, will never know. What we do understand is that copyists added their views, words, and even their theology to their texts of Mark's Gospel. And this is the copy of the Bible that the preacher holds up claiming that it is "the inerrant, infallible Word of God, every jot and tittle." What we have today is not an inerrant text. Thankfully, it is not commanded or even suggested that we "take up serpents." Amen to that!

The Fallacy of the "Slippery Slope" and the "Domino Effect"

So why do preachers and theologians argue so passionately about inerrancy? It's due at least in part to what they allude to as "the slippery slope" or the "domino effect." The "slippery slope" theory involves the fear that if we acknowledge a single error in the approximately 774,746 words of the Bible copied by hand multiple times over hundreds of years then a slippery descent will ensue and continue unabated until it destroys the entire biblical revelation. The "domino effect" theory encompasses the fear that if a single error is acknowledged then the entirety of biblical truth will come crashing down like a setup of cascading dominos. Still another analogy has to do with a house of cards: if even one card is removed then the basis for the whole Christian faith will fall apart. Regardless of the metaphor used, all of this fear relates to the core belief that if a mistake is acknowledged at any point then it becomes possible that the Bible is wrong on other matters. The rationale for the entire Christian faith could collapse if a single error is acknowledged anywhere in the Bible. If there is a textual error here or there or in Mark's or John's Gospel then perhaps Jesus didn't die on the cross; maybe He didn't rise from the dead; conceivably Jesus never really existed at all. Any of these notions is abhorrent to and absolutely untenable for any passionate, dedicated Christian believer.

Slippery slope? Falling Dominos? House of cards? I promise you that the Bible text and the Christian faith have been proven to be far more substantive and reliable than those phantom fears. Can we acknowledge that there were errors made in copying and some of them are seen in our modern versions of the Bible, and yet maintain the integrity of Scripture? Absolutely. The church, you, and I have nothing to fear from acknowledging that there are errors in the Bible. The trustworthiness of the biblical revelation is built on a foundation far more substantial than the precise accuracy of some incompetent or weary copyist who reproduced a manuscript a dozen centuries ago in a remote, dimly lit monastery.

The Integrity of Scripture and the Message of the Gospel

The integrity of Scripture is found not in an inerrant text, but in its historical factuality. Of the thousands of textual changes in over 5,400 manuscripts or parts of manuscripts, the overwhelming majority are insignificant and inconsequential. The differences reveal nothing other than perhaps an ancient scribe couldn't spell or stay on the same line of text any more than we can today if we were to copy long manuscripts by hand. No important fact or doctrinal position is called into question in the majority of these textual differences. The truth is that so many documents only slightly differing in places and yet all affirming the fundamental truths of the Christian faith, is in fact a *validation* of the Bible's message. The textual evidence proves that the revelation of God found in the biblical record is reliable and trustworthy beyond any doubt. It's just not inerrant.

There are some textual questions, however, that can influence our understanding of Jesus and the Christian life. Did Jesus actually let an adulteress off with the mild warning? "I do not condemn you, either. Go. From now on sin no more" (John 8:11). Is this how God treats sinners? I accept this as a valid part of the text and Jesus' ministry. Why? Not because it brings me personal comfort for my own sins and failings (which, by the way, it does), but because it fits Jesus' life. It sounds like something the God of grace would say. This story is a precious part of my understanding of Jesus and the deep reach of amazing grace. Yet, I can understand how some copyist could view it as too dangerous and omit it from the Gospel of John. If it were, however, proven that this story is false, my understanding of Jesus would not be altered in the slightest. Why? Because my understanding of God as a God of amazing grace is based on the entire revelation of God as Jesus "explained" Him (see John 1:18): that God is a God of unconditional love, forgiveness, and acceptance. My understanding of God, Jesus, and the Christian faith do not stand or fall on any lone passage of Scripture or in an inerrant text.

On the other hand, did Jesus say "they will pick up serpents, and if they drink any deadly poison, it will not hurt them" in Mark 16:18? I don't think so. Why? Not because I don't like snakes, but because it doesn't fit Jesus' life. From His temptations in the wilderness at the beginning of His ministry and frequently throughout His ministry, Jesus refused to test God and warns us against doing so. Handling poisonous snakes or drinking poison is an example of putting God to the test. Further, there is nothing similar to this passage anywhere else in the four Gospels, or in rest of the New Testament for that matter. Therefore, I have no problem rejecting the text as spurious. It is an add-on to Mark's Gospel and not part of the biblical revelation. This does not mean that we can just accept the texts we like and disregarding those we do not like. I promise you there are many other verses I do not "like"—such as the ones mandating we love your enemies, turn the other cheek, and so on—but I accept the Bible as the Word of God. We read it in light of Jesus Christ, the living Word of God, and acknowledge the truth about what we consider to be a highly reliable written work.

When textual differences influence our understanding of the Bible's message, how are we then to interpret scriptural truths? "Let Scripture interpret Scripture" is always a wise guide. We were taught in seminary that it is never prudent to build a theology on a single verse or passage. To be theologically sound the truth has to be part of the overall teachings of the Bible. The entirety of the New Testament can guide our understanding when a particular passage has a textual variance. The same is true when we face passages difficult to understand or that seem to contradict one another. The final criteria for comprehending Scripture is Jesus Himself. Given the revelation of Jesus in the four Gospels, does a questionable or difficult biblical text sound like something Jesus would say or teach? In passages that seem to contradict, what would Jesus do or say? What would be in keeping with His character and teachings? Forgiving a woman taken in adultery sounds like something Jesus would do. Picking up poisonous snakes does not.

The questionable passages from John and Mark are two examples where textual differences can influence our understanding of Jesus and the Christian faith; one positively, the other negatively. Yet, Jesus' central message, the message of God's love, grace, and redemption for all humankind is unaffected. Taken all together, the differences in texts and manuscripts have no effect on the heart of the New Testament message.

Do we have the original autographs of the New Testament? No. The papyrus on which they were likely written disintegrated long ago. We do, however, have reliable documents from within a few years of the time the originals were written, and these are attested to by thousands of manuscripts and portions of manuscripts unequaled to any other source documents from the ancient world. If God intended us to have the original autographs, He could have preserved them as readily as He inspired them. If God wanted our faith to be in a text or a manuscript of Scripture, He would have preserved those manuscripts. That He did not is a clear indication that He wants our faith to be in Him, and not in words, manuscripts, or a book. While some texts were altered across 1,500 years of copying that occurred prior to the invention of the printing press, God and His truth have not changed. The foundation of our faith is Jesus Christ who "explained" (see John 1:18) the unseen Father to us. This foundation stands unalterably secure. As precious as "The Holy Bible" may be to us, our faith is in the Living God, not a book.

Why Are We Pledging Allegiance to the Bible?

Pledging allegiance to a book, even if it is the Bible, is something more akin to Islam than Christianity. Consider that:

> In Islam, the purpose of the man—Muhammad—is to give us a book, the Koran.
>
> In Christianity, the purpose of the book, the Bible, is to give us *the Man*—Jesus Christ.
>
> In Islam, the purpose of the Koran is to reveal the *laws* by which Muslims are to live.
>
> In Christianity, the purpose of the Bible is to reveal *God* in Christ Jesus, through whom all can live. (The Koran makes no claim to reveal Allah.)
>
> Moslems are committed to a *book*—the Koran.
>
> Christians are committed to a *Person*—Jesus Christ.

Unfortunately, many Christians treat the Bible like Moslems treat the Koran. Moslems consider the Koran to be the literal, verbatim words of God dictated to Muhammad by the angel Gabriel which must be read in the original Arabic text. The individual words themselves are considered holy. The book itself contains the literal words of God. This is why Moslems will kill and go to war over treatment of the Koran: the *literal, holy words* of God have been defiled.

Historically, this is not how Christianity has always regarded Scripture. Even though the Bible is labeled or called the "Holy Bible," God is not revealed in the actual individual words themselves but in the historical events recorded in the Bible; first in the life of Israel and then ultimately, "suitable to the fullness of the times, that is, the summing up of all things in Christ" (Eph 1:10). For the Christian, God is revealed in the person of Jesus of Nazareth; through His life, interaction with people, His teachings, parables, and instructions, and through Jesus' death and resurrection. God is not revealed in the individual words of the Bible, but in the message of truth contained in the Bible. Thus, traditionally, Christianity has held that the Bible is "the record of the revelation of God."[5] The wording is precise here. The Bible is not "the revelation of God." (As the Koran is the revelation of the rules.) The Bible is "*the record* of the revelation of God" [emphasis mine]. For Christians, the revelation of God comes through Jesus, not in the individual words of a book. The book is *the record* of that revelation. "In the beginning God" (Gen 1:1) and "for God so loved the world" (John 3:16) are not words to be worshipped. The God who began it all and who offers eternal life is to be worshipped.

This is not an instance of splitting hairs. The distinction is important, and overlooking it has led many Christians to approach the Bible as Muslims approach the Koran. This virtual worship of the Bible, more than causing untold conflicts that have brought enormous pain and suffering, is a subdued idolatry. It is called "bibliolatry." I know of no one who advocates bowing down to the Bible or singing hymns to the Bible or praising the Bible the way we praise God. It is more subtle, like making the Bible into a demi-god; something divine, just as God is divine; infallible, just as God is infallible; inerrant, just as God is inerrant; revered, just as God is revered; worshipped, just as God is worshipped. And we teach our children to pledge allegiance to the Bible? As Christians, we worship the God of the Bible, not the Bible. We honor the Book, but we worship God alone. Christians are not idolaters. I have the highest view of Holy Scripture, but I do not worship the Bible the way Muslims worship the Koran. I do not believe in inerrancy, but I do believe that the message of the Bible is the record of the revelation of God and the truth about God, humankind, and life. The B-I-B-L-E is still the book for me.

---

[1]"Exposition, Transmission and Translation," *The Chicago Statement on Biblical Inerrancy with Exposition* <www.bible-researcher.com/chicago1.html>.

[2]Ibid, Article X.

[3]Bart D. Ehrman, *Misquoting Jesus: The Story Behind Who Changed the Bible and Why* (San Francisco: Harper Collins, 2005) 52.

[4]*The New English Bible* (London: Oxford University Press, 1970) 143.

[5]*The Baptist Faith and Message* (Nashville: The Sunday School Board of the Southern Baptist Convention, 1963) 7.

CHAPTER 8

"I Believe in God the Father Almighty, Maker of Heaven and Earth"...and in Evolution

WHEN I WAS A CHILD IN PUBLIC SCHOOL, we learned about the development of humans. I remember the pictures in my science textbook stretching all the way across the top of two pages of the book, wider than tall. Next to the outside margin of the left page was a picture of a hairy ape, like the ones we see at the zoo: ape-shaped head, stooped back, and long arms with knuckles dragging the ground. Over the developing series of pictures, the ape gradually straightened up, until the last picture next to the outside margin of the right page contained an image of a modern man: standing upright, arms at a natural human length, and nowhere near as hairy. These series of images depicted the evolution of mankind. We were told about the Big Bang and how the universe began millions upon millions of years ago with an enormous explosion somewhere in a vast void. In those days, students loved their teachers and what they taught was sacrosanct. A fifth grader did not doubt the teacher or the science book. Most of us accepted without question the images portraying human evolution and the big bang explanation of creation.

During Sunday school and morning worship we were told, "In the beginning God created the heavens and the earth" (Gen 1:1), that He created Adam from the dust of the ground, and He made Eve from Adam's rib. Moreover, we were told God created the entire universe, including the apes, Adam, and the always fascinating dinosaurs in six,

125

twenty-four hour days. Wow! Anything that came from church, Sunday school teachers, or the preacher was sacrosanct as well. What was a ten-year-old supposed to do when the two institutions he had been taught to love, respect, believe, and obey taught two totally different perspectives? I don't recall giving much thought to it at all. It was not a great problem for me, most likely because I was neither a good student nor a deep thinker. When at church, I believed what the church taught. When in school, I believed what I learned there. (My teachers were almost all devout Christians themselves, and I can only now assume they soft-peddled the evolution material. I honestly don't remember.) As a ten-year-old boy, I wasn't terribly inquisitive about what books contained anyway, whether science books or Sunday school quarterlies. I preferred exploring the deep woods behind Aunt Lyba's house on the weekends or playing Davy Crocket with my coonskin cap, hatchet with leather carrying case, and my BB gun. Out there I was "king of the wild frontier." It was not a problem because I remember thinking that these two teachings must, somehow, fit together, and one day, I would figure it out. I mean, they *had* to go together: this is what two trusted institutions were teaching me.

What was not a problem for me in the fifth grade is still not a problem for me today (though it is a massive problem for many people). It is a conflict between the biblical story of creation and the discoveries of modern science. It is a needless conflict often caused by the church, one that's unnecessary because the biblical and scientific accounts of creation actually do fit together. We can believe what the Bible says and what modern science says about creation of the universe and the origin of life. Properly understood, they do not contradict. We can believe in God as the "Maker of heaven and earth" (Ps 115:15) and in evolution. Allow me to explain.

Four Examples of the Conflict Today

First, a popular evangelical seminary in Florida forced the resignation of a distinguished Old Testament scholar over a statement he made that was quoted in *USA Today*: "If the data is overwhelmingly in favor of evolution, to deny that reality will make us a cult...some odd group that is not really interacting with the world."[1] Although this respected scholar had taught at the seminary for over twenty years, he was dismissed because he called on the church to take seriously the findings of modern science, warning the church that if it did not, it would be relegated to something akin to the Flat Earth Society.

Second, an evangelical university in Ohio included this statement in its fourteen-point doctrinal credo: "We believe in the literal six-day account of creation." Every member of the faculty must sign the creedal statement as a condition of employment.

Third, when a newly installed president of a Baptist college in Georgia was asked if he believed, "God literally created the world in six days," he answered, "Oh yes."

Fourth, Christian organizations fill the Internet with arguments for a six-day creation. One attractive, well-done website on Christian doctrine says that anyone who does not believe in a literal, six-day creation does so because they are probably not saved:

> How many of those who say they are Christians but who refuse to accept the Biblical account of a literal six-day creation as true, are actually saved? I suggest very few. Belief in a literal six-day Creation is a litmus test for all who claim to belong to Christ.[2]

In the preface I referred to types of situations that cause people to consider the church irrelevant or outright dangerous. The four above are but a few examples.

Nowhere have I have read the Apostle Paul saying, "If you confess with your mouth Jesus as Lord, and believe in a literal, six-day creation, you will be saved" (see Rom 10:9). Yet this is how visceral the issue has become for too many Christians. In a noble attempt to remain faithful to the Bible amid an increasingly secular culture, many Christians—from professors in the academy to pastors in the pulpit to church members in the pew—continue to demand belief in a preposterous notion. As is often the case, the more strident the voice (see the quote cited above from the Internet), the weaker the argument. The danger of such demands reaches far beyond an interpretation of Genesis 1. The greater peril is the impression these statements give about the church itself. The Old Testament professor I mentioned above is correct in his assessment. Such beliefs make the church sound vapid, stodgy, disengaged, and withdrawn in the face of a real world with scientific discovery and honest inquiry. Can any organization that insists on an outdated tradition despite a contradicting corporeality be counted on to deliver truth about anything? We are cutting our own throats.

Take a field trip to the Museum of Natural History in New York City. Visit the Hall of Ornithischian Dinosaurs, the Hall of Saurischian Dinosaurs, and the Hall of Human Origins. See (and touch) some of the five million fossilized specimens that extend back some 500 million years. Some are plaster replicas, but many are real fossilized remains of beings that actually existed. Follow the meticulous development of the world from millions of years ago until now. How someone can ignore such evidence—proof—and still claim the world was created in six twenty-four hour days is mindboggling. There's so much "none-sense" being advocated by Christian colleges, universities, seminaries, pulpits, and churches. Why should anyone believe anything the church has to say on other matters such as God, His love for humankind, salvation, life after death, heaven, hell, or anything else? If the church discounts the evidence and still demands belief in a literal six-day creation, why should those *outside* the church believe in God as the "Maker of heaven and earth" (Ps 115:15). Why would they not doubt or discount everything else the church says? If the church consistently and insistently gets it so wrong on this matter, perhaps it is just as wrong on all other matters. Why should anyone believe what we have to say about a God of grace? Anyone, any institution (church, school, university, seminary) that believes and teaches the world was created in six, twenty-four hour days, would be disqualified from speaking with authority on any subject. It is tantamount to asking people to believe in the factuality of Grimm's Fairy Tales, the historicity of Aesop's Fables, that the tooth fairy gives money for a tooth placed under a pillow, or that "Once upon a time...they all lived happily ever after." (I am aware of the many notable and respected Christian exegetes past and present who advocate a literal six-day creation. I know that the Larger Catechism of the revered Westminster Confession of Faith states, "God in the beginning, by the word of his power, made of nothing the world, and all things therein, for himself, within the space of six days, and all very good." I also know that the Westminster Confession of Faith was written in 1646 long before we discovered so much of what we now know.)

It is not my intent to be harsh or offensive. Credibility, however, is critical for the church. Nothing is more important than being believed, and for that, the church must be believable. Further, evangelicals believe that people's eternal destiny rests in believing the message we bring. Those days in which, if the preacher said it, it must be true, are long gone. Today the culture is much more secular, believers are much more discerning, and information is much more readily available. (If you cannot make it to New York, visit the website for the Museum of Natural History.) If people cannot believe what we say, the mission and message of the church is forfeited. If the church has it *so wrong* on matters of creation, turns a blind eye and a deaf ear to overwhelming scientific proof, and asks people to believe in a biblical interpretation of creation that contradicts massive amounts of historical and scientific evidence—all in the name of blind faith—perhaps the church is just as wrong in its interpretation and understanding of everything in the Bible. Even worse, perhaps *the Bible* itself is just as wrong on everything else as it is on a six-day creation. The Bible is relegated to an archaic text of an antiquated religion for an ancient people from a faraway time and place. It surely must be of no account for this time and place.

As you can see, this is not an ancillary issue.

Genesis 1

The expansive sweep and extensive scope of this book is raw beauty in words and staggering in apprehension. The same could be said of the creation story in Genesis 1. Its expansive sweep reaches from heaven to earth. It speaks of God and His creation, of humankind and human destiny. Its extensive span bridges an infinite space between a "weltered waste"[3] where nothing existed to an ordered world of all that became. Genesis 1 is "raw beauty in words and staggering in apprehension"[4] whose portrayals extend beyond the research of scientific discovery and are exceptionally more expressive than factual history could ever be. Genesis 1 is a confession of faith, not a chronicle of history or an axiom of science.

The first eleven chapters of Genesis are often referred to as prehistory. These chapters (along with all the Bible) pre-date science. Galileo, the father of modern science, and Copernicus would not be born until centuries later. The creation story is not about science or history. Yet much of the conflict and confusion surrounding the interpretation of the creation stories arise when either the church or the scientist seek to make the Genesis accounts of creation either historic or scientific accounts of creation. They are neither. They do not correlate with modern history or science. They cannot. They should not. It is not their purpose. Though Genesis and scientists share a fascination with the beginnings of the cosmos and of life, the purpose and approach of each is completely different.

I use the pluralized "accounts" of creation because Genesis contains two versions of the creation story. The first is found in Genesis 1:1–2:4a, and the second account follows in Genesis 2:4b-25. Vocabulary, order of creation, and style of writing are different in the two accounts. They need not be reconciled.

A bit of background provides pertinent insight. Many scholars believe Genesis was written during the Babylonian Captivity when both Israel's national identity and faith in God was in serious jeopardy. (Biblical scholarship almost unanimously agrees that Moses did not write Genesis and nowhere does the text of Genesis attribute authorship to Moses. The belief in Moses as the author comes from a long, mistaken tradition.) The great prophets had warned Israel about impending judgment if the nation did not repent. Israel did not repent, and judgment fell in 587-586 BCE. The Babylonian army marched into Jerusalem and utterly destroyed both city and nation. The Temple of Solomon (viewed at the time as God's dwelling place) was leveled to the ground and the walls of Jerusalem were razed. Zedekiah, King of Israel, and his entire family were brought before Nebuchadnezzar, king of Babylon. Zedekiah watched as every member of his family was slaughtered, and with that being the last image he would ever see, they gouged out his eyes. As the holy city of Zion lay in smoldering ruins, blind Zedekiah and his defeated people were bound and marched to Babylon where a pagan king and a pantheon of pagan gods ruled. From all appearances the gods of Babylon had defeated the God of Israel, His king, and His chosen people. Their pitiable plight is recorded in the pathos of Psalm 137:1-4:

> By the rivers of Babylon,
> There we sat down and wept,
> When we remembered Zion.
> Upon the willows in the midst of it
> We hung our harps.
> For there our captors demanded of us songs,
> And our tormentors mirth, saying,
> "Sing us one of the songs of Zion."

Chapter 8

> How can we sing the LORD'S song
> In a foreign land?

Genesis 1 is not an abstract statement, incidental musing, or detached rumination about the origins of the world. It is not a "scientific description but a theological affirmation"[5] about Israel's all-powerful God in light of their destroyed nation and in the face of Babylonian hegemony. It is a pastoral message of courage for a hopeless people whose nation and religious treasures had been decimated. When the Genesis narrator writes in the second verse that the earth was "formless and void"—one marginal translation reads "welter and waste"[6]—those who saw their city, temple, king, and nation destroyed saw the welter and waste firsthand. Their homeland and nation were destroyed and their lives were hollow and hopeless. To these defeated and discouraged exiles, what is contained in Genesis declared that although defeated by Babylon, their God created the entire universe and still rules over all, including Babylon, its king, and its gods. Out of the turmoil and emptiness of their existence, the God of creation revealed order in the face of chaos and provided courage when all hope had been lost. Their God—greater than Nebuchadnezzar, his armies, and his gods—is the Creator of all that is!

Genesis 1 remains a message of hope to all people for all times, especially to those facing catastrophic circumstances. This message offers every generation a hope far grander than scientific discovery or factual history. New discoveries alter science and our understanding of history. The foundational truths of God, however, are unchanging. As Old Testament scholar Dr. Walter Brueggemann writes:

> When the text is heard as news in a theological idiom, it leaves open all scientific theories about the origin of the world. The Bible takes no stand on any of these. The faith of the church has no vested interest in any of the alternative scientific hypotheses. The text is none other than the voice of the evangel proclaiming good news.

For over a hundred years fundamentalist Christians have tried to make the book of Genesis a battleground in a war with science. For too long, many ardent Christians have gone along. I hope I can show that the message of Genesis is more majestic than anything science might discover. The greatest truths of life transcend science. Genesis was never written to address the questions of modern science. It is impossible and unnecessary to try to reconcile Genesis with modern science. Enormous, destructive, and needless conflicts arise when Christians try to make the biblical stories of creation either scientific or historic accounts of creation. They are neither.

The Story of Creation

Genesis was written to convey grand truths in images we can grasp, images far greater than scientific discovery or factual history. Genesis 1 is the language of confession and praise, the language of poetry and liturgy. The structure of Genesis 1:1-31 reveals much of the intent of the author. The refrains follow stanzas similar to our modern hymns:

"Then God said...then God said...then God said...then God said."

"Let there be...let there be...let there be...let there be."

"And it was so...and it was so...and it was so...and it was so."

"And God made...and God made...and God made...and God made."

"And God saw that it was good...and God saw that it was good...and God saw that it was good...and God saw that it was good."

"And there was evening and morning...and there was evening and morning...and there was evening and morning...and there was evening and morning"

This is the language of liturgy. The repetition enables the congregation to remember the story and be part of the confession and celebration of worship. Genesis 1 was written during a time of utter defeat for the nation of Israel. It was written to remind Israel who their God truly was and to enable the congregation to worship and praise their God, the God who created heavens, earth, light, darkness, vegetation, animal, and human life. Their God is the God of all creation. He is Lord over

Babylon. Can you imagine the encouragement that the repetition of these refrains would bring to a defeated people in a pagan land, suffering the mockery of their captors?

This is the language of poetic rhythm, of verse and refrain, of symmetry and beauty. The narrator reaches heights of truths about creation and life via melodic lyrics in ways scientific facts could never hope to achieve. Using word-pictures, the creation story reveals profound truth we can see, feel, and understand. It is truth that could never be found in the equations of science or the documents of history. Refrain after refrain reveals the dynamics of life in the truths of each stanza. The creation stories in Genesis are inspired poetry.

A more recent example of beautiful truth expressed in poetic verse rather than in either historic or scientific fact is Shakespeare's play, *As You Like It*. Shakespeare wrote about "tongues in trees, books in the running brooks, sermons in stones and good in everything."[7] A literal reading of this Shakespeare excerpt would lead a person to say something like, "That is nonsense. The writer is confused. Trees don't have tongues, books are not in brooks, and sermons are not in stones. Everyone knows that sermons are in books and stones are in running brooks." Literally, that rationale is accurate, but who cares? Such mundane comments are worthless unless you are on a nature walk with a three-year old. One author said of these verses in Shakespeare, "In terms of raw facts, they are not true; in terms of the living meaning they convey, they are true to the point of inspiration."[8]

This is how Genesis 1 is written. It is a poem, a psalm, a hymn celebrating the Creator and His creation. More than a scientific or historic description of creation, it is a poetic celebration of creation. Trying to make Genesis 1 about science or history misses the entire point; it misses the joy, the thrill, and the celebration. It is not science. It is not history. It is a hymn of celebration intended to inform, delight, and inspire. The creation story is about joy: the joy of God's people because of both the Creator and the creation.

The first chapter of Genesis is alive with the joy of creation. Both the rhythm of poetry and the revelation of joy are seen in the refrain, "… and God saw that it was good":

"God said, 'Let there be light'; and there was light. God saw the light was good" (vv3-4).

God created the firmament and the dry land; "and God saw that it was good" (see vv6-11).

"The earth brought forth vegetation...and God saw that it was good" (v12).

God made the sun and the moon, "and God saw that it was good" (vv16-18).

God created every living creature, "and God saw that it was good" (vv24-25).

The doxology over all that God created appears in Genesis1:31, "God saw all that He had made, and behold, it was very good."

Genesis 1 reveals a God who delights to create, a God for whom life and living is a joy. This is not science. It does not sound like or resemble science. It is poetry, a hymn of joy complete with the refrain, "God saw that it was good." Like all poetry, whether Shakespeare or the Bible, taking it literally distorts both the beauty and the meaning. All attempts to make this about a literal six-day creation obscure the meaning and miss the joy. Any effort to reconcile the creation story in Genesis with science overlooks the purpose, the message, and beauty of the story. More than a literal scientific or historic description of creation, Genesis 1 is a paean of celebration of the Creator and all His creation.

Interpreting the creation story as a scientific account is like being invited to a party featuring a lavish dinner given in our honor. The menu is the finest cuisine prepared by a world-class chef. Behold the magnificent table set before us for our enjoyment! As we sit down at the table to enjoy the feast, one of the guests provides us with a detailed description of what we are about to eat. He talks of the fertilizers needed to grow the fruits and vegetables and their dangers and toxicity. He tells how the crops would be destroyed if it were not for the insecticides used to kill the destructive pests. He entices us with an explanation of the poisonous herbicides necessary to kill unwanted weeds. Then to top off such scintillating mealtime conversation, he describes for us—in detail no less—the workings of the slaughter houses necessary for us to enjoy the delicious meats prepared for our delight.

A host has prepared an exquisite meal for us to savor, and rather than enjoying the meal, we are subjected to conversation about manure and poisons and the bloody slaughter of animals. I cannot imagine anything more rude, inappropriate, and disgusting for all the guests. And, what must the host think? It misses the host's intent and everyone fails to enjoy what has been prepared for our delight. The party is ruined.

This is what the church does when it dissects the creation stories of Genesis in terms of modern science or history and insists on things like a literal, twenty-four hour, six day creation. Sure, the Hebrew word for "day" (*yom*) as used in Genesis 1 means precisely a twenty-four hour period from sunrise to sunrise. "And there was evening and there was morning, one day" (Gen 1:5). Insisting, however, that we interpret the story literally misses the intent of the narrator. It distorts the meaning and purpose of the story. Dissecting the story in light of science, we lose the flavor, beauty, and joy of what is set before us.

Just for the record, it is not only the church that can confuse these things and spoil the story. Scientists, too, have done their part. Just as it is unwise for the church to make *scientific* statements about the *theology* of creation, the same is true when scientists make *theological* statements about the *science* of creation. Gifted scientists are often poor theologians who stumble when they step out of their field and make theological statements. One of the most sensational is Carl Sagan's famous quote, "The cosmos is all that is or ever was or ever will be."[9] Oh? And the late Professor Sagan knew "all that is?" Wow! We should have crowned him *something*: king, potentate, tsar of the world. To have among us one who knows "all that is" is rare indeed. (I know sarcasm is unbecoming, but sheesh! Isn't it a bit warranted this time?) Dr. Sagan was an eminent astronomer, astrophysicist, cosmologist, and scientist. He was internationally renowned in his field. This famous quote, however, is a theological or philosophical statement. It is not founded in scientific inquiry. It is somewhere between poor science and no science at all. It is personal opinion parading as absolute fact. And just because an eminent scientist says it, does not make it true. Sensational statements such as this are foolish, misleading, and just a tad infuriating to some people. They further confuse the issue.

An Analogy

The Bible and modern science are speaking of the same world but from two totally different perspectives and for two completely different reasons. When people of faith and people of science understand this, most of the conflicts between the Bible and science and between the church and the scientific community will be resolved (at least over the origins of the universe). An illustration will reveal how we can believe both the Genesis story of creation and at the same time believe modern science; it reveals how we can "believe in God the Father almighty, maker of heaven and earth"[10] and in evolution.

Compare *the story* of creation in Genesis 1 to the performance of a Broadway play such as Victor Hugo's *Les Miserables*. Most who attend the play are captivated by the story of redemption and revolution set in 19th century France. Jean Valjean is released from prison after serving 19 years for stealing bread to feed his sister's starving children. Our emotions are stirred to the depths when Fantine sings the beautiful and haunting *I Dreamed A Dream* and by the score and lyrics of *Bring Him Home*. The story, drama, score, script, acting, orchestra, splendid singing, and spectacular scenery transport us to that time in which high hopes were lost and sweet dreams were shattered. It is passion and romance, drama and tragedy; it is all together inspiring, uplifting, and exhilarating. It is like the wonder and beauty of Genesis 1.

Yet before we ever sit down in the theater and the lights are dimmed to begin the performance, an unimaginable amount of work had to be done with meticulous attention given to every detail so we could enjoy the play. Victor Hugo's novel had to be adapted to the modern stage. Claude-Michel Schonberg had to write his exquisite score. Choreographers had to choreograph the graceful movements of dozens of actors so that it could all occur simultaneously on a small stage. Actors and vocalists had to be auditioned, hired and rehearsed. The costumes had to be envisioned, sketched, and designed; fabrics and colors selected, and seamstresses had to put them together. Elaborate staging had to be imagined in someone's mind. Engineers, then, had to figure the details and architects had to draw blueprints. Building materials had to be purchased and carpenters had to construct the staging. Artists had to paint it all in period colors. And this is merely the beginning.

The sets had to be built in such a way that they could be moved easily for quick scene changes. Of course, before a piece of fabric or lumber was purchased months and months of enormous research was necessary to make it appropriate for the period and believable to the audience. Then there are critical technical matters of sound and lightening, budgets and financing, union compliance, renting a theater, coordination between construction and rehearsal schedules. Minute attention on the most mundane details is critical if the play is to be successful. Then after all the pieces are in place (staging, music, orchestra, actors, singers, sound, lighting) we sit down in an air conditioned theater, the lights come down and we are enthralled by the play. Much later, we walk out having had a deep and moving experience.

What does all of this have to do with the creation account in Genesis? Compare attending the play to reading the story of creation. Reading Genesis 1 is like sitting down in the theater: the lights come down and the creation story is played out before us. It is moving, enthralling, inspiring, and enlightening. We read it and acquire deep and profound insights into our God: His power to create, His involvement with the universe, and His relationship with humans, the crown of His creation. We read Genesis 1 and are captivated by the story of unimaginable omnipotence that speaks the world into existence. Wow, indeed!

Just as the play is not about the details of staging and rehearsing, costumes and construction, story lines and set designs, so the creation story is not about the details of creation: Big Bangs and fossil records, radiometric dating and geologic calendars, solar systems and expanding galaxies, nanoseconds and light-years, and all other scientific stuff akin to these. The Genesis story is not about the scientific details or the factual history of how it happened. It is not about believing in a literal, six-day, twenty-four hour creation. It is the beautiful and moving story of God and His creation, written to encourage a forlorn people during a desperate time. Properly understood it encourages and informs people of all times. And the science of creation has nothing, *nothing* to do with the story.

While the biblical story is not about the details (How detailed can it be? The entire creation is covered by one chapter containing 31 verses!), there are those attending the play who are interested in the details of the play. Engineers and architects notice the specifics of how the movable staging was designed to work so efficiently. Fashion designers notice intricate designs in the costuming that the rest of us miss. A rhetorician's trained ear hears the inflections and diction of the actors. Choreographers are impressed at the precision of multiple actors rushing around the stage without running into each other. Producers, scouting for new talent, take note of the pristine voices of the vocalists. A CPA thinks of what it cost, how it was financed, and how much money the play is making.

In the same way, scientists look at the world and wonder how it all came together. Are the scientific details important? Not only are they important, they help us understand our world. Scientists study geology, sedimentary rock formations, dinosaur bones, and fossils and try to date and interpret their discoveries. They look through the telescope and study the mind-altering space of an ever-expanding universe where billions of galaxies with innumerable stars are separated by untold light years. They study black holes, supernovas, and nebulae. Other scientists look through the microscope and study quarks and hadrons, composite particles that make up all matter. (None of which I understand.)

Just as the details of the Broadway play are critical in making the play enjoyable, so scientists who study the details of creation make the universe understandable. Space exploration, physics, chemistry, biology, medicine, and genetics are just a very few of the many fields whose advancement make modern life both easier and more enjoyable. Air conditioning keeps me cool on hot, humid days. I spoke with my family in the United States via cell phone from a subway in Beijing, China, and it sounded like they were next door. Satellites in geostationary orbits circle the earth and bring events as they are happening in New York City or Tehran to my living room. Medical science has extended both the length and quality of life. A surgeon can now make a minor incision to the abdomen, insert a tiny camera and instruments, and perform surgery without the risks and complications that can accompany a larger opening. Scientists provide us with invaluable benefits about the science of creation and an advanced understanding of our world. At the same time the biblical account of creation provides people of faith with profound truths about God and the entire cosmos, providing definition, meaning and purpose in life. So long as each understands and respects the other, there is no conflict or contradiction between the two. Neither is there any need to reconcile them. The two are looking at the drama from different perspectives, for different reasons.

Chapter 8

The Ever-Changing Science and the Never-Changing God

The Bible reveals truths that are far beyond science, truths that science could never discover in a telescope or microscope. Though scientific discoveries change our understanding of the universe and facts of history are refined in every generation, the Bible and the creation accounts in Genesis do not change. They deal with the great and grand eternal themes of life in timeless ways, providing a deeper understanding of God and His creation than can never be found in scientific discovery or in historical record. People of faith who believe in the truths of the Bible, as I do, need never cower before scientific facts or be intimidated because of our faith in God and our belief in the story of creation. The biblical creation story answers questions that can never be discovered by scientific inquiry or ever be answered via a lab, test-tube, microscope, or telescope. The Genesis account of creation is not about science; it transcends science. The creation story reveals the joyful story and celebration of both the Creator and the creation. Implicit in the creation story is the message: Enjoy God! Enjoy creation!

Finally, it would behoove all of us, people of faith and trained scientists, to remember that we are dealing with an infinite and eternal God and an ever expanding, perhaps even an infinite universe. By definition, this means that there is far more about both that we do not know than what we do know. There is an infinite amount still to be learned on both fronts. Thus, when any of us ventures to speak of such grand matters, we need a deep appreciation for the mysteries of both God and the universe He created. Therefore, speak with great humility and respect and value the mystery of both.

No better description of the wonder of God and His creation can be found than the characteristic prose offered by the great African American preacher, S.M. Lockridge:

> Where did God come from? When heaven and earth were yet unmade, when there was empty blackness and void formlessness, and darkness was on the face of the deep, when time was yet unknown, Thou in Thy bliss and majesty did live and love alone. He called

light out of darkness; He called cosmos out of chaos; He called order out of confusion. But the question still clamors for an answer: Where did God come from? The answer is that He came from nowhere. That is theologically correct and it is biblically sound. The reason God came from nowhere is there wasn't anywhere for Him to come from. And coming from nowhere, He stood on nothing. And the reason He stood on nothing is there was nowhere for Him to stand. And standing on nothing He reached out where there was nowhere to reach, and caught something when there was nothing to catch, and hung something on nothing and told it to stay there. And standing on nothing He took the hammer of His own will and He struck the anvil of His omnipotence, and sparks flew from there, and He caught them on the tips of His fingers and flung them out into space and bedecked the heaven with stars. And God said, "That's good."

In chapter five I quoted the final verse of Henry van Dyke's lyrics for Beethoven's *Ninth Symphony*. The first two verses call us to celebrate the joy of God's creation.

> *Joyful, Joyful We Adore Thee*
> Joyful, joyful, we adore Thee, God of glory, Lord of love;
> Hearts unfold like flowers before Thee, Opening to the sun above.
> Melt the clouds of sin and sadness; Drive the dark of doubt away;
> Giver of immortal gladness, Fill us with the light of day!
>
> All Thy works with joy surround Thee, Earth and heaven reflect Thy rays,
> Stars and angels sing around Thee, Center of unbroken praise.

Chapter 8

Field and forest, vale and mountain, Flowery meadow, flashing sea,
Singing bird and flowing fountain Call us to rejoice in Thee.[11]

[1]Charles Honey, "Adamant on Adam: Resignation of prominent scholar Bruce Waltke underscores tension over evolution," *Christianity Today*, 25 May 2010 <www.christianitytoday.com/ct/2010/june/1.14.html>.

[2]K.B. Napier, "Why Christians Don't Believe in Literal Six-day Creation," *www.christiandoctrine.com*, 20 July 2012 <www.christiandoctrine.com/index.php?option=com_content&view=article&id=964:why-christians-dont-believe-in-literal-six-day-creation&catid=105:science-and-environment&Itemid=477>.

[3]Robert Alter, *Genesis: Translation and Commentary* (NY: W.W. Norton & Company, 1996) 3.

[4]Ibid, *Baptist Faith and Message*, 7.

[5]Walter Brueggemann, *Interpretation, A Bible Commentary for Teaching and Preaching: Genesis* (Louisville, KY: John Knox Press, 1982) 25.

[6]Alter, *Genesis*, 3.

[7]William Shakespeare, "As You Like It," Act II Scene I, "The Forest of Arden."

[8]Walter Russell Bowie, *The Interpreter's Bible 12 Vols*, vol. 1 (Nashville: Abingdon Press, 1952) 463.

[9]Carl Sagan, *Cosmos* (NY: Random House Publishing Group, 1980) 1.

[10]"The Apostle's Creed," *The Book of Common Prayer According to the use of The Episcopal Church* (NY: The Church Hymnal Corporation) 53.

[11]Dyke, "Joyful, Joyful" (1911).

CHAPTER 9

God, the Gospel, and Gays

TOGETHER WITH HER TWO BROTHERS, Michelle was raised in the church by her parents. They were third-generation members of a church where I served as pastor. Her entire family—parents, grandparents, siblings, aunt, uncles, nieces, and nephews—along with Michelle, were active in every phase of church life: singing in choirs, leading as church officers, teaching in Sunday school, participating in children and youth ministries, participating in mission trips and choir tours, and so on. Michelle also happened to be lesbian. Michelle wasn't abused as a child, raised in a dysfunctional family (any more than the rest of us), co-opted by other lesbians, or the victim of date-rape or disappointing male/female relationships. She has two heterosexual brothers. There was nothing abnormal about her upbringing or life. Something about Michelle was different. One could search her history or psyche in vain to discover why.

Her mother said, "From her earliest years, we knew Michelle was different." Michelle told me that she never "chose" or "decided" to be lesbian. "No one caused me to be this way. It's not a choice. Who would choose this manner of living?" Michelle is attracted to girls and not boys. It's been that way for as long as she can remember. That's simply a part of who she is, and she knew it before she understood how to give it a name. In grade school and throughout high school she struggled with what she felt made her different from a lot of other girls. Allow me to clarify "struggled." Michelle has the confidence and strong sense of self that any caring parent hopes for their children to have. She did not need or seek the affirmation of others and was never offended by the views and opinions of others, be it her family, friends, or preacher. Still, it is human nature not to want to be unlike those around us; feeling and knowing she was a bit different from other girls was a struggle. "Not until college did things come together," she says. Like most of us who struggle through the awkwardness of adolescence, we don't begin to fully understand and accept ourselves until our young adult years.

Michelle said that part of her struggle was having no one to whom she could talk. When she was twenty-two her dad asked her to stop by his workplace so that he could talk with her. When she dutifully arrived, he told her that after speaking with her mom and both brothers they were all in agreement that she must choose between her same-gender orientation and her family. From his standpoint, she could not have both. He gave her thirty days to decide. Michelle was devastated. Imagine the agony! How does one choose between their family and being true to self? (It saddens me greatly that she was even put into a position of having to choose.) As it turned out, the thirty days passed, then sixty, and then ninety. The subject was not brought up again between father and daughter. After he died, Michelle asked her mom and brothers about the agreement. As it turns out, none of them knew anything about any sort of agreement. Her father was a devout Christian and member of the church. He had been wrestling with how to deal with an issue that suddenly had become very personal. Given his religiously rigid background, he responded in the only way he knew. If intimidating his daughter with the threat of losing her family could force her to "straighten up," then all would be well and he could resume life as he had known it.

By the time Michelle was twenty-four she had fully accepted her sexual orientation. Throughout life, she had been active in her church and participated in much of what many church-goers do as preschoolers, children, teenagers, and young adults. "The church was a great source of comfort to me," she said. Michelle also realized that what was said about homosexuality by me, her preacher, and by others in the church, was not the entire story. She said she knew we were just ignorant, talking about something about which we knew nothing. Church had become a dichotomy: despite the comfort she found there, the condemnation brought great distress.

In addition to seeking the comfort of church, she began finding closer friends—gay and straight—in bars. She tried for years to reconcile her church life with whom she knew herself to be. She kept coming to church. Through it all she was exposed to my harangues against the social ills of the time, which always include a condemnation of homosexuality.

"Your preaching made me feel so small. I wanted to say, 'Preacher, you are so wrong. It's not that away. I'm not that person you preach about.' Everything I was living, you were preaching against. I tried not to take it personally. If all the gays and lesbians sitting in church on Sunday morning turned purple, you would be shocked."

At the beginning of chapter one I mentioned that I was the type of preacher about whom the prostitute was talking ("Why would I ever go there [church]? I was already feeling terrible about myself. They'd just make me feel worse."[1]) I was not speaking figuratively. Eventually my preaching forced Michelle out of the church. She hasn't attended church for years. "I just can't go to church," she says. Michelle still loves God and knows that He loves her and her partner of twenty-one years. Together they have a son. She still prays. "I don't understand why God does the things He does. But I know He loves me." I have asked if she's considered going back to church. She's told me that if she does, it won't be to her previous church or denomination.

I apologized to Michelle long ago for my caustic and arrogant attitude, for not seeing her and caring for her, and for driving her out of church. Above all, as an ordained minister of the gospel of Jesus Christ who was supposed to at least try and be like Jesus for, I have apologized for not assuring her of the "good news" of God's love for all people; even those whose sexual orientation with which I or the church may disagree. She, of course, was and continues to be most forgiving, understanding, kind, and gracious to me. She is that way to everyone, which is also a part of who she is. Michelle has been far more like Jesus to me than I ever was to her, even as her pastor. When I asked if she would be willing to be interviewed and for her story to be told in a book, she replied, "I'd love to. Maybe it will help."

There are so many more people like Michelle and preachers like me out there. How many people wish their preacher saw them—not their "sort," but them—and genuinely cared for them even if they could never agree about homosexuality? That's what Jesus did. How many struggle to stay in a church that doesn't know the pain of the rejection and condemnation it heaps on them. Doesn't know the struggle of trying to love God, serve, and be loyal to the church, and yet be true to who they know themselves to be? How many preachers would be shocked to learn how many closeted gays and lesbians are in their congregations? How much regret might ministers feel if they truly knew that some of the same people they love as parishioners are suffering silently from their preacher's needless tirades against homosexuality?

I know that what I write in this chapter is not going to resolve any conflicts. I can't say that it is fully resolved in my own heart. I am at peace biblically, spiritually, and personally with the explanations given and conclusions drawn here. At the very least, I hope to provide a bit of perspective. I hope it can open the door for credible and meaningful discussion among some in the church and in the gay and lesbian community.

Homosexuality is mentioned in the Bible seven times, four in the Old Testament and three in the New Testament. The most well-known account involves the destruction of Sodom in Genesis 19. The city was already under divine judgment before the two messengers (i.e., angels) arrive. You may recall Abraham bargaining with God in Genesis 18. God agreed to spare the city if 50 righteous men could be found in Sodom. Abraham bargained from that number to 45, 30, 20 and then finally 10, but to no avail. Not even ten righteous men could be found in an entire city. (By the way, what does it say about us that we focus more on God's judgment on Sodom than on God's willingness to spare everyone in a city if but ten righteous people could be found.) Sexual perversion pervades the entire passage: the townsmen demand sexual encounters with the strangers, Lot offers his two daughters to the townsmen to satisfy their demands, and the townsmen threaten to rape Lot. The attempted sexual offence with the two strangers, however, is not homosexuality per se but aggravated sexual battery: homosexual gang rape. Treating men as women was the ultimate insult, humiliation, and offence. Modern experts are in agreement that rape is never about the desire for sexual pleasure, but is about dominating, humiliating, and controlling another person.

Keeping this in mind, a careful reading indicates that the sin in this instance is not sexual in nature. The sin here is the insult, abuse, and attempted assault of the visitors. In the ancient Near Eastern world there existed an inviolable, sacred code of hospitality to strangers. In Genesis 18:1-15 Abraham extends deferential hospitality to these same strangers before they arrive in Sodom. Lot does the same when they come to his house in Genesis 19:2-3. Even the term for the "outcry" of Sodom in

Genesis 18:21-22 and 19:13 is used elsewhere to refer to the cries of the victims of social and economic injustice. The term is never used to refer to sexual abuse. So great is the offence of such injustice to strangers that Lot, with no expressed biblical condemnation, prefers giving the mob his two daughters to use as they please if they would give up their goal of assaulting the two visitors.

Given the prevailing treatment of this account—one with which we are all likely quite familiar if we've been raised in church—I understand that my interpretation is difficult indeed to consider. Even our modern term "sodomy" is taken from the word "Sodom" and often brings to mind a variety of sexual behavior. Moreover, in the New Testament, only Jude 7 associates Sodom with "immorality and...strange flesh." In the remainder of the Old Testament, however, every other time Sodom is referenced, sexual sins are never mentioned. *Never.* The offence is always the violation of the code of hospitality: refusing to care for those living among us who are in need or for strangers whose sojourn brings them across our path. Consider Amos 4:11: "'I overthrew you, as God overthrew Sodom and Gomorrah, and you were like a firebrand snatched from a blaze; Yet you have not returned to Me,' declares the LORD." What sin rivaled that of Sodom and Gomorrah? Amos makes it plain in 4:1 by noting clearly those "who oppress the poor, who crush the needy." From the prophet Isaiah, 3:9, "The expression of their faces bears witness against them, and they display their sin like Sodom; They do not even conceal it. Woe to them! For they have brought evil on themselves." What is the sin and evil that Isaiah compares to Sodom? "'It is you who have devoured the vineyard; The plunder of the poor is in your houses. What do you mean by crushing My people, And grinding the face of the poor?' Declares the Lord GOD of hosts" (Isa 3:14-15). (See Genesis 18:19 for the importance placed on "righteousness and justice.") The prophet Ezekiel clearly identified the sins of Sodom in Ezekiel 16:49, "Behold, this was the guilt of your sister Sodom: she and her daughters had arrogance, abundant food, and careless ease, but she did not help the poor and needy." Beyond Genesis 19, nowhere else in the entire Old Testament is Sodom associated with sexual sin of any kind. In every other instance Sodom's sin is described as mistreatment of the poor and the needy.

On the several occasions when Jesus speaks of Sodom, He never attaches anything of a sexual nature one way or the other. He does, however, warn cities that refuse to extend hospitality to His disciples.

"Truly I say to you, it will be more tolerable for the land of Sodom and Gomorrah in the day of judgment than for that city" (see Matt 10:14-15). The importance Jesus attaches to the care for the disadvantaged and those in need is seen in the parable of the sheep and goats. Jesus says that on the day of judgment the nations will be judged by their treatment of the stranger, the hungry, the thirsty, the naked, and the prisoner (Matt 25:31-46). So far as the biblical record is concerned, Jesus never mentions same-gender relationships. It seems plain that the treatment of the stranger, the poor, the helpless, and the disadvantaged was far more important to Jesus than speaking about same-gender relationships.

While many may disagree about the sin of Sodom, the Bible itself does not agree that their sin was homosexuality. The sin of Sodom was the abuse of power, the neglect of the poor, and the attempted brutalizing of the stranger. Before the two strangers ever arrived, the city was a society of organized oppression, violence, and corruption that was diametrically opposed to God's *shalom* (Hebrew, meaning peace, completeness, prosperity, and welfare). The sexual perversion of Sodom is one aspect of the city's overall social disorder. Social immorality more than sexual immorality is the sin of Sodom, and "that issue is presented in a way scarcely pertinent to contemporary discussions of homosexuality."[2] Violation of the code of hospitality may not amount to much for us today, but it was paramount in Near Eastern biblical times. The Bible is often misinterpreted and then misapplied, particularly on homosexuality. This occurs when God's judgment on ancient Sodom is used to condemn contemporary homosexual relationships. Those looking to the Bible to condemn same-sex relationships must look elsewhere.

The other two Old Testament references do unquestionably condemn same-sex relationships. Leviticus 18:22 refers to it as "an abomination" and 20:13 demands death for anyone involved. The New Testament instances are found in Romans 1:26-27, 1 Corinthians 6:9, and 1 Timothy 1:10. From Paul's perspective, it appears that heterosexuals were "leaving," "giving up," and "exchanging" what is "natural" for them and engaging in "unnatural" homosexual behavior.

First of all, it is without debate that the Bible does condemn same-sex relationships when the subject is mentioned. This, however, is not the end of the discussion. As is the case with every matter discussed in the Bible, it is important to consider Scripture in the context of its day and then interpret it in light of our own time. We do this on a regular

Chapter 9

basis without realizing it. Consider, for example, that in numerous passages God orders the wholesale slaughter of entire cities, including all men, women, children, infants, and livestock (note 1 Sam 15). This sort of act is abhorrent to us today and is inconsistent with the God that Jesus "explained" (see John 1:18) to us in the four Gospels. Can anyone imagine Jesus ordering such travesties? Such horrific slaughter supposedly demanded by God must be understood in the context of the time and then interpreted in light of clearer revelation and modern understanding. The Deuteronomic Law demanded that anyone committing adultery be put to death, both the man and woman. We understand these passages in the context of that time and then interpret them in the light of our day. We do not obey these scriptural commands. Levirate marriage (a deceased husband's brothers taking his widow in order to help propagate the family name) was demanded by the Law. We don't obey this command either.

In the Bible, slavery is never explicitly condemned, and even as late the first century CE, Paul commands, "slaves, be obedient to those who are your masters" (Eph 6:5). An entire book in the New Testament (Philemon) instructs a slave-owner how to treat his slave. Even in more modern times, the Bible has been used to advocate for and defend slavery. During the early history of the United States, the Bible was used by opponents of the abolition movement to defend slavery. Reverend E.W. Warren, pastor of the First Baptist Church of Macon, Georgia, preached a sermon in 1861 called, "Scriptural Vindication of Slavery," taking as his text Ephesians 6:5-8. The town's local newspaper printed the entire sermon. Note the following excerpt from Reverend Warren's message:

> A sermon on a topic so unusual to a Southern audience may need a word of explanation to justify it. Two reasons will be sufficient for this purpose:
> 1. Slavery forms a vital element of the Divine Revelation to man. Its institution, regulation, and perpetuity, constitute a part of many of the books of the Bible. God instituted it in the days of Noah, and gave it His sanction again at Mt. Sinai. His Son commended it during his ministry on earth. The holy apostle Paul, exhorted his son Timothy to preach it; and Peter teaches a most important precept as to its obligations.

2. The public mind needs enlightening from the sacred teachings of Inspiration [sic] on this subject.³

Interpreting Scripture to advocate slavery is abhorrent and beyond belief for us today. Any rational Christian would cringe if a minister tried to twist the Bible in such a way and then attempt to convince us that we are justified in treating a group of people so terribly. Yet, this is the exact same argument used to condemn same-sex relationships by those who proclaim, "It is biblical." The biblical revelation must be understood in the context of its time, and each generation is responsible for interpreting the Bible in the light of its own day. In every example I have cited above, the overly-simplistic argument "because the Bible says so" doesn't necessarily mean that it is so for us today. If it were, we would all be responsible for obeying every one of the commands noted above; commands that few (if any) of us agree are still applicable today.

The old adage, "God said it; I believe it; that settles it," is not as settled as some would like to think. Given the examples above (several others could be cited), it is obvious that the Bible contains some things we do not believe, accept, or practice. The Bible and human relationships are far more complicated than the simplistic statement, "God said it; I believe it; that settles it." Each of us understands that the Bible demands what we in our time would never obey. Moreover, it also prohibits practices in which we readily engage. We ignore commands that are now obviously obsolete and do so without a second thought. Similarly, the sexual ethics of the Bible have changed over the more than 1,200 years during which it was written. One of the most obvious examples is that Moses permits divorce while Jesus prohibits it. How do we, therefore, interpret the biblical teaching on divorce for today? Conservatives do interpretive gymnastics to get around the plain teachings of Jesus, while liberals plainly say they simply no longer believe it. Either way, though Jesus prohibits divorce, divorce is regularly accepted in most Protestant churches and denominations today. So, just because "the Bible" or even Jesus "says it," does not resolve the issue. People have long interpreted Scripture for their time, and rightly so.

The plain fact is that we disagree with most of the Bible's sexual ethics. Here are some examples, though this is not an exhaustive list.

1. Leviticus 18:19 forbids having intercourse with a woman during her menstrual period. There is no prohibition or restraint on such practice today.

2. Deuteronomy 22:22 demands that adulterers be stoned to death. We obviously do not practice this.

3. Nudity was strictly forbidden and considered sinful. Appropriate nudity is not considered sinful today.

4. Polygamy, having more than one wife at the same time, was regularly practiced in the Old Testament (see 1 Kings 11:3; 2 Chron 11:21). We disagree with this practice, and it is forbidden by law in the United States today.

5. Concubinage, having women as unmarried sexual partners, was accepted in the Old Testament (see 2 Sam 5:13; Song 6:8, 9). Such treatment of a woman is anathema in our culture. (Solomon, the so-called "wise one," had seven hundred wives and three hundred concubines. A glaring example that the Scriptures do indeed require interpretation.)

6. Deuteronomy 25:5 demanded levirate marriage. This is not practiced today.

7. Semen and menstrual blood renders all who touched it "unclean." Today we do not follow the biblical notions of "clean" and "unclean."

8. Moses allows for divorce. Jesus forbids divorce. Most Protestant churches are accepting of those whose lives have been touched by divorce.

9. Prostitution, while frowned upon, was permitted in the Old Testament (see Gen 38:15; Lev 21:14; Prov 29:3). Today it is illegal in most of the United States, and most consider it immoral.

10. In the Old Testament, female slaves were used for sexual pleasures. Slave owners in antebellum America treated female slaves the same way. Even today, with some modern armies, women are part of the spoils of war and are treated similarly. For most of the modern

world, however, such treatment of defenseless women is considered heinous.

There are four Biblical sexual prohibitions with which most agree today: incest, adultery (without the death penalty), rape, and bestiality. (If one were keeping score, that would make it 10 to 4.) We disagree with the Bible's ethical teachings on more matters than we agree.

So, what's the purpose for all my reasoning? My point is, we feel at liberty to reject most of the Bible's sexual ethics without a second thought, while at the same time honing in on those few passages of Scripture that address same-gender relationships. Though we readily reject most of the Bible's teachings on sexual behavior, we want to lift out the select passages on homosexuality and try to enforce them. At the very least, this is cherry-picking Scriptures (picking the verses we like and disregarding those we don't). This practice of using what we like and discarding what we don't is blatantly inconsistent.

A second important consideration regarding our understanding of the biblical passages on same-sex relationships is that, in the Bible, everyone is considered to be heterosexual. You won't find in the Old or New Testament the concept of *sexual orientation* only of *sexual behavior*. Sexual orientation was something beyond Paul's frame of reference, something Paul could not consider. There have been same-sex relationships throughout history, and the New Testament writers were surely familiar with it, but their understanding was limited to sexual behavior without any concept of sexual orientation. Sexual orientation, in contrast to sexual behavior, is something which was unknown before modern psychology could distinguish it, if not fully explain it. This has given us a far better understanding of human sexuality than was available in biblical times. Gays and lesbians no more *decide* to be gay or lesbian than heterosexuals *decide* to be straight. It is just the way we are wired. (If you are heterosexual, did you ever "decide" to be heterosexual? No. It is just who you are and what you've always been.) Thus, it is sinful for heterosexuals, abandoning what is "natural" for them, to engaging in "unnatural," homosexual relationships. Notice—for it is significant—that the passages in which Paul mentions homosexuality are heavy laden with references to lusts other than same-sex relationships. The 1 Corinthians passage cites "fornication" and "adulterers" in its list of sins (see 6:9). Romans 1:27 says they "burned in their desire toward one another." These are not adults in a committed, loving, same-gender relationship. They are lustful heterosexuals engaged in homosexual behavior.

Third, the Christian's understanding of living in the spirit rather than under the law must be considered in our understanding of a biblical sexual ethic. Critical to the fundamental theology of the Apostle Paul is that Christians are no longer under the Law of Moses. "For Christ is the end of the Law for righteousness to everyone who believes (Rom 10:4) is one of many passages that can be cited. The entire letter of the Apostle Paul to the Galatians addresses this very issue. He argues that if we intend to live under the Law, we must accept it all and live under it all: "For as many as are of the works of the Law are under a curse; for it is written, 'Cursed is everyone who does not abide by *all things written in the book of the law, to perform them*'" [emphasis mine] (Gal 3:10). Paul then uses Leviticus 18:5 to show that the law is based on doing, not believing, "He who practices them [the law] *shall live by them*" [emphasis mine] (Gal 3:12). So, if you are going to demand living under the law, you must live under all of it. Paul's point, however, is that living under every demand of the law is impossible. (See Paul's own struggle with obedience to the law in Romans 7:14-25.) What, then, is Paul's answer to the impossible demands of the law? "It was for freedom that Christ set us free; therefore keep standing firm and do not be subject again to a yoke of slavery" (Gal 5:1). The impossibility of living according to the law drives us to Christ where we find mercy, grace, and freedom.

Those who condemn all same-gender relationships do so by appealing to the biblical law. Yet, while they insist on the application of the law regarding same-gender relationships, they, at the same time, easily and readily disregard the application of the law to other matters of sexual ethics such as divorce, polygamy, concubinage, prostitution, and so on. Once again, cherry-picking Scriptures to condemn some sexual behavior while completely and inexplicably disregarding other scriptural teaching is nothing short of hypocrisy. Picking and choosing which laws or verses to obey while knowingly disregarding others is a sham that belies the very premise upon which the biblical argument rests: "The Bible says it. That settles it." All who demand obedience to portions of the law, must include the whole law, which they obviously do not.

Fourth, does this mean that anything goes, that there are no biblical, ethical demands made on us? It does not. There is a biblical ethic we are to follow in all relationships. Jesus gave it in Matthew 22:37-40:

And He said to him, "You shall love the Lord your God with all your heart, and with all your soul, and with all your mind." This is the great and foremost commandment. The second is like it, "You shall love your neighbor as yourself." On these two commandments depend the whole Law and the Prophets.

The law we are to follow is the law of love. The good news is not about rules and regulations, laws and commandments, "thou shalts" and "thou shalt nots." There is no inner, life-transforming dynamic in the law. The good news, the law of love, however, can and does transform the heart and set us free (see Gal 5:1 above). Augustine said, "Love God and do what you will."[4] The thought is that if we truly love God, we are set free to do what is pleasing to God. Let's be honest: none of us obeys this law of love either. None among us truly loves God with *all* our heart, soul, mind, and (as Mark's account adds) strength. Thus, even with the law of love, we are still and always dependent upon the mercy and grace of God. The law of love is, however, the foundation upon which the entire gospel is built. Love is the heart of God.

Is it possible for someone to love God with heart, soul, mind, and strength and at the same time love another person of their same gender? It is not only possible, it happens. There are gays and lesbians who love God as much as Billy or Franklin Graham, Rick Warren or Benny Hinn, Mother Teresa or the Pope or any other heterosexual, and yet find fulfillment in a committed, loving relationship with another adult of the same gender. One might say, "That can't happen." It does happen whether or not we acknowledge it, and whether or not we understand it. Michelle is just one example. For the record, Michelle is far more Christ-like—loving, forgiving, accepting, kind, gentle, and so on—than are many heterosexual Christians (preachers included) who viscerally ridicule, judge, and condemn her and others like her. Though I drove her out of the church with my censorious pontificating on something about which I understood little, Michelle, in her Christ-like gentleness, has never been unkind or even discourteous toward me. Even as I condemned her, she always treated me with respect and continues to live by the law of love.

Finally, some claim that condemning same-gender relationships and marriage is a way of defending the institution of marriage. It's utterly illogical to argue that same-gender marriage will somehow encourage or influence people to become homosexual. Given the stigma attached to it, as Michelle says, no one would readily choose to be gay. In what way would same-gender marriage deface, diminish, or detract from traditional marriages? How much destruction do gay marriages (or the concept of gay marriage or even the legalization of same-gender marriage) cause families compared to the damage caused by the divorce and extra-marital affairs of heterosexuals? The disintegration of homes and families is tragic and there are multiple reasons for this cultural malady that have nothing whatsoever to do with same-gender relationships.

In C.S. Lewis's *The Screwtape Letters*, the senior devil, Screwtape, advises his apprentice, Wormwood, to divert Christians' attention from real problems. "The game is to have them all running about with fire extinguishers whenever there is a flood."[5] In trying to defend traditional marriage by opposing same-gender marriage, the church brings a fire extinguisher to a flood, and the emotional rhetoric keeps it from facing real problems that have nothing to do with homosexuality. Traditional marriages are facing a flood of problems. Same-gender marriage is not one of them.

The largest Protestant denomination in the world, the Southern Baptist Convention (SBC), changed its historic constitution to prohibit membership to churches that "affirm, approve, or endorse homosexual behavior." In 1995 "messengers" (voting delegates) to the annual convention had to sign a statement affirming their church's compliance with this provision in order to receive credentials at official convention gatherings. In recent years, Southern Baptists have ousted churches who accept and minister to gays and lesbians. I wonder, What would have happened if Southern Baptists, who ardently and proudly claim to believe that the Bible is the "divinely inspired, inerrant, and infallible Word of God," had taken the same stand against divorce that Jesus took. Jesus' stand against divorce is clear and unequivocal, while He never mentioned homosexuality. What if the SBC had prohibited membership to churches which "affirm, approve, and endorse..." *divorce* rather than homosexuality? I imagine membership (and money) in both the convention and the churches would have dropped off sharply. Just wondering. This is another example of how duplicitous people (and denominations) can be in applying biblical teachings to modern life.

Is it not worth asking how Jesus might have treated these churches? Would He have rejected them for ministering to His own or would He have dined with them as He did with Matthew and all his thieving, tax collecting friends? As I said in the Preface, Christians acting in this manner is one reason so many people today conclude that the church is:

> ...judgmental, anti-homosexual, and too political. And young people are quick to point out that they believe that *Christianity is no longer as Jesus intended.* It is unChristian.[6]

How then should the church and Christians respond to gays and lesbians? Though I have tried to provide biblical reasons why loving, committed, same-gender relationships among adults are not always sinful or a violation of Scripture, I am sure many (most) are not convinced. So, if you still consider all same-gender relationships to be sinful and wrong, what then is a good way to respond? Personally, I think a Christian and a church should respond the same way if it were anyone else. The message of the church of Jesus Christ is the gospel of God's grace: an unconditional love, forgiveness, and acceptance of all people. Thus, if anyone disagrees with me and still considers same-gender relationships to be sinful and wrong, it is incumbent upon you by the life and message of Jesus to obey His command to "Follow Me" (see Matt 16:24; Mark 1:17; Luke 5:27; John 10:27). Follow Christ in loving all of humankind, especially your enemies (and certainly if you consider gays and lesbians to be your enemies or the enemies of the church or God). Jesus never mentioned same-gender relationships, but He did command us to love our enemies. Unconditional love is the coin of the realm, and if you claim to be a citizen of the Kingdom of God, loving all people is your obligation. Follow Christ in forgiving. The object of forgiving is the restoration of relationships. Follow Christ in accepting people just as they are. Be honest enough with yourself and don't take the easy way with a "I love the sinner, but hate the sin" cop out. Do you? Do you love the sinner? Do you love the gay or lesbian person whom you believe to be a sinner? Where is the evidence of that love, forgiveness—restored relationship—and acceptance?

Moreover, if you see homosexuality as a sin far greater than your own sins, then you must acknowledge that *greater grace* is extended by God to *greater sins* (see Rom 5:20). It is also important to review the lesson of Jesus in the parable of the Pharisee and the tax collector (see

Luke 18). Jesus told the parable "to some people who trusted in themselves that they were righteous, and viewed others with contempt" (Luke 18:9). The religious Pharisee thought his sin was far less than those of the thieving tax collector standing next to him. Jesus said the Pharisee's sin remained. The tax collector knew his sin and, "standing some distance away, was even unwilling to lift up his eyes to heaven, but was beating his breast, saying, 'God, be merciful to me, the sinner'" (18:13) Jesus applies the parable: "This man went to his house justified rather than the other; for everyone who exalts himself will be humbled, but he who humbles himself will be exalted" (18:14).

You may still see gay and lesbian persons as terrible sinners, but the more important matter is, "How do you see yourself?" Are you a Pharisee or a tax collector? Are you hyper-spiritual or a humble sinner? Are your sins less than those you condemn? How so? Are you so righteous that you can be the judge and voice of condemnation to others? Do you hold them in contempt? If so, you are like the Pharisee. On the other hand, are you humble enough to receive God's love, mercy, forgiveness, and grace, and having been loved and forgiven, then extend love, mercy, forgiveness and grace to others, including those with whom you disagree? If so, you are like the tax collector—a sinner, but a grateful and forgiven sinner. How will you treat gay and lesbian persons? Are you like the tax collector? Are you so concerned with *your* own sins that you cannot even look up to see the sins of others? Or are you like the Pharisees, so confident with your righteousness that you think you can sit in judgment of others? Jesus said these people remain in their sins and are far from the kingdom of God.

Mrs. Turpin is the right, proper Christian woman in Flannery O'Connor's short story, *Revelation*. She and her husband Claud have a small farm where they raise cotton and hogs.

> Sometimes at night when she couldn't go to sleep, Mrs. Turpin would occupy herself with the question of who she would have chosen to be if she couldn't have been herself. If Jesus had said to her before he made her, "There's only two places available to you. You can either be a nigger or white-trash," what would she have said?[7]

While waiting for Claud to see the doctor, Mrs. Turpin evaluates the other patients in the waiting room. There is the blond child in the dirty romper with a runny nose, a lean stringy old fellow with rusty hands, the stylish, well-dressed lady, an ugly fat girl with purple acne reading the book *Human Development*, a leathery old woman in a print cotton dress, and a lank-faced woman with snuff stained lips and dirty yellow hair. Mrs. Turpin is proud of who she is, and, in none too subtle ways, she disparages everyone in the waiting room but the well-dressed lady with whom she is talking.

> If it's one thing I am, it's grateful. When I think of who all I could have been besides myself and what all I got, a little of everything, and a good disposition besides, I just feel like shouting, "Thank you, Jesus, for making everything the way it is!" I could have been different.... O thank you, Jesus, Jesus thank you![8]

Just as she was thanking Jesus, WHAM! The *Human Development* book was hurled across the room striking Mrs. Turpin in the face. The girl with purple acne then jumped over a coffee table, knocked Mrs. Turpin to the floor, climbed on top, and began choking her. Everyone scurried to rescue Mrs. Turpin from the girl. After a few minutes Mrs. Turpin was able to sit up and gather her senses before looking at her assailant.

> She leaned forward until she was looking directly into the fierce brilliant eyes. There was no doubt in her mind that the girl did know her, knew her in some intense and personal way, beyond time and space and condition. "What you got to say to me," she asked hoarsely and held her breath, waiting, as for a revelation.
> The girl raised her head. Her gaze locked with Mrs. Turpin's. "Go back to hell where you came from, you old wart hog," she whispered. Her eyes burned for a moment as if she saw with pleasure that her message had struck its target.[9]

Back home later that evening Mrs. Turpin attempted, without much success, to convince herself that she was not a wart-hog from hell.

Chapter 9

The girl's eyes and her words, even the tone of her voice, low but clear, directed only to her, brooked no repudiation. She had been singled out for the message, though there was trash in the room to whom it might justly have been applied.[10]

As dusk falls, still shaken by the encounter, Mrs. Turpin stood on the bottom rail of the hog pen—much closer to the filth than she ever imagined—watering the hogs, when the sun began to fall below the line of trees on the horizon.

At last she lifted her head. There was only a purple streak in the sky, cutting through a field of crimson and leading, like an extension of the highway, into the descending dusk. She raised her hands from the side of the pen in a gesture hieratic and profound. A visionary light settled in her eyes. She saw the streak as a vast swinging bridge extending upward from the earth through a field of living fire. Upon it a vast horde of souls were rumbling toward heaven. There were whole companies of white-trash, clean for the first time in their lives, and bands of black niggers in white robes, and battalions of freaks and lunatics shouting and clapping and leaping like frogs. And bringing up the end of the procession was a tribe of people she recognized at once as those who, like herself and Claud, had always had a little of everything and the God-given wit to use it right. She leaned forward to observe them closer. They were marching behind the others with great dignity, accountable as they had always been for good order and common sense and respectable behavior. They alone were on key. Yet she could see by their shocked and altered faces that even their virtues were being burned away.[11]

Mrs. Turpin then stepped off the rail, turned off the water, and returned to her house hearing only "the voices of the souls climbing upward into the starry field and shouting hallelujah."[12]

On that great day, the Day of the Lord, it may very well be that Michelle along with a host of gay and lesbian persons, will be leaping, dancing, and shouting for joy on the upward swing that leads to heaven. The self-righteous, religious crowd who has judged, ridiculed, and condemned may well be walking a long way behind, listening to the grateful shouts of hallelujah from those ahead. Jesus said to the religious crowd of His day, "Truly I say to you that the tax collectors and prostitutes will get into the kingdom of God before you (Matt 21:31).

By the way, the girl who assaulted Mrs. Turpin in O'Connor's short story was given an interesting name by the author: Mary Grace. Grace has a way of putting the top rail on bottom and the bottom rail on top.

Merry grace!

---

[1]Yancey, *What's So Amazing*, 11.
[2]Brueggemann, *Genesis*, 164.
[3]Bruce Gourley, "Baptists and the American Civil War: January 27, 1861," *www.civilwarbaptists.com* <www.civilwarbaptists.com/thisdayinhistory/1861-january-27>.
[4]John Bunaby, ed., *Augustine: Later Works* (Philadelphia: Westminster Press, 1955) 316.
[5]C.S. Lewis, *The Screwtape Letters* (San Francisco: HarperSanFrancisco, 1996) 138.
[6]Kinnaman, *unChristian*, dust jacket.
[7]Flannery O Connor, *Flannery O Connor: The Complete Stories* (NY: Farrar, Straus, and Giroux, 1971) 491.
[8]Ibid, 499.
[9]Ibid, 500.
[10]Ibid, 502.
[11]Ibid, 508.
[12]Ibid, 509.

CHAPTER 10

The Greatest Challenge Facing the Church Today: Believing the Gospel

I WAS IN MY FRESHMAN YEAR of college when the April 8, 1966 issue of *Time Magazine* hit the newsstands. Emblazoned on the black cover in big, bold, red letters was the question that dominated the religious discussion for the remainder of the decade: "Is God Dead?" I still have my copy. Debuting only two days before Easter, it was scheduled to coincide with the most sacred day of the Christian calendar. The story set forth the musings of the death-of-God theologians, principally Thomas J.J. Altizer, then Professor of Religion at Emory University, a Methodist-affiliated school in Atlanta. The Methodist student magazine ran a notice of God's death in the obituary style of newspapers including the dateline:

> ATLANTA, Ga., Nov. 9—God, creator of the universe, principal deity of the world's Jews, ultimate reality of Christians, and most eminent of all divinities, died late yesterday during major surgery undertaken to correct a massive diminishing influence.[1]

This was all big news in 1966. It provided preachers fodder for our sermonic cannons for months on end, especially that Easter Sunday morning as we celebrated the resurrection of the living God. The editorial pages of newspapers around the nation were flooded with angry replies from both clergy and laity. *Time* received some 3,500 letters, the largest number at that time for any single story. Billy Graham expressed the views of most church-going Americans: "I know that God exists because of my personal experience. I've talked with him and walked with him."[2]

Throughout the ensuing controversy, the most poignant and pragmatic response came from theologian and Oxford University scholar, Dr. R.T. France in a little book called *The Living God*. Professor France's evaluation is truer today than it was when published in 1970.

> It is perfectly true that for the vast majority of the church-going American population (and America is not alone in this distinction), God *is* dead.... The "death-of-God" theologians...are describing the true character of much contemporary Christianity. As far as the ordinary man in the pew is concerned, God is dead. His daily life runs its predictable, gilt-edged, humdrum course without reference to God. He would, of course, be scandalized by the suggestion that God is dead, but if it were true, it would make no practical difference to his life. His work, his home, his sport, his politics, yes, and even his church life, would run on very much the same. They have no place for God; not practically, at any rate. God is a useful philosophical postulate, a comforting abstraction, a vague, nebulous word for what is solemn and serious and irrelevant to daily life. But He does not come into the reckoning when decisions are made, and the thought that He could have any practical effect on the way things turn out never disturbs the even flow of secular life.[3]

Believing Jesus

Christians believe in God and that Jesus is the Savior, and many go to church on Sundays. They are basically orthodox in their faith and accept, at least in theory if not fully in practice, the Christian ethic of the Ten Commandments, the Sermon on the Mount, and the ethical sections of the Pauline epistles. The greatest challenge facing the church

Chapter 10

today, however, is not whether we believe correct theology, but whether we believe Jesus. Oh, I know we believe who Jesus was, and that He was...

> ...conceived by the Holy Spirit, born of the Virgin Mary; suffered under Pontius Pilate, was crucified, dead, and buried; He descended into hell; the third day He rose again from the dead; He ascended into heaven, and sitteth on the right hand of God the Father Almighty; from thence He shall come to judge the quick and the dead.[4]

This reflects a belief *in* Jesus, that He lived at a time and place in history. The challenge we face, however, is: Do we believe Jesus? I'm not talking about believing in what Jesus did (turning water to wine, feeding five thousand people, etc.), what He said (to Nicodemus, to the woman at the well, etc.), or what is recorded in any particular biblical chapter and verse. I am not even talking about believing what Jesus said about being born again so that we can go to heaven. (And despite what I was taught as a kid, that is not the purpose of salvation. The purpose of salvation is not to get people out of earth into heaven, but to get God out of heaven into people. God is concerned with *now*, with how we live right now.) What I want us to consider is, "Do you believe Jesus: his life and message comprising all the things He said and did? Do you believe "the Jesus way" (see John 14:6) is the right way, the best way and the truth about life?"

Consider what precedes "I am the way, and the truth, and the life; no one comes to the Father but through Me" (John 14:6) in the magnificent prologue of John's Gospel:

> But as many as received Him, to them He gave the right to become children of God, even to those who believe in His name, who were born not of blood nor of the will of the flesh nor of the will of man, but of God (John 1:12-13).

The redeemed have been "born...of God," and that has consequences. We are the "children of God," and that should make a difference in how we live. Does it? While you may be a theoretical Christian, are you at the same time a practical atheist? What I mean is this: do you believe in the Jesus of history (His life, ministry, and teachings), yet there's no noticeable difference that He influences your work, home, sports, politics, or even your church?

Throughout this book I have attempted to emphasize through various examples what grace means. God loves, forgives, and accepts us all unconditionally, which is the heart of the gospel and the heart of God. Believing all of this *will* make a difference in how we live. By "believe" I do not mean merely accepting facts (e.g., Apostles' Creed), I mean the sense of belief described in John's writings: *an affirmation that is binding on all of life*. This sort of believing changes the way we live, not simply how we spend our Sunday mornings. It changes who we are pragmatically not just what we believe historically or how we think theologically. Does your believing Jesus make a difference in your life? Or to use R.T. France's terminology, does God "come into the reckoning when decisions are made,"[5] or is God just "a useful philosophical postulate, a comforting abstraction, a vague, nebulous word for what is solemn and serious and irrelevant to daily life?"[6] Is it the case for you that your "daily life runs its predictable, gilt-edged, humdrum course without reference to God?"[7] Are you a confessing Christian and yet, without realizing it, a practicing atheist?

Allow me to pose four questions where the subject of the dependent clause (each is underlined) goes a long way in describing the Jesus way and what it means *practically* to believe the gospel.

1. Do you believe that <u>love</u> is a greater power than hate? Jesus did.

2. Do you believe that <u>forgiveness</u> is a greater power than vengeance? Jesus did.

3. Do you believe that <u>kindness</u> is a greater power than cruelty? Jesus did.

4. Do you believe that <u>goodness</u> is a greater power than wickedness? Jesus did.

Making the questions even more practical rather than theoretical, consider the following. What do you believe to be the best option for countering the hatred that drives radical, Islamic terrorism? Do you think military action, improved airport security, a foreign policy change, or more secure borders will solve the problem? How about the love of God? What do your casual comments and conversations about terrorism indicate? I know the problem is multifaceted, but is God even part the solution for us as Christians? Are spiritual or theological components part of your perspective? Does God enter the equation or "Is God Dead" for all practical purposes? The message of Jesus, the gospel, and the New Testament is that only God's love is can change the kind of hatred that breeds terroristic attacks.

Consider that the entire apparatus of the U.S. government and the billions of dollars are being spent to protect us from truck and car bombings, suicide attacks, and jetliners flying into skyscrapers. All of this has thwarted many attacks, and for that we are grateful. The government can track down, arrest, try, convict, and incarcerate terrorists. However, after the billions spent and the effort expended, the only change of heart that will have occurred is intensifying the terrorists' hatred toward our country and Christianity.

We are quite clear about the task of the government regarding terrorism, but what is the task of the church? How would Jesus respond? How should His church respond? It is our task to embody the love, forgiveness, kindness, and goodness of God to all humankind, including radical terrorists sworn to kill us. I think that is what Jesus would do. How would terrorists respond to God's love? Probably the same way people responded to Jesus 2,000 years ago and the same way some people in our neighborhoods respond to Jesus today. Some believe and are transformed by His love, while others continue to hate and kill. Their reaction, however, is not the church's responsibility. Embodying God's love to the world is the church's responsibility.

Realistically, though, most of us will never personally encounter a terrorist. So, let's make things more practical. How do we live day-in-and-day-out with the people we actually do encounter? How do we act where we live, go to school, work, and shop? Does being born of God and being a child of God make a practical difference in how you live every day? Does being born of God make any difference in who you are, how you live, and how you interact with those you encounter in your home, at the office, in the factory, on the campus, in the classroom, at the grocery store, in the bank, in a restaurant, at a ballgame, or waiting in line at the DMV? In places and at times such as these, do God and the gospel influence your actions and reactions or, for all practical purposes, "Is God Dead" in your life?

The greatest challenge facing the church today is not theological—beliefs about inerrancy, creation, hell, atonement, and so on. Most people, Christian or not, do not care about your theology and likely will not be influenced by your church's doctrine. What they do see and what will influence them is how you live, how you treat them, and how you relate to them and other people. This is the essence of the church's challenge: are Christians Christ-like? Are we loving, forgiving, kind, good, and gracious like Jesus, or are we harsh, bitter, mean-spirited, resentful, and vengeful? At the intersections of life, does God matter to you? Do *you* truly believe Jesus? *In your relationships with other people:* Do *you* trust love to be greater than the power of hate? Do *you* trust forgiveness to be greater than the power of vengeance? Do *you* trust kindness to be greater than the power of cruelty? Do *you* trust goodness to be greater than the power of wickedness? Are *you* loving, forgiving, good, and kind? By the way *you* treat other people in your attitude, words, and actions, does God "come into the reckoning when decisions are made,"[8] or is God just "a useful philosophical postulate, a comforting abstraction, a vague, nebulous word for what is solemn and serious and irrelevant to daily life?"[9] Is it the case for you that your "daily life runs its predictable, gilt-edged, humdrum course without reference to God?"[10] This is the greatest challenge facing the church.

The church is presently failing its challenge. This is an example of bad Christianity. It is a primary reason that millions are abandoning the church and millions of others have never darkened its doors because they deem the church irrelevant. This is the reason for the "de-converts," the "leavers," and the "nones" noted earlier in this book. As David Kinnaman found out, "Young people are quick to point out they believe that *Christianity is no longer as Jesus intended.* It is unChristian."[11] The reason for this sad condition rests at the feet of Christians.

Jesus and the Segregated South

I was born in the American South during its time of prevailing segregation. Schools were segregated and stores had separate water fountains bearing "White" and "Colored" signs. The "White" water fountains were refrigerated. The "Colored" fountains consisted of exposed pipes protruding through a wall that were attached to a white porcelain basin. I remember noticing the difference, but it said more than a kid could realize at the time. The lunch counter at Woolworths was segregated. There were segregated bathrooms, medical waiting rooms, neighborhoods, and churches. Whites and blacks lived in separate neighborhoods. And, unbelievably, I was in college before I came to understand how truly offensive the language we used was to my brothers and sisters of color. As a kid and teenager, I never knew that any offence was intended. Our offensive terminology was used freely everywhere by everyone including at home, in my extended family, in my church, and in the culture. It was a segregated way of life to which I sadly gave no thought.

Once when daddy needed some help doing work at our house, he hired a black man to help him for the day. When lunch time came, I remember momma taking his lunch to him on a paper plate, with plastic utensils. His sweet tea was in a Mason jar and he ate on the steps of the back porch. After he had finished and gone back to work, momma used a paper towel to carefully pick up the plate and utensils and throw them in the garbage can *outside*. With another paper towel, she did the same with the Mason jar. She would neither touch them with her bare hand nor let them be brought back into the house. Not a word was spoken, but a lot was communicated.

There were thousands of Christians who were not racist. There were many Christian clergy and laity, black and white, who marched shoulder to shoulder in the civil rights struggle of the 1960s. I was not one of them. At the time, my alma mater Mercer University was affiliated with a state Baptist convention. Members of the faculty were active in the civil rights movement both in the classroom and on the streets. The administration made every effort to attract minority students and provide an opportunity for an outstanding education. As a young adult, I heard an interview with internationally known evangelist Billy Graham. Some asked him, if it was possible to eliminate one sin, which one would he eliminate? He instantly replied, "racism."

Racism is our shame and embarrassment. It has been historically perpetuated by many in the Christian church and by the church itself. I recall one particular Sunday sermon where I blasted away at some ruling of the U.S. Supreme Court. It had nothing to do with racism, and I have no memory of the point I was attempting to make. What I do remember is receiving a call the next morning from a member of my church inviting me to lunch. Dr. Roberts was a college professor in American history and whenever he invited me to lunch I knew I had blown it. I had either been wrong about or misinterpreted historical facts. He referred to what I did ignorantly on occasions as "lawyer's tricks." I might have had some of the facts right, but I twisted them to suit my liking. It was always a humbling experience. I recall how he began at the particular lunch in question:

> Steve, I was interested in your take on the Supreme Court in your sermon Sunday. You were very critical of the Court. Pastor, I have always had a great respect for the Court. May I remind you that it was not the Christian church that led the fight for equality and civil rights and an end to segregation in the nation and the South. It was the Supreme Court.

I had never thought about it, but he was right. My views about the U.S. Supreme Court changed that day. If all who claim to be Christian—regardless of race or ethnicity—truly believed Jesus and embraced the gospel, the racial animosity in America would diminish dramatically.

While circumstances regarding race have dramatically altered since the passage and enforcement of effective civil rights legislation, there remains in our country a level of racially-tinged animosity and suspicion. Dr. Graham's wish has not come true. The worn and hackneyed cliché is "The most segregated hour of the week is eleven o'clock Sunday morning." But that's not the problem, and is not even a symptom of it. The reasons for differing Sunday morning church choices have nothing to do with racial animosity. It is a matter of preference in type and style of music, worship, preaching, and so on; none of which are right or wrong, just different. The problem is not segregated churches, though for whatever reasons most churches of the South are still segregated. The problem is the hearts of Christians of whatever color regarding people of another race. How can Christians reconcile the gospel with the cruel and wicked forces of racism that still plague the hearts of so many? I think it is because Christians do not believe Jesus. They do not believe the gospel.

The core of the problem is that the gospel of love, forgiveness, kindness, and goodness is not always shaping our opinions, conversations, attitudes, and actions. For too many Christians and churches, the culture shapes our attitudes and actions rather than the gospel working through us to shape the attitudes and actions of both the church and culture. Many Christians have overcome racial hatred and prejudice, and it has taken decades to do so. The battle, however, is not over. Some think it may never be. Timothy Tyson is the son of a Methodist preacher and a senior research scholar at Duke University. He developed a gripping documentary about the racism he experienced in 1970 North Carolina. In *Blood Done Sign My Name*, he refers to slavery as America's original sin and doesn't think we will ever get over it. Racial prejudice, hatred, and cruelty have been built into the American experience since slave ships brought Africans here with the accepted belief, even among Christians and churches, that it was okay for one person to own another. The gospel must constantly challenge our attitudes and actions.

While I was in seminary, a prominent Texas pastor had been dismissed from his church because of his conciliatory views on race. His termination became a springboard for classroom discussions led by godly and gifted Bible scholars. In ethics and pastoral ministries classes we read the writings of such prominent civil rights leaders as Dr. Martin Luther King, Jr. I discovered that he was not the communist or rabble rouser we had been led to believe he was. Dr. King was an intelligent, educated, Baptist preacher with a social conscience akin to Old Testament prophets and a non-violent, turn-the-other-cheek philosophy like Jesus. A Methodist pastor with whom I became friends years later actually marched with Dr. King. After one of their non-violent protests they were resting in a home when a shotgun blast blew out the front picture window. They all hit the floor. When they thought it was relatively safe, they all began to rise from the floor. My friend said, "Martin, I'm tired of this, I'm not going to take it anymore," and gripped with fear and rage he ran out the back door. (He told me he had no idea what he would do, but his anger had taken over.) Dr. King was fast after him, wrestled him to the ground, and said, "If you do that, you are no different from them."

Dr. King's "Letter From Birmingham City Jail" was a reasoned, thought-provoking, impassioned, and kind plea for freedom, justice, and equality. It sounded more like Amos, "Let justice roll down like waters and righteousness like an ever-flowing stream" (5:24). It seemed more like Micah, "And what does the Lord require of you but to do justice, to love kindness, and to walk humbly with your God" (6:8)? It sounded nothing like Trotsky, Stalin or any of the other communists we were told he was like. It sounded like the teachings of Jesus. His plea for biblical values was irrefutable and made more sense than all the opposing arguments I had heard over my lifetime. Those discussions in seminary pricked my conscience about my attitudes on race.

Every Christian decides consciously or not: is the gospel of Jesus of Nazareth going to guide my life or am I going to live by other principles? There are as many excuses and reasons given as there are people as to why we don't actually follow Jesus. "That's just the way I was raised." "The Johnsons have always had a short fuse and a hot-temper." "I never have liked anyone telling me what to do." "That just won't work around here. "You can't run a business that way." "I have to look after myself and my family." All of these statements reflect ways we can be Christian yet not believe the gospel. We believe the stories of Jesus and that He is the Savior. We are theologically orthodox. But when it comes to living for Jesus day by day we don't believe the gospel. To our shame, Professor France describes the church so well,

> God is a useful philosophical postulate, a comforting abstraction, a vague, nebulous word for what is solemn and serious and irrelevant to daily life. But He does not come into the reckoning when decisions are made, and the thought that He could have any practical effect on the way things turn out never disturbs the even flow of secular life.[12]

The gospel is what changed my views on race. "That's just the way I was raised," could not withstand the gospel. Either "God so loved the world" or He didn't. If Jesus is "our peace, who made both groups into one and broke down the barrier of the dividing wall" (Eph 2:14), then racial attitudes of the past could not remain either in my heart or in my church.

Racism, the Church, and Jesus

My first ministry role beyond seminary was serving as associate pastor for the church I attended from my infancy until I left for college. The heat of the civil rights movement occurred during my teen years. During that era, my home church (the largest in the city) stationed ushers at the doors to forbid entrance to blacks who might try to attend, an action in which the church took great pride. Years later, even after pragmatic realities caused that policy to be dropped, I was preaching one Sunday night. Toward the conclusion of my sermon, a note was slipped over the pulpit to me. It read: "No invitation. Blacks in the back." The church didn't want to take the chance that blacks might want to join. (The irony and symbolism of such a note being slipped over a *Christian* pulpit is appalling.) In promoting revivals or special church programs, a printed advertisement never read, "Everyone Welcome" because some people weren't welcome.

One of my most cherished ministry opportunities was returning to pastor the church of my childhood. This church had raised me so I came with instant credibility. I would often chide them playfully, "If you had done a better job raising me, I would be making you a better pastor." It was a wonderful relationship for everyone involved. The great Baptist leader of yesteryear, Dr. Louie D. Newton, had an oft repeated phrase: "Happy pastor; Happy people." We were happy indeed. Yet, even when I arrived as pastor in the mid-1980s the church was still segregated.

I answered the telephone one afternoon and a Mr. George Foster asked for an appointment to see me. I didn't know until he arrived that he was black. He was a doctoral candidate in communications from New York and was now working in our city. "Pastor, I've been watching your church on television and have been blessed by the services. I don't want to cause you or the church any problems, but would you or others be offended if I began to visit?" I assured George that I and most of the church would welcome him. "However, I must tell you that not everyone will be glad to have you in church. Some will be offended by your coming, and I don't want them to offend you." George began attending regularly. Standing about six feet, three inches, with a salt and pepper gray beard, and the only black person in the congregation, he was not difficult to see.

After several months, George came back to see me. "Pastor, I've enjoyed attending, and everyone has been most cordial. Again, I don't want to cause you any trouble, but I would like to join and become a member. Would that be okay with you and with the church?" I again assured George that I and most of the members would be glad for him to join and would welcome him as a brother in Christ. Once again, I noted that it would not be a unanimous opinion.

The next Sunday when my sermon was over and the congregation was singing the hymn of invitation, George left his pew and walked forward. I stepped off the platform, greeted him with a handshake, and invited him to have a seat on the front pew where those who come forward are always seated. After the invitation I asked the congregation to be seated and George to stand with me. I told the church of our two meetings and of George's desire first to attend and now to join. Then I said,

> Ladies and gentlemen, the gospel invitation of the New Testament is, "Whosoever will let him come." How could I in a thousand years ever explain to anyone who wanted to join this church that I really didn't mean what I said when I said, "Whosoever will let him come?" And, if I had all eternity, how could I ever explain it to God? From this point forward we are going to welcome everyone Jesus would welcome, and we are going to kick out everyone Jesus would kick out. As of this moment this church has an open door policy. Whosoever will let him come.

The church as one body rose to their feet in thunderous applause. I turned and looked at George. Tears were not only streaming down his cheeks, they were on mine and many others, too! It was a glorious day for the church, for the gospel in our midst. This was an instance of the church truly believing Jesus and the gospel. George had a booming baritone voice and became a wonderful addition to our choir, regularly voicing recitations in choir specials and serving as narrator when needed. A marvelous Christian, faithful member, and wonderful addition to the church family, George was elected to serve as a deacon. Within a few months, two biracial couples came to join, and when the church gladly accepted them I knew we had turned the corner on racism.

Racism is just one example of the challenge to believe the gospel. Are we going to believe the gospel, or for all practical purposes is God just "a useful philosophical postulate...[who] does not come into the reckoning when decisions are made?"[13] I used to wonder why God or the gospel doesn't determine more of our actions and reactions. I learned long ago that it's because we think our ways are better. Martin Luther defined sin as, *cur incurvatus od sed*: "the heart curved in on itself." Too often Christians really do think that their hate achieves more than God's love. We think that getting revenge is a better response to an insult than forgiveness. Jesus won't get even, so I must. We really believe that harshness is a better response to hostility than kindness. They must be taught a lesson. We believe that meanness is a better response to antagonism than goodness. Jesus will just let them get away with it; I won't. Though they would deny it, many really believe that these vices serve our personal ambitions, objectives, purposes, and crass cravings better than the Jesus way, the gospel way. Can a person be a Christian and not believe Jesus, the Jesus way and the gospel? They can. I've known hundreds who are exactly that way. They trust Jesus for salvation, but not for living. Too many Christians consider our turned-in-on-self is better served by our turned-in-ways than by being loving, forgiving, good and kind like Jesus. Jesus and the gospel often get in our way. "Is God Dead?" No. *For many Christians, however, it seems as if it simply does not matter that He is alive.* This is why believing the gospel is the greatest challenge facing the church today.

Living the Gospel

Believing the gospel means living the gospel. Tony Campolo is one of the most engaging and insightful leaders of our generation. He is a university professor, a sociologist, a prodigious author, and an ordained Baptist minister. If you ever hear him speak, you will never forget it. I heard Tony tell the story of being in Honolulu to speak at a conference. The time zone difference had him wide awake and hungry in the middle of the night. He got up and was out on the streets looking for something to eat at three o'clock in the morning. He came across a dingy little diner, the kind where the only seats are stools bolted to the floor at a counter. Harry was unshaven and wore a dirty apron when he came out of the kitchen to take Tony's order. When Tony asked for a cup of coffee and a doughnut, Harry poured coffee, lifted the plastic top of the cake plate with one hand, and wiped his other hand on the dirty apron before picking up the doughnut and putting it on a plate. You get the picture of what sort of place Tony found himself.

He was eating his doughnut and drinking his coffee when around three-thirty that morning the door opened and nine prostitutes entered. "I mean, the dress and conversation," Tony exclaimed, "You knew they were prostitutes!" The diner was small with only the one counter, so they were crammed in and sitting all around him. He told us, "A preacher and nine prostitutes in a greasy spoon at three thirty in the morning!"

One of the girls sitting next to Tony said, "Tomorrow is my birthday, I'm going to be thirty-nine." Another girl, talking across Tony, said, "So, what do you want me to do? Sing 'Happy Birthday?' You want me to give you a cake or something?" "Why do you have to be so mean," said the birthday girl, "I've never had a birthday cake in my whole life. I don't expect to have one now. I was just telling you, that's all."

Tony told us that right then he decided what he was going to do. After the prostitutes left, Tony learned from Harry that the same girls come in every night. "It's Agnes' birthday tomorrow, Harry. What do you say we decorate this place, and when she comes in tomorrow night we throw her a party. She's never had a party."

Harry said, "Mister, that's beautiful! That's beautiful!" He called Jan, his wife out from the back. "Tomorrow is Agnes's birthday and this guy wants to throw a birthday party for her." Jan said, "Oh, mister, that's grand! Nobody ever does anything for Agnes and she is one of the good people in this town. She gives so much to other people." Tony didn't want to think about what she gave other people. He offered to decorate the place and Harry volunteered to do the cake.

The next morning Tony was at the diner at two-thirty with streamers, decorations, and a big "HAPPY BIRTHDAY AGNES" sign that he placed over the mirror behind the counter. Word had gotten out on the street and by three o'clock, Tony said, "Every prostitute in Honolulu was squeezed into that diner. It was wall-to-wall prostitutes and me!"

When Agnes and her friends walked through the door at three-thirty, everyone shouted, "HAPPY BIRTHDAY, AGNES!" She was totally stunned as everyone cheered like mad. Her knees almost buckled before her friends steadied her and helped her over to one of the stools. Harry came out with the cake and everyone sang the Happy Birthday song to Agnes as she broke down in tears. She was crying so hard that Harry had to blow out the candles for her. Excited, Harry said, "Cut the cake, Agnes! Cut the cake!"

Agnes just sat there for a moment before saying, "Harry, is it okay if I don't cut the cake right now? I ain't never had a birthday cake before. I just live a couple of blocks away. I want to take the cake and show it to my mother. I'll bring it right back, Harry. I promise. I just want to keep it a little while and show it to my mother."

Harry looked at Tony, and Tony nodded his approval. Tony told us, "Agnes picked up that cake like it was the Holy Grail." She carefully made her way through the crowded diner, opened the door, and walked out into the night. In the awkward silence that followed, everyone stood crammed in the small diner with their eyes lowered. Then, at three thirty in the morning and surrounded by a bunch of Hawaiian prostitutes, Tony announced, "Let's pray."

They all bowed their heads and Tony prayed for Agnes. He prayed for her safety and protection; that God would heal the scars of her soul and hurts of her heart; that God would make her new, for her family and all her friends in the diner. Afterward, Harry said, "You didn't tell me you was a preacher. What kind of church you belong to?" In a moment of divine inspiration, Tony says he replied, "I belong to a church that throws birthday parties for whores at three o'clock in the morning." "No you don't," said Harry, "No you don't. I'd join a church like that." Tony then concluded the telling of his story:

> Wouldn't we all! Wouldn't we all! I've got news for you: that is the kind of church Jesus came to create. He came to bring celebration into the lives to those who have nothing to celebrate. This is true religion, says the Epistle of James, to visit the fatherless and the widows in their affliction and bring celebration into their lives. The Christ that saves you from sin and fills you with His joy, commissions you to go out and to spread that joy. *Joy to the world because the Lord has come. The Lord has come!*

Tony Campolo shows us what it is like to live the gospel.

Believing the Gospel

We all can't be like Tony Campolo, but all of us can believe and live the gospel. It is impossible to read about the life of Jesus in the four Gospels without understanding that Jesus wanted to transform our lives. The Sermon on the Mount alone makes this as clear as crystal. It is not enough not to kill our enemies, we must not even hate them; but even more, we are to love them. Properly understood, the theology of the

New Testament—what we believe—is not an end in itself. The Pharisees, of which Paul was one, had a proper theology, but they cared little for people and received Jesus' most scathing rebuke (see the "seven woes" Jesus pronounced on the Pharisees in Matthew 23:13ff). Our theology—the gospel—is a means to an end: transforming our lives. And transformed people live the gospel wherever they go.

In the verses of Scripture we refer to as the "salvation formula" (John 3:16, 14:6; Rom 10:9-10), the "believe" involves more than accepting the historicity of the biblical story of creation or the precepts of the Apostles' Creed. It is more than believing in the inerrancy of Scripture, in heaven, hell, or atonement. Believing is more than believing the salvation formula. Jesus followed up His words in John 14:6, "I am the way, the truth, and the life; no one comes to the Father but through me," by explaining practically what the Jesus way is: "Truly, truly, I say to you, he who believes in Me, *the works that I do shall he do also*" [emphasis mine] (vs. 12). Believing the gospel means doing the gospel, doing "the works that I do." The reason I love Tony's story about throwing a birthday party for a prostitute named Agnes is that this is something Jesus would do.

This is the kind of difference the gospel makes: it transforms us within. The experience of the love and forgiveness of God can change our heart. Paul says it best in 2 Corinthians 5:17, "Therefore if any man is in Christ, he is a new creature; the old things passed away; behold, new things have come." Being "in Christ" (this phrase with its variations is used 164 times by Paul) means we are an entirely "new creation" (NIV, ESV). This makes a difference. Paul describes that difference in verses 18-19,

> Now all these things are from God, who reconciled us to Himself through Christ, and gave us the ministry of reconciliation, namely, that God was in Christ reconciling the world to Himself, not counting their trespasses against them, and He has committed to us the word of reconciliation (2 Cor 5:18-19).

The basic meaning of the word "reconciled," used as either a verb or noun four times in these two verses, is "to make other than it is" or "to effect a change." Believing the gospel makes us other than what we were before we believed. It effects a change in our lives. The transformed

Chapter 10

heart ("new creation") leads to a transformed life ("reconciliation"). Jesus was not interested in us changing our theology. For Paul, a proper theology should produce a transformed life. (Most of Paul's letters are clearly divided between the theological portion in the first half, and the ethical portion in the second half. For example, Ephesians 1-3 is the theological part, and chapters 4-6 are the ethical. Ephesians 4:1 begins, "Therefore..." Because of what you believe—theology—this is how you are to behave—ethics.) The purpose of salvation is not so we can go to heaven when we die. It is to make us new creatures now so we can live. Experiencing the love of God makes us more loving. It transforms the way we think, live, and relate to other people. The absence of obvious change in the lives of so many who claim to be Christian is why R.T. France says that if God were dead it would make no practical difference to millions of Christians.

One of my mentors in ministry says, "We behave what we believe. All else is just religious talk." Believing the gospel means *behaving* the gospel. Believing the gospel means that we...

> ...believe that the Jesus way of love is a better way to live than the way of hate. Therefore, we do not hate people; we love people.
> ...believe that the Jesus way of forgiveness is a better way to live than seeking revenge. Therefore, we forgo revenge and forgive those who offend us.
> ...believe the Jesus way of kindness is a better way to live than the way of malice. Therefore, we repudiate maliciousness and treat people with kindness.
> ...believe the Jesus way of goodness is a better way to live than the way of wickedness. Therefore, we spurn wickedness, and we treat people, even our enemies, with goodness.
> ...love, forgive, and accept all people. It means that we throw parties for whores at three-thirty in the morning.

How, you ask, is this possible? It's like the example of the lemon in chapter one. Whatever is on the inside is what comes out when life puts the squeeze on you. You are "in Christ" and Christ is in you. You testify to this every time you partake of the Lord's Supper. His body, His blood,

His life are now in you and are part of your life. Jesus is as present with you as the wafer you hold in your hand, a wafer that becomes part of your body. You have experienced the love, forgiveness, and acceptance of Jesus. This is what should come out when you are "squeezed." What, then, can we do when these things do not come out? We *remember*. The Apostle Paul has one imperative verb throughout the first three chapters of Ephesians. "Remember" (2:11). We go back and remember, as the poet said, "the pit from which you were dug" (Isa 51:1). We remember where we were when God loved, forgave, and accepted us; where we are yet when God continues to loves, forgives, and accepts us. Remembering and renewing the experience enables us to live the gospel.

"Is God Dead?" No, He is not. But does it make any difference to you that He is alive?

[1] Anthony Towne, "An Obituary for God," *The News and Courier*, 14 March 1966, sec. A, p. 6 <http://news.google.com/newspapers?nid=2506&dat=19660314&id=uMdJAAAAIBAJ&sjid=hwoNAAAAIBAJ&pg=2870,3087409>.
[2] Patrick Allitt, *Religion in America Since 1945: A History* (NY: Columbia University Press, 2003) 76.
[3] Richard Thomas France, *The Living God* (London: Inter-Varsity Press, 1970) 9.
[4] *Book of Common Prayer*, 53.
[5] France, *Living God*, 10.
[6] Ibid, 10.
[7] Ibid, 10.
[8] Ibid, 10.
[9] Ibid, 10.
[10] Ibid, 10.
[11] Kinnaman, *unChristian*, dust jacket.
[12] France, *Living God*, 10.
[13] Ibid, 10.

CHAPTER 11

Grace Above All.
Then, More Grace

WITHOUT EQUAL, the greatest explanation of the gospel that I have ever read outside the New Testament is found in the Heidelberg Catechism. A catechism is an instructional tool for teaching the major tenants of Christian doctrine. Catechisms are often written in a question and answer format. The question inquires about an important aspect of the Christian faith and is followed by the answer. Each word in the answer has been meticulously and purposefully chosen and syntactically arranged to articulate and preserve the truth from generation to generation. The Heidelberg Catechism was written in 1563 in Heidelberg, Germany, amid the Protestant Reformation.

The sixtieth question and answer give an expression of the gospel unequaled (in my view) in the voluminous writings of the church:

Q: How art thou righteous before God?

A: Only by a true faith in Jesus Christ; so that, though my conscience accuse me, that I have grossly transgressed all the commandments of God, and kept none of them, and am still inclined to all evil; notwithstanding, God, without any merit of mine, but only of mere grace, grants and imputes to me, the perfect satisfaction, righteousness and holiness of Christ; even so, as if I never had had, nor committed any sin: yea, as if I had fully accomplished all that obedience which Christ has accomplished for me; inasmuch as I embrace such benefit with a believing heart.[1]

Read the question and answer again, thoughtfully and slowly. If you rush through it, you might miss it. Allow me to separate the answer into phrases that I have found helpful.

> Only by a true faith in Jesus Christ;
> So that, though my conscience accuse me, that I have grossly transgressed all the commandments of God,
> And kept none of them,
> And am still inclined to all evil;
> Notwithstanding,
> God,
> Without any merit of mine,
> But only of mere grace,
> Grants and imputes to me,
> The perfect
> Satisfaction,
> Righteousness and
> Holiness of Christ;
> Even so, as if I never had had, nor committed any sin:
> Yea, as if I had fully accomplished all that obedience which Christ has accomplished
> For me;
> Inasmuch as I embrace such benefit with a believing heart.

Now, allow me to unpack what I think this means for everyone who embraces "such benefit with a believing heart." This can reveal how deep amazing grace truly reaches.

Chapter 11

Here Is the Wonder of the Gospel of Grace

Q: How art thou righteous before God?

"Only"

This is the most important word in the entire reply. "Only" sets the gospel of Jesus Christ apart from all other religions, especially the Christian "religion." Religions tell us the multiplicity of things we need to do for God, so He will forgive us and like us. "Only" the gospel tells us everything God has already done for us: He loves us, He has already forgiven us. We are righteous, but not because of what we have done, will do, or by believing an orthodox theology. We are righteous "only" through one thing. When we add anything to the "only," we do not deflate or destroy the gospel (we cannot destroy the gospel); we simply render it ineffective in our lives, and we continue on the religious treadmill trying to earn by performance what we already have by grace.

"By a true faith in Jesus Christ"

One thing is necessary to be righteous before God: "true faith." I am referring to genuine faith where God is the type of God Jesus "explained" (see John 1:18) to us throughout His life, teachings, and ministry. We must be careful not to turn our belief into another work, something that we try to do to earn God's favor. Recall for a moment the example I offered in chapter one about my house falling down for lack of repair. In that analogy, my house gets repaired by friends when I am injured and unable to work. The house gets repaired and though I can only see pictures from my hospital bed, I still believe that the work occurred. Though I did nothing to fix it, it is mine nonetheless to enjoy. Life in Christ is like this. We can simply believe and rest, knowing it is true. Faith is the antithesis of performance. "True faith," however, is neither flippant nor casual. It is *an affirmation that is binding on all of life*. It is the foundation upon which a person's life is built, even if the building is terribly flawed. It is not the quality of one's faith that determines its strength; it is the object of faith. "Mustard seed" faith in Jesus Christ can move mountains (see Matt 17:20).

"So that, though my conscience accuse me, that I have grossly transgressed all the commandments of God"

A healthy conscience can be a good barometer for behavior and an indicator of moral failures that need to be rectified. While the conscience is culturally conditioned, it can be used by the Holy Spirit to bring conviction of sins against God (see Ps 51:17). Unhealthy or neurotic guilt and irrational shame that come from unrealistic expectations, however, can be debilitating, even life-threatening. In one study, almost 80% of adults attempting suicide had histories of guilt or shame. Demanding perfection from ourselves, feeling responsible for the misfortunes of others, excessive remorse over a past that cannot be changed, and even failure to obey God's laws (see Gal 2:19), can create unhealthy guilt. In one way or another most have in fact "transgressed all the commandments of God," and our conscience accurately accuses us of doing so.

Any proper appreciation for the purity of the thrice holy God ("Holy, holy, holy is the Lord of hosts" from Isa 6:3, see also Rev 4:8), contemporaneously exposes our sins that are not merely causal peccadilloes or minor shortcomings. Minor mistakes can be corrected through explanation and negotiation. Great sin requires God's grace. An accusing conscience is a debilitating weight that robs us of joy, limits our potential, and drives us to discouragement, defeat, depression, and some even to death. "True faith" is the solace to an accusing conscience.

"And kept none of them"

If our breaking of the law had occurred in but one or two places, we would merely be rendered sinful. However, we have "kept none of them." You might say, "Steve, I know I'm not perfect, but I also know I have not broken all the law." Did not James say in 2:10 that breaking a single commandment renders us guilty of all? We might not have broken the sixth commandment and committed murder, but we have been hateful, envious, jealous, or resentful. We may not have broken the seventh commandment and committed adultery, but we have lusted and entertained certain thoughts and feelings for another person. We may not have broken the ninth commandment and born false witness, but we have gossiped behind another's back and flattered someone to their face, and both are lies and sins of the heart. Finally, who among us has loved God with *all* our heart, soul, mind and strength? Jesus went beyond the written law to address the condition of the heart. There, all stand guilty.

Chapter 11

"And am still inclined to all evil"

Before his tragic and untimely death, Mike Yaconelli wrote in *Messy Spirituality*:

> Pretending is the grease of modern nonrelationships. Pretending perpetuates the illusion of relationships by connecting us on the basis of who we aren't. People who pretend have pretend relationships. But being real is a synonym of messy spirituality, because when we are real, our messiness is there for everyone to see.[2]

We like to pretend that our penchant to sin has been relegated to the past. We dress up for church on Sunday mornings and can manage to behave ourselves for a couple of hours in order to impress people with how spiritual we are. We try to present ourselves as if we really don't struggle with sin like others. Hogwash!

When our three children were younger, on Sunday mornings Connie would do all she could to get them and herself ready for Sunday school and church. I, of course, was segregated in another part of the house sanctifying myself so I, as the man of God, could bring "the word of God" to the people that morning. My contribution to getting us to church on time would be to go to the car when time came to leave and honk the horn so the neighbors would know that it was not me making us late to church. Not infrequently, Connie and I would argue on the way to church about whatever it was that made us late that day. I would be seething by the time we arrived at church. I would find a parking space, ram the car in it, jam the brakes, get out with Bible and sermon in hand, and slam the door just as some dear old lady would walk by and say, "Good morning, Pastor. How are you?" My reply? Well, of course, "Oh, I'm great, sister! Praise the Lord! It's so good to see you this morning." All I was doing was pretending that I wasn't struggling with sin when I actually was.

The pull of sin—greed, selfishness, impurity, lying, jealousy, impatience, anger, and envy—is within the best of us. In Romans 7, the great Apostle Paul confesses his own intense struggle with sin:

> I am of flesh, sold into bondage to sin. For that which I am doing, I do not understand; for I am not practicing what I would like to do, but I am doing the very thing I hate.... So now, no longer am I the one doing it, but sin which dwells in me. For I know that nothing good dwells in me, that is, in my flesh; for the willing is present in me, but the doing of the good is not. For the good that I wish, I do not do; but I practice the very evil that I do not want. But if I am doing the very thing I do not want, I am no longer the one doing it, but sin which dwells in me. I find then the principle that evil is present in me, the one who wants to do good (Rom 7:14-21).

First Timothy is one of the last letters attributed to Paul. There, at the end of his life, he designates himself "the worst" of sinners (see 1 Tim 1:15, NIV).

Like Paul, though redeemed and indwelt by the Holy Spirit, we are all still inclined to evil. Dostoyevsky was correct: though the redeemed enjoy the "Madonna" within us, we still struggle with the indwelling "Sodom."[3] Recall Martin Luther's *simul justus et peccator*: "At the same time, righteous and sinner."[4] C.S. Lewis reminds the redeemed, "One essential symptom of the regenerate life is a permanent and permanently horrified perception of one's natural and (it seems) unalterable corruption. The true Christian's nostril is to be continually attentive to the cesspool."[5] *Strong language from all four authors!*

"Notwithstanding, God"

"Notwithstanding" is a contrasting conjunction. It signifies the demarcation contrasting the bad news and the good news about to be described. It introduces us to the subject who acts to make us righteous: God. The *what* that makes us righteous is a *Who*, and the Who is God. Our salvation, our redemption is God's work. It is all God's work. Despite all that *we* have done, we are now told of all that *God* has done.

Chapter 11

"Without any merit of mine"

This phrase further explains the "only," and is critical to our understanding of the entire gospel message. This is the difference between God's gospel of grace and humankind's religions of works. All too often what we hear from Christian pulpits is about *all we need to do for God or for the church*. We need to attend church weekly, serve in the program life of the church (sing, teach, be on a committee, change diapers, keep the preschoolers, usher, greet, etc.), keep the Ten Commandments, follow the Golden Rule, and abide by other denominational expectations. Most of all, we are to tithe and give money to the "special offerings" taken up periodically. Neglect any of this and your faithfulness and loyalty both to God and the church is called into question. Neglect more of this, and it is doubtful if you are "really saved." All of this is performance religion that far too often passes for Christianity.

In contrast to religion, the gospel is about *all that God has done for us*. He has made us righteous "without any merit of mine." No longer are we like ecclesiastical hamsters running a treadmill of religious performance, trying to earn or merit God's favor. Everything that we are attempting to earn via religious pursuits is already ours by grace.

One thing that shocked me as I began advocating the radical nature of God's grace was the level of resistance I encountered from other preachers. Church members—other than the legalists and the moral police—loved it, but not so the preachers. Ministers, supposedly ordained to proclaim the gospel of grace, are often the most averse to the practical application of that grace. Actually, it is an occupational hazard. If the church is to keep its doors open and modern programs staffed then the bills and salaries must be paid. This requires people giving money, and quite a lot of it. If we educate church members, someone must teach at every age level from preschool to senior adult. If worship is to meet today's modern standards, excellent music is expected. All of this and more takes a supreme commitment of numerous volunteers every week. A church cannot operate without the faithful service of its members. The degeneration and denial of the gospel begins to occur when pastors (often out of utter frustration) stoop to viewing their congregants as obstinate, distracted, or lazy people who must be motivated with threats of God's displeasure and judgment—both temporal and eternal. I suppose it doesn't help that I am attempting to assure their members that God loves them whether or not they tithe, participate in the life of the church, and so on. The resistance of preachers is understandable. The result is, as one of my insightful mentors has said, "Preachers are not the key to the church, they are the lock."

Philip Yancey ends his book, *What's So Amazing About Grace* by talking about the way everyone "thirsts for grace." I believe what he's saying, but not everyone does. If your preacher tries to guilt you into service, understand that he may be attempting to keep the church functioning because he knows that you demand it of him. It is just that he is going about it the wrong way. Try to help him understand the gospel. Paul says that "the love of Christ compels us" (2 Cor 2:14, NKJV) to faithful obedience and loyal service, not guilt. If he is intransigent, it may be time to find a new preacher or a new church. If both pastor and people are not very careful, our method of operating the church can degenerate into a denial of the gospel that pastors are ordained to proclaim.

If our righteousness has nothing to do with our works, religious deeds, and performance, how then are we made righteous? The next phrase with which we are dealing in the Heidelberg Catechism points the way.

"But only of mere grace"

If "only" is the most important word in the answer, "mere" is the most descriptive. "*Mere* grace." With God, it doesn't take great grace or a greater grace or the greatest grace. In fact, grace is not a noun that should be qualified with degrees of comparison such as great, greater, or greatest or much, more, or most. There are no positive, comparative, or superlative degrees of grace, no great grace or greater grace or greatest grace; not theologically at any rate. Not only are they not necessary; they would diminish the meaning of grace. There is just "mere grace."

With God, grace is always "mere," and "mere grace" is always enough. "Mere grace" is forever abundant. The attributes of God are like God Himself. Just as God is both eternal and infinite, so is God's grace. Eternal means not only that there is no end, but also that there is no beginning. Looking to the past, there has never been a time when God has not been gracious toward you. Looking to the future, there will never be a time when God will not be gracious to you. God's grace, like God, is eternal. God's grace is infinite (meaning endless, without limit) and, like God, God's grace never ends. His grace has no limits. This is the deep reach of grace. The preacher's letter said, "Grace runs out." No.

Religion runs out. Second chances run out. New leaves to turn over run out. Warnings and threats run out. Reproaches run out. However, mark this down for the peace of mind and soul: *grace never runs out.* Our salvation, our righteous standing before God is "without any merit of mine, but only of mere grace."

As we continue to proceed through unpacking the Heidelberg Catechism phrases on which we are focusing, let's pause to remind ourselves of the original question: "How art thou righteous before God?"

"God Grants and Imputes to Me"

This begins the heart of the gospel. "How art thou righteous before God?" "God grants and imputes to me...." Righteous, our standing before God, is forever the gift of God. He "grants and imputes to me...." The term "grant" is readily understandable; it means a gift or a transfer of something from one person to another. It means to *bestow on another* (example: the student was granted or bestowed the foundation's scholarship) and *to give* (example: the governor granted or gave the petition for clemency). The word "impute" is not a word used with regularity today, but it means "to credit someone with." It was used by the Apostle Paul in Romans 4:

> For what does the Scripture say? "Abraham believed God, and it was *credited* to him as righteousness".... To the one who does not work, but believes in Him who justifies the ungodly, his faith is *credited* as righteousness [emphasis mine] (Rom 4:3, 5).

The word "credited" has the meaning of this term "impute." Paul borrowed the word (Greek, *logizomai*) from the accounting terminology of his day and used it to describe how God redeems us. It means "to enter into the account book." Through faith in Christ, God makes an entry into our accounting ledger. It means that God credits to us the virtues of Jesus specified in the next phrase. (Paul is using a revealing metaphor to explain our salvation. God does not keep ledgers on us. Remember, God is not a bookkeeper. He is a lover.)

God granting and imputing is what sets the Christian gospel apart from all religions, even the Christian religion. Always remember, religion is about *all that you need to do for God*, so hopefully God will love you, forgive you, accept you, and He will take you to heaven when you die (or, for some, so you can con Him out of some blessings while you live). In contrast, the gospel is about *all that God has done for you.* What has He done for you? He "grants and imputes" to you.

What specifically does God grant and impute to us? The Heidelberg Catechism offers insight that is not to be missed. Find here the deep reach of amazing grace.

"The Perfect Satisfaction, Righteousness and Holiness of Christ"

What does it mean that God grants, imputes, credits, and accounts to us *the satisfaction of Christ*? Are you ready for it? *It means that God is as satisfied with you as He is with Jesus.* I know that sounds implausible even impossible, yet this is the gospel, the good news. And, this is only part of the wonder of mere grace. Without any merit of our own, but *only by true faith,* God finds in us the same satisfaction that He finds in His Son, Jesus. The word "satisfaction" in Scripture means a state of contentment. God is just as content with you now as He was with Jesus then. How satisfied was God with Jesus? Partially? Mostly? Completely? Hebrews 1:3 tells us:

> He is the radiance of His glory and the exact representation of His nature, and upholds all things by the word of His power. When He had made purification of sins, He sat down at the right hand of the Majesty on high.

This verse states three things Jesus did. First, He radiated the glory of God as the sun radiates rays of light. The term "radiance" is "effulgence" (the only time this word is used in the New Testament); it is not a reflected light, but light in itself. Jesus does not reflect the light of God. He *is* the light of God. Second, He is "the exact representation of His nature." As I have maintained throughout this book from John 1:18, Jesus "explained" the Father to us. Third, He made purification for our sins. "Purification" is the word from which we derive our English word "catharsis," which means "a purging or a cleansing." God's glory and nature are seen most clearly when God cleanses us from sin. Having done all of this, Jesus' work is complete and He is accepted by the Father: "He sat down at the right hand of the Majesty on High." The Father was satisfied with the Son.

God is as satisfied (content) with you as He is with Jesus. Take a moment to think about this reality. This is the deep reach of amazing grace. This is why John could write in 1 John 4:17, "By this, love is perfected with us, that we may have confidence in the day of judgment; because *as He is, so also are we in this world*" [emphasis mine]. For so many the thought of judgment is a fearful prospect. After all, we know ourselves and how we pretend. We know our hidden thoughts, secret motives, and untoward ways. We can identify with Paul's struggle with sin. Deep inside, in those places we let no one else visit, those places we even seldom visit ourselves, we know that, like Paul, we have a dark side.

J.R.R. Tolkien's *The Lord of the Rings* is a fine example of the inner conflict between the good and evil that is common to all of us. After an epic journey of unrelenting struggles and unimaginable threats to his life, Frodo finally arrives with the evil ring to Mordor, the only place where the ring can be destroyed. We wait with great anticipation for the climactic moment when the book's hero figure casts the ring into the fires of Mount Doom. Tolkien, however, is much too insightful for such wistful fantasy. We are stunned when Frodo, after so many life-threatening events involving the ring, is overcome by the ring's evil and refuses to destroy it. The noble, faithful, and virtuous Frodo has become infected with radical evil. In Frodo, Tolkien demonstrates what Ralph Wood calls the juxtaposition of radical good with radical evil. Tolkien knew that the human heart is the locus of both virtue and villainy, and does a masterful job of portraying that reality in his well-known story.

Knowing that deep inside rests a corruption about which we seldom talk, it can be difficult for some to conceive that God finds satisfaction in us. Yet, it is because of such radical evil that our only hope for God to be satisfied with us is His granting and imputing to us His satisfaction as a gift of "mere grace." Why can we have confidence in the day of judgment? "Because *as He is, so are we* in this world"—right now, right here. This is the gift of God's grace through faith. This is the deep reach of amazing grace.

Not only does God grant and credit us with the satisfaction of Christ, He grants and imputes to us the perfect righteousness of Christ.

"...the perfect... righteousness...of Christ;"

Though our conscience may condemn us for all our sins of the past and we know that we will sin again in the future, God nonetheless grants and imputes (credits) to us the righteousness of Christ. This means that God sees us as righteous as Jesus, and the orthodox doctrine of the church says that Jesus was without sin.

In my pastoral ministry, I have known many people deeply burdened with the guilt of past sins. Though they had already claimed salvation and were in the church, they still labored under the weight of the sins and failures of their life. One of the most difficult obstacles I encountered was trying to convince them that their sins have been completely forgiven and that God does not hold their sins against them. God in Christ has forgiven the sins of the world (see 1 John 2:2). Through the gift of God, He no longer "sees" or relates to us as sinners. He has given each of us the "*perfect righteousness of Christ,*" and this is how God relates to each one of us.

The wisdom contained within the Heidelberg Catechism continues. We note that God grants and imputes to us the perfect holiness of Christ.

"...the perfect... holiness of Christ;"

We know that God is satisfied with us and views us as righteous as Christ. However, it gets better: God declares that we are as holy as Christ. Knowing that God is satisfied with me is wonderful, and realizing that God sees me as righteous as Jesus is amazing. But "holy" is the term used throughout Scripture to describe God Himself. God based the entire foundation of biblical ethics on His own character when He told Moses in Leviticus 19:2 "Speak to all the congregation of the sons of Israel and say to them, 'You shall be holy, for I the Lord your God am holy.'" Why are we to live holy lives? Are we to do so because our God is holy? Holy is the preeminent term used in the Old Testament to describe God.

Fifteen hundred years of Old Testament history, however, has proven that it is impossible to keep that commandment. Now, however, there is a new covenant (see Luke 22:20) and we don't have to worry about the impossibility of trying to holy or worthy enough to merit God's love. This new covenant is not about obedience to the laws of the old covenant. This brings death, because we simply are incapable of achieving it (see Rom 7:24). The new covenant is about the Spirit of God working in the inner person to bring new life, making them new people (see 2 Cor 3:6). The new covenant says that by simple faith in this loving, forgiving, kind and gracious Jesus of Nazareth, "the exact representation of His (God's) nature," grants and imputes to us the holiness of God Himself.

Humans never become God or gods. We are always human with all the innate and inherent flaws that accompany being human. We are forever creature, never Creator. Yet we become like God in holiness! We are granted and it is imputed to us, the satisfaction, righteousness, and holiness of Christ.

Notice that it is "*the perfect* satisfaction, righteousness and holiness of Christ." Like the term "grace," there are no degrees of comparison in "perfect." Nothing is more perfect or most perfect; it is either perfect or it is flawed. What God grants and imputes to us is *the perfect* satisfaction, *the perfect* righteousness and *the perfect* holiness of Christ.

Hear the gospel, my friends! This is what makes the good news so wonderful: the good news works right here in the midst of the bad, and despite the bad news of our sins, God grants and imputes to us the perfect satisfaction, righteousness, and holiness of Christ. God is as satisfied with you as He is with Jesus and sees you as perfectly righteous and holy as Jesus. Every time I say or write that, it gives me pause, and I have to ask myself, "Steve is that right? Are you sure?" I go back to the New Testament and can only conclude again that, yes, based on the clear teachings of Scripture, this is correct. The Heidelberg Catechism captures this reality and eloquently expresses it. This is the deep reach of amazing grace.

The catechism, however, is still not finished.

"Even so as if I never had had, nor committed any sin."

When I say that one of the implications of grace is that God doesn't count our sins but forgives us of them, this is how thorough God's forgiveness is: it is as if we've never had any sin or even committed any sin. "That cannot be," you say. Yes! It be! This is how full, how complete God's salvation is. It could not be otherwise with the God explained to us in the Bible, even in the Old Testament. My favorite psalm is Psalm 103:

He has not dealt with us according to our sins, nor rewarded us according to our iniquities. For as high as the heavens are above the earth, so great is His lovingkindness toward those who fear Him. As far as the east is from the west, so far has He removed our transgressions from us (Ps 103:10-12).

People relate to us based on our performance, but not God. The basis of His dealing with us is not our sins and iniquities, but His grace. With God, just as the east never meets the west, we will never again meet our sins. Our sins are gone, and they are gone forever. All of our sin has been removed, erased, blotted out, and taken away. Using the imagery Paul portrays in Colossians 2:13-14, our transgressions have been lifted up and carried off, they are no more. The prophet Jeremiah takes it even further: "For I will forgive their sin and *will no longer call to mind the wrong they have done*" [emphasis mine] (31:34). People can forgive, but the psychologists tell us that we rarely ever forget anything. However, the omniscient God who knows all things does forget; He forgets our sins. The old hymn, "The Love of God" expresses profound truth:

> *The Love of God*
> The love of God is greater far
> Than tongue or pen can ever tell;
> It goes beyond the highest star,
> And reaches to the lowest hell;
>
> The guilty pair, bowed down with care,
> God gave His Son to win;
> His erring child He reconciled,
> And pardoned from his sin.[6]

The song was written by Frederick M. Lehman. In 1948 he wrote a pamphlet called, "History of the Song, The Love of God." Here is an excerpt from that pamphlet:

> One day, during short intervals of inattention to our work, we picked up a scrap of paper and, seated

upon an empty lemon box pushed against the wall, with a stub pencil, added the (first) two stanzas and chorus of the song....Since the lines (the third stanza from a Jewish poem) had been found penciled on the wall of a patient's room in an insane asylum after he had been carried to his grave, the general opinion was that this inmate had written the epic in moments of sanity.[7]

Apocryphal or not, here is what that third stanza says,

> Could we with ink the ocean fill,
> And were the skies of parchment made,
> Were every stalk on earth a quill,
> And every man a scribe by trade;
> To write the love of God above
> Would drain the ocean dry;
> Nor could the scroll contain the whole,
> Though stretched from sky to sky.[8]

God's love reaches from the farthest stars to the lowest hell. Even the endless skies are not large enough to contain a written expression of His love for us. This love is the reason for His redemption and why He relates to us as if we had never sinned. That is the negative side. Here is the positive side.

"As if I had fully accomplished all that obedience which Christ has accomplished for me"

In the Book of Common Prayer, the daily confession in the Morning Prayer acknowledges, "We have left undone those things which we ought to have done; And we have done those things which we ought not to have done."[9] How much have you left undone today? How much have you left undone in the last week or year, or throughout your life? The omissions are beyond number, impossible to recount or to rectify. How much have you done that you should not have done? This matters in human religion, *but not with God and His gospel.* God's perfect satisfaction, righteousness, and holiness is credited so thoroughly to you that it is as if you have already lived in perfect obedience to God's will and have done everything God ever asked you to do. God relates to you as if you had accomplished all that He ever asked or expected of you. All those expectations have been accomplished for you by Christ, then granted and imputed to you by God. This is the deep reach of amazing grace.

How does all of this radical, outlandish, and amazing grace become ours? One final time, we gain insight from the Heidelberg Catechism.

"Inasmuch as I embrace such benefit with a believing heart."

How does God's perfect satisfaction, righteousness, and holiness become ours? We embrace it. The term "embrace" connotes a warm-hearted, affectionate cheek-to-cheek and heart-to-heart hug. We choose to believe from our hearts that God is the Father Jesus "explained" to us to us in John 1:18, a God of outlandish grace. The only thing we can do is to embrace it. Tillich wrote that we accept our acceptance,[10] and this is the essence of the "true faith" mentioned above. "Believing" means accepting the truth that God accepts us, and we embrace this truth with a believing heart. Therein we are righteous before God. All of this is the wonder of the gospel and the deep reach of amazing grace.

The Struggle to Believe the Gospel of Grace

Why is it that we struggle to believe the pure, unalloyed grace of God? Why is it that those in the church resist the "good news"—the "best news"—the world has ever received? Amazingly, it seems that the more religious the person, the more resistance there is. There are many reasons: human pride (we think we can do something to merit redemption), it threatens the status quo (we are motivated by personal fears and ecclesiastical intimidation), shame and guilt (we feel bad about ourselves and want to pay back God), we do not understand Jesus' message (we can quote Scripture, but we miss the message), and so on. One of the main reasons we struggle to believe the gospel is that grace is so rarely ever modeled for us. The culture uses the term, but grace is never modeled in daily life. Law enforcement officers do not model grace when they catch me speeding on the highway. They give me a ticket. Detectives do not model grace when they catch criminals. They arrest them. The courts do not model grace. They try, convict, and sentence the guilty. The mortgage company does not model grace when someone defaults on a loan. They foreclose. The U.S. military does not model grace to terrorists. They kill them. Every one of these institutions are fulfilling their designated functions. Their officers, representatives, and employees are doing their jobs. None were ever designed for the purpose of modeling grace. Grace is not part of their function, description, or responsibility.

There is only one institution in the world that has ever been organized and commissioned to model grace to the world: the church of the Lord Jesus Christ. Sadly, more often than not, the church preaches like, talks like, looks like, and acts like the rest of the world's peoples and institutions. The main reason we do not believe grace is that the church so rarely models grace. The church can be just as unloving, unforgiving, rejecting, condemning, critical, harsh, vengeful, and damning as the secular world. As a result of all of this, it is not always easy to know what grace looks like. Then, when we do see it or hear it, it is so different from our understanding of Christianity, that we do not recognize it; we conclude that someone is just being "soft on sin," or "they just don't know the Bible" or "They have lost their mind."

The Church: A Sanctuary

In the Old Testament there were cities of refuge where one accused of involuntary manslaughter could find protection from immediate eye-for-an-eye vengeance. There were also other places of sanctuary that provided a safe haven for fugitives. English law—from the fourth to seventeenth century—later acknowledged churches as places of sanctuary where fugitives could be protected from authorities and be immune from arrest. The church came to be a place of sanctuary, a safe place from harm, abuse, seizure, or arrest. I cannot recall where, but there is a painting of a priest standing on the steps of the church and staring down secular authorities. He is protecting his besieged parishioners who are laying down in distress behind him. In that painting, the priest is refusing entrance to the king's threatening army that is fully armored with banners unfurled and swords flashing. Behind the army are others struggling to make it to the church where they know they will find sanctuary.

What a wonderful portrayal of the church! The church needs to be a sanctuary, always. It should be known as a place of refuge and a safe haven for anyone. The church should be a place where all can find love, forgiveness, and acceptance. And, because of that, find security, rest, encouragement, support, guidance, and peace. In church, people should be defended from the attacks from the external world and find comfort and healing from the assaults of their own besieged and weary hearts. "If I can just get to church, I'll be safe. If I can get to the people who love me, forgive me, and accept me I will find refuge. There I'll find rest for my soul and peace from the struggles. They will help me and support me; if I can just get to church. In church, I'll find sanctuary." WOW! Who wouldn't want a church like this? I do not view this as an unrealistic or overly romanticized notion of what can be. This is the kind of church grace produces. Oh, that the church would model grace to the world!

So, what do we do until the church becomes a sanctuary? When virtually no one models grace to us, including the church, it is difficult to believe and remember that God is a God of grace. This is why Martin Luther said, "Preach the gospel to yourself every day." He knew that unless we do that, we will forget the only unique message the church has: the message of the grace of God. Every day tell yourself, "God loves me, forgives me, and accepts me unconditionally. No matter what I do or leave undone, regardless of my failures, weaknesses, and sins, no matter what others say or think about me, or how they treat me, God loves me, forgives me, and accepts me unconditionally. Then engage other people out of the vast reservoir of grace—the love, forgiveness, and acceptance—that fills your heart.

Do not forget the gospel. Preach it to yourself every day.

[1]Herman Hoeksema, *The Triple Knowledge: An Exposition of the Heidelberg Catechism*, vol. 2 (Grand Rapids: The Reformed Free Publishing Association, 1971) 316.
[2]Mike Yaconelli, *Messy Spirituality: God's Annoying Love for Imperfect People* (Grand Rapids: Zondervan, 2002) 27.
[3]Dostoyevsky, *Karamazov*, 97.
[4]McGrath, *Theology Reader*, 443.
[5]C.S. Lewis. *The Inspirational Writings of C.S. Lewis*. (Edison, NJ: Inspirational Press, 1994) 307.
[6]Frederick M. Lehman, "The Love of God," *Songs that Are Different*, Vol. 2 (Pasadena: Lehman Songs Company, 1919).
[7]Frederick M. Lehman, "History of the Song, The Love of God," 1948, <http://biblestudycharts.com/HH_The_Love_Of.html>.
[8]Lehman, "Love of God."
[9]*Book of Common Prayer*, 41.
[10]Tillich, *Foundations*, 163.

Epilogue

DANISH THEOLOGIAN Søren Kierkegaard wrote, "The most dreadful sort of blasphemy is that of which 'Christendom' is guilty: transforming the God of Spirit into...ludicrous twaddle."[1] This summary of the Christian church was written his book, *Attack Upon Christendom*. Kierkegaard died in 1855. As a Lutheran, he went on to say:

> O Luther, thou hadst 95 theses—terrible! And yet, in a deeper sense, the more theses, the less terrible. This case is far more terrible: there is only one thesis. The Christianity of the New Testament simply does not exist. Here there is nothing to reform; what has to be done is to throw light upon a criminal offense against Christianity, prolonged through centuries, perpetrated by millions (more or less guiltily), whereby they have cunningly, under the guise of perfecting Christianity, sought little by little to cheat God out of Christianity, and have succeeded in making Christianity exactly the opposite of what it is in the New Testament.[2]

The struggle to keep the gospel of God's grace from becoming simply another religion and reducing profound truth to "ludicrous twaddle" is nothing new. Christendom, religious denominations, and local churches all wrestle with it. The most critical place, however, where this battle is waged is in the hearts and minds of the individual Christian; those of us who call ourselves followers of Jesus.

Do you believe the gospel? I am not referring to the creeds and doctrines of the church, ethical instruction, or the stories of the Bible. Do you believe the gospel of the grace of God? Do you believe that God:

1. Loves *you* and everyone else unconditionally?

2. Has already forgiven *you* and each of us for all our sins, whether past, present, or future?

3. Accepts *you* and all others right now, just as we are?

This is the God Jesus "explained" to us (see John 1:18).

I have been highly critical of the church, and it deserves the criticism. It has, in many ways, turned the astonishing "good news" into "ludicrous twaddle." It has complicated, confused, distorted, and denied the simple, unalloyed truth of God's grace. And millions of people are flat out weary of it. They agree with Kierkegaard: "The Christianity of the New Testament simply does not exist."[3]

All of this, however, is *too* critical. The gospel of grace *does exist*, and it is being presented by pastors, preachers, teachers, authors, and theologians. We just have to find them and distinguish their message from those who are substituting amazing grace with a religion of Christian performance, which is not Christianity at all.

In these pages, I have tried to refocus our attention on the gospel of Jesus Christ, unencumbered by religious clutter. The gospel of God's grace is still the hope of humankind. It is still marvelous light in dreadful darkness, and the God of grace remains wonderful and beautiful beyond any poet's or psalmist's skill to describe. True faith in Jesus Christ is still soul-stirring, heart-lifting, life-changing, and earth-shaking. I hope those who have given up on the church do not give up on God. I hope those discouraged with the church will be encouraged by the gospel. I pray *The Deep Reach of Amazing Grace* can reveal the outlandish nature of God's grace. Most of all, I hope you can discover the deep reach of amazing grace in your own life. Once again, "Merry Grace!"

[1] Søren Kierkegaard, *Attack Upon Christendom*, trans. Walter Lowerie (Princeton: Princeton University Press, 1968) 110.
[2] Ibid, 32.
[3] Ibid, 32.

Works Cited

Allitt, Patrick. *Religion in America Since 1945: A History* (Columbia Histories of Modern American Life). Copyright © 2003 Columbia University Press.

Alter, Robert. *Genesis: Translation and Commentary.* Copyright © 1996 by W.W. Norton & Company.

Bainton, Roland H. *Here I Stand: A Life of Martin Luther.* Copyright © 1977 by Penguin Books.

The Baptist Faith and Message. 1963. The Sunday School Board of the Southern Baptist Convention.

The Book of Common Prayer According to the use of The Episcopal Church. "The Apostles Creed." The Church Hymnal Corporation, NY.

Bowie, Walter Russell. *The Interpreter's Bible 12 Vols.* Vol.1 General and Old Testament Articles, Genesis, Exodus. Copyright © 1952 by Abingdon Press.

Brueggemann, Walter. *Interpretation, A Bible Commentary for Teaching And Preaching: Genesis.* Copyright © 1982 by John Knox Press.

Bunaby, John. Editor. *Augustine: Later Works* (Library of Christian Classics). "Homilies on I John." Copyright © 1955 by Westminster Press.

Calvin, John. *Institutes of the Christian Religion.* 2 Vols. John T. McNeill, Ed. Ford Lewis Battles, Trans. Copyright © 1960 W.L. Jenkins by Westminster Press.

Campolo, Tony. *The Kingdom Is A Party.* Copyright © 1990 by Tony Campolo, "A Party In Honolulu," and from my recollections of personally hearing Mr. Campolo tell the story. Used by permission of Tony Campolo's office, October 24, 2012. All rights reserved.

Capon, Robert Farrar. *The Mystery of Christ and Why We Don t Get It.* Copyright © 1993 by William B. Eerdmans Publishing Company. All rights reserved. Used by permission.

Capon, Robert Farrar. *The Parables of Judgment.* Copyright © 1989 by William B. Eerdmans Publishing Company. All rights reserved. Used by permission.

Chesterton, G.K. Cited by Brennan Manning in *The Ragamuffin Gospel: Embracing the Unconditional Love of God.* Copyright © 1990 by Multnomah Books.

Chicago Statement on Biblical Inerrancy. Copyright © 1978 by ICBI. All rights reserved. Published with permission from the Dallas Theological Seminary Archives, Repository of ICBI Archives. For information, contact: The Coalition on Revival, Inc., P.O. Box 1139, Murphys, CA 95247

Dyck, Drew. *Christianity Today.* "The Leavers: Young Doubters Exit the Church." <www.christianitytoday.com/ct/2010/november/27.40.html>.

Edersheim, Alfred. *The Life and Times of Jesus the Messiah.* 2 Vols. Copyright © 1969 by William B. Eerdmans Publishing Company. All rights reserved. Used by permission.

Edwards, Jonathan. *Sinners in the Hands of an Angry God.* University of Nebraska-Lincoln DigitalCommons@University of Nebraska-Lincoln. Electronic Texts in American Studies Libraries at University of Nebraska-Lincoln.

Ehrman, Bart D. *Misquoting Jesus: The Story Behind Who Changed the Bible and Why.* Copyright © 2005 by Harper Collins.

Falwell, Jerry and Pat Robertson. "The 700 Club." *The Christian Broadcasting Network,* Inc. 13 September 2001 <www.youtube.com/watch?v=H-CAcdta_8I>.

Ferguson, Niall. *The War of the World, Twentieth-Century Conflict and the Descent of the West.* Copyright © 2006 by Penguin Press.

France, R.T. *The Living God.* Copyright © 1970 Inter-Varsity Press. Used by permission of InterVarsity Press, PO Box 1400, Downers Grove, IL 60515. (www.ivpress.com). All rights preserved.

Gourley, Bruce. *www.civilwarbaptists.com*<www.civilwarbaptists.com/thisdayinhistory/1861-january-27>.

Hoeksema, Herman. *The Triple Knowledge: An Exposition of the Heidelberg Catechism.* 3 Vols. Copyright © 1971 by The Reformed Free Publishing Association.

Honey, Charles. "Adamant on Adam: Resignation of prominent scholar Bruce Waltke underscores tension over evolution." *Christianity Today.* 25 May 2010. <www.christianitytoday.com/ct/2010/june/1.14.html>.

Huxley, Aldous. *The Perennial Philosophy: An Interpretation of the Great Mystics, East and West.* Copyright © 1947 by Chatto and Windus, London.

Kinnaman, David and Gabe Lyons. *Unchristian: What A New Generation Really Thinks About Christianity...And Why It Matters.* Copyright © 2007 by David Kinnaman and Fermi Project. Baker Books. All rights reserved. Used by permission.

"Land of Hope And Dreams" by Bruce Springsteen. Copyright © 2012 Bruce Springsteen (ASCAP). Reprinted by permission. International copyright secured. All rights reserved.

Lewis, C.S. *The Inspirational Writings of C.S. Lewis.* Copyright 1994 by Inspirational Press.

_____. Cited by Alan Jacobs in *The Narnian: The Life and Imagination of C.S. Lewis.* Copyright © 2005 by Harper San Francisco.

_____ *The Pilgrim's Regress: An Allegorical Apology for Christianity, Reason and Romanticism.* Copyright © 1992 by William B. Eerdmans Publishing Company.

_____ Cited by Scott Hoezee in *The Riddle of Grace: Applying Grace to the Christian Life.* Copyright © 1996 by William B. Eerdmans Publishing Company. All rights reserved. Used by permission.

_____ *The Screwtape Letters.* Copyright © 1996 by HarperSanFranscisco.

Luther, Martin. *Three Treatises: An Open Letter to the Christian Nobility; the Babylonian Captivity of the Church; the Freedom of a Christian.* Copyright © 1960 by The Fortress Press.

McGrath, Alister E., Ed. *The Christian Theology Reader.* Third Edition. Copyright © 2007 by Blackwell Publishing.

Moltmann, Jürgen. *The Crucified God: The Cross of Christ as the Foundation and Criticism of Christian Theology.* Copyright ©1993 by Fortress Press. All rights reserved. Used by permission.

Napier, K.B. *www.christiandoctrine.com.* "Why Christians Don't Believe in Literal Six-day Creation," 20 July 2012. <www.christiandoctrine.com/index.php?option=com_content&view=article&id=964:why-christians-dont-believe-in-literal-six-day-creation&catid=105:science-and-environment&Itemid=477>.

Works Cited

Newbigin, Lesslie. *The Gospel In A Pluralistic Society.* Copyright © 1989 by William B. Eerdmans Publishing Company. All rights reserved. Used by permission.

"No Man's Land" ("The Green Fields of France") by Erick Bogle. Copyright © by Erick Bogle. All rights reserved. Used by permission.

Nouwen, Henri J. *The Return Of The Prodigal Son: A Story Of Homecoming.* Copyright © 1992 by Henri J. Nouwen. Used by permission of Doubleday/Random House. All rights reserved.

O'Connor, Flannery. *Flannery O'Connor: The Complete Stories.* Copyright © 1971 by The Estate of Mary Flannery O'Connor. Farrar, Straus, and Giroux. "Revelation." All rights reserved. Used by permission.

Public Broadcasting Service. "Instructions for the Last Night." *Frontline* <www.pbs.org/wgbh/pages/frontline/shows/network/personal/instructions.html>.

Putnam, Robert D. and David E Campbell. *American Grace: How Religion Divides and Unites Us.* Copyright © 2012 By Simon and Schuster.

Sagan, Carl. *Cosmos.* Copyright © 1980 by Random House Publishing Group.

Santayana, George. *The Life of Reason* (Great Books in Philosophy). Copyright © 1998 by Prometheus Books.

Stott, John R.W. *The Contemporary Christian.* Copyright © 1992 by John R. W. Stott. Used by permission of InterVarsity Press, PO Box 1400, Downers Grove, IL 60515. (www.ivpress.com). All rights reserved.

Strobel, Lee. *The Case for Faith: A Journalist Investigates the Toughest Objections to Christianity.* Copyright © 2000 by Zondervan.

Thoreau, Henry David. *Walden; Or, Life in the Woods.* Copyright © 1994 by Dover Publications.

Tillich, Paul. *The Shaking Of The Foundations.* Copyright © 2012 by Wipf and Stock Publishers. Used by permission of Wipf and Stock Publishers. (www.wipfandstock.com). All rights reserved.

Towne, Anthony. "An Obituary for God." *The News and Courier,* 14 March 1966, sec. A, p. 6 <http://news.google.com/newspapers?nid=2506&dat=19660314&id=uMdJAAAAIBAJ&sjid=hwoNAAAAIBAJ&pg=2870,3087409>.

Willard, Dallas. *The Divine Conspiracy: Rediscovering Our Hidden Life in God.* Copyright © 1998 by HarperCollins.

Yaconelli, Mike. *Messy Spirituality: God's Annoying Love for Imperfect People.* Copyright © 2002 by Zondervan.

Yancey, Philip. *What's So Amazing About Grace?* Copyright © 1997 by Philip Yancey. Used by permission of Zondervan. (www.zondervan.com). All rights reserved.

www.ingramcontent.com/pod-product-compliance
Lightning Source LLC
Chambersburg PA
CBHW070741160426
43192CB00009B/1530